CHIEF RABBI NATHAN MARCUS ADLER

Also by Derek Taylor

British Chief Rabbis, 1664–2006

Don Pacifico: The Acceptable Face of Gunboat Diplomacy

Jewish Parliamentarians

Solomon Schonfeld: A Purpose in Life

The Sunderland Beth Hamedresh

'Thank You For Your Business': The Jewish Contribution to the British Economy

Hillel House – A Lesson in Tolerance

Chief Rabbi Hertz: The Wars of the Lord

Defenders of the Faith: The History of Jews' College and the London School of Jewish Studies

Chief Rabbi Nathan Marcus Adler

The Forgotten Founder

Derek Taylor

VALLENTINE MITCHELL
LONDON • CHICAGO, IL

First published in paperback in 2021 by *Vallentine Mitchell*

Catalyst House,
720 Centennial Court,
Centennial Park, Elstree WD6 3SY, UK

814 N. Frankllin Street
Chicago, Illinois
60610, USA

www.vmbooks.com

first published in cloth 2018

British Library Cataloguing in Publication Data:
An entry can be found on request

ISBN 978 1 912676 58 3 (Paper)
ISBN 978 1 910383 68 1 (Ebook)

Library of Congress Cataloging in Publication Data:
An entry can be found on request

Contents

List of Illustrations

Preface and Acknowledgements

Should we welcome immigrants into the country? If we do, should they assimilate or try to retain their individual cultures? These are hot topics, widely discussed and even influencing the voting on Brexit.

Now the fact is – unpalatable as it may be to many – that almost everybody in the country can trace their ancestry back to an immigrant from somewhere overseas, and almost all the ethnic communities have assimilated. Where are the Norman conquerors, the Flemish weavers, the eighteenth-century Huguenots, the freed black slaves and the refugees from the 1848 uprisings on the Continent? They may have left relics of themselves behind – Norman Churches in Norfolk, the records of the Flemings in the archives of the Worshipful Company of Weavers, the surnames reflecting their overseas origins, and that part of Bradford which is still called Little Germany. Overall, though, they have vanished.

Except for one ethnic minority which has been in this country since Cromwell's time and hasn't vanished. There may be only 270,000 Jews in Britain, but they still follow their faith, while playing a full part in every aspect of the country's life. This, in spite of the fact that if they gave up Judaism, social acceptance for hundreds of years would have been easier. Which, of course, meant that tens of thousands did. Also in spite of the fact that Judaism is a very demanding religion, and there are still well-funded organizations trying to get Jews to convert.

Observing the tenets of Orthodoxy is the more demanding kind of Judaism, rather like the Catholics being required to be more observant than the followers of the Church of England. The majority of Jews in many countries have, indeed, adopted a less rigorous version of the religion. That didn't happen in Britain, and why it didn't happen is the subject of this book; Chief Rabbi Nathan Marcus Adler.

It always amazes me how kind and helpful complete strangers are when I need information and advice. Top of my list of thanks on this occasion is Rabbi Raymond Apple, the former Av Beth Din in Australia and minister of the Great Synagogue in Sydney for many years. He has been a tower of strength, and went through the draft manuscript with a tooth comb, to its great advantage.

I'd also like to thank Dr Peter Schulze, the archivist of the Jewish community in Hanover, Professor David Meola of the University of Alabama, an expert on early nineteenth-century German Jewish history, Elkan Levy, Rabbi Jeffrey Cohen, Rabbi Reuben Livingstone, Professor Geoffrey Cantor, Warren Klein of the Jewish Theological Seminary in New York, the staff of the Jews' College Library, Charles Tucker, the record keeper of the archives of the office of the Chief Rabbi and the United Synagogue, the staff of the London Metropolitan Archives, Dr Jeremy Schonfield, Terry Bridger, Richard Cooper, and Jonathan and Léonie Cowan.

My ever-patient wife, Diane, has once again lived with endless talk about a long forgotten historical character for months on end; this time Nathan Marcus Adler. What would I do without her?

Derek Taylor, OBE
London 2017

Foreword

I am happy to commend Derek Taylor's biography of Nathan Marcus Adler for at least two good reasons. First: it is a fine piece of work, well researched, lucidly written, and historically important. Second: it is a book which I had dreams of writing myself, but other things got in the way, including the pressures of public life. I actually assembled a sheaf of material on the subject, partly thanks to a study subvention enabling me to investigate the Adler collection at the Jewish Theological Seminary of America, and I was happy to pass some of my material to Derek.

The book he has written places a great rabbi in the context of his period and addresses some of the mysteries that seem to attach to Adler's rabbinate. On the broad canvas of Anglo-Jewish history I and others have long wondered whether and why Adler apparently allowed others to receive credit for policies, plans and projects which were really his, and I for one am satisfied that Derek has found the answer. Historians have also wondered how and why Adler was so adamant that Anglo-Jewry and its ministry had to be so tightly centralized and controlled, and once again Derek has found an explanation.

Cecil Roth called Adler the grandfather of the Anglo-Jewish pulpit - an encomium that does not entirely fit, once again for reasons that Derek investigates - but if we borrow Roth's terminology we are entitled to call Adler the grandfather of historic Anglo-Jewry or at least everybody's uncle. He was a nice kind man whose beam encompassed young and old, native-born and immigrant, ministry and lay leadership. As someone once said, one felt better to be in his company.

It is true that since Adler's time the community has changed dramatically – but its centralized institutions survive and are still quite strong and there is still a uniquely disciplined pattern of Jewish life in Britian. Much of this is the outcome of Adler's incumbency. The Adler name seems to have more or less receded, but Anglo-Jewry owes the Adlers an immeasurable debt.

Derek's book tells a good story and tells it well. I am delighted to commend it.

Rabbi Dr. Raymond Apple, AO RFD
Emeritus Rabbi of the Great Synagogue, Sydney
Past president of the Australian Jewish Historical Society

1

The Story So Far

Who was Nathan Marcus Adler? On Yom Kippur, the most important Jewish fast day, there is a prayer said in many British synagogues for the former chief rabbis, and at that annual point Nathan Marcus Adler emerges from obscurity. His ministry in Britain ran from 1845 to 1890, the longest Chief Rabbinate on record to this day. Even so, he died 127 years ago and his influence on the development of the Jewish community in Britain is long forgotten. That contribution was, in fact, massive.

During the first half of the nineteenth century Jews were at last given civic equality in many European countries. It was the result of the movement called the Enlightenment, and Jews were, with some exceptions, finally able to go to universities, hold public office, live where they chose, be taxed at the same level as everybody else, and be treated like any other citizen. It was finally worth their while addressing their lack of a secular education which they would need to take their place in society.

With this new freedom, however, came another movement for change, an attempt to 'modernise' Judaism, which developed into the Reform, Conservative and Liberal movements. Pioneered in Germany and the USA, these movements became popular because, among other factors, they were more flexible than Orthodoxy and were more to the taste of Christian governments because they adopted some of the principles of church architecture, terminology and administration.

In Britain, however, these movements have made very little progress over the years, and the man responsible for ensuring that the Jewish community remained traditionally Orthodox was Nathan Marcus Adler.

Chief rabbis don't, of course, spring to life, ready-made, like the phoenix from the flames. When, in 1845, Nathan Marcus Adler was installed as Chief Rabbi of Britain and the Empire, he was 42 years old. He had spent his entire life up to that time in Germany. That was where his upbringing, education, ministerial experience and beliefs had all been formed. So it is in Germany that any account of his life must start.

Adler was the Chief Rabbi of Oldenburg in Germany in 1829 and of Hanover from 1830–45 (Hanover is both the town and the state.) As he was born in Hanover in 1803, he spent half his life in Germany. Now, there are military families and political families; there are farming families and families of scientists. There were also families of rabbis in Germany and the Adlers were among them. They were *Cohanim*, descended from the Biblical priestly tribe, and they lived for centuries in Frankfurt. Like the families of other rabbis, they also intermarried with each other.

Germany, up to 1807 and Napoleon's conquests, was made up of 333 small states, all of which owed allegiance to the Holy Roman Emperor. These small principalities were run by Electors, Dukes, Princes and Bishops. Many of them might only control their castle and a few surrounding villages, but they had laws in common and they also had their own traditions and ethos.

Their treatment of the Jews was not uniform, but it had in common that the Jews were not accepted on a par with other citizens. Jews were not allowed to even live in many states. Others expelled them, some rioted against them, there were pogroms and massacres, and every ruler had the objective of converting them to Christianity. How then did they survive? Only by sheer dogged determination on the part of enough of them to keep Judaism alive, generation after generation, century after century.

The Adlers came to Frankfurt, probably from Crete, in the early 1200s, though Jews are on record as living there for 300 years before that, when it was simply a market town. The first German rabbi in the family was Simeon Hadarshan, 'The Preacher'. As was often the case, the Jews in Frankfurt were useful to the rulers when they needed money, as they all did, either by imposing additional taxation on the community, or by using the banking skills possessed by a few of the Jewish leaders. The latter were called money lenders but they were, in today's nomenclature, merchant bankers. They could also obtain luxury goods from other countries from fellow Jewish merchants because they had far more sophisticated international contacts than the provincial rulers. They also had voluminous rules for carrying out international trade, set down in the Talmud and codes. The system could be used wherever Jews lived, and there was also a network of Jewish law courts (*Batei Din*) who could settle disputes between Jewish merchants.

Whenever the Jews weren't useful to the state, they would be discriminated against, periodically persecuted, treated – at best – as second-class citizens and despised and humiliated. In 1241 a Jew in Frankfurt refused to be baptised and more than three quarters of the community were murdered as a reprisal. Imagine being suddenly arrested and condemned to death because some complete stranger refused to be baptised.

In 1349 when the plague struck, they were accused of poisoning the wells, leading to another massacre, as well as their expulsion. Without Jews, however, Frankfurt's trade declined markedly and so, within a few years, Jews were encouraged to come back.

Jews still weren't allowed to own land, though, and they had to pay taxes that were only imposed on their community. They were also barred from membership of a guild, which effectively prevented them from taking part in the normal commerce of the state in which they lived. There were minor humiliations as well; in some towns, like Frankfurt, they were always at the mercy of drunken mobs, they weren't allowed to use public parks or walk on the pavement, and they had to tip their hats to any non-Jew who demanded obeisance when he cried out 'Jud mach mores' – 'Jew show your manners'. In later years even most of the favoured Jews were only allowed to wear high white wigs, rather than the upper-crust powdered ones.

A typical example of oppression came in 1614 when the community in Frankfurt was expelled during a revolt led by a rabble rouser called Vincent Fettmilch, an unpleasant character who described himself as the new Haman of the Jews (Haman was the ancient anti-Semitic fanatic whose infamous story is told in the Biblical Book of Esther). The Emperor eventually decided that Fettmilch had overstepped the mark and had him arrested and hanged. Thereupon the Jews of Frankfurt celebrated by making the day they returned to the city in 1616, the 20th of their month of Adar, 'Purim Vincenz'. Defeating their oppressors was a rare occurrence and worthy to be duly commemorated.

That day, leading the Jews back into the city from which nearly 1,500 had fled, was the rabbi, carrying the imperial flag, on which was a black eagle – the Reichsadler. From that time on the family took the name Adler, instead of the original Kahn. The end of Fettmilch did not, however, presage an improvement in the lot of the Jews in Frankfurt. In the early seventeenth century a new set of regulations was approved which restricted the numbers of Jews who could live in the town to 500. The community was only permitted twelve marriages a year and couldn't open shops. All or some of these oppressive dictates also applied to the other German states. If he was involved in a court case, a Jew would have to swear the De More Judaico, which was imposed throughout Germany. In this oath he had to call down on himself all the curses in the Biblical books of Leviticus and Deuteronomy if he didn't tell the truth. Plus the ten plagues of Egypt, the leprosy of Naaman and Gehazi in the Second Book of Kings and the Biblical fate of Dathan and Aviram when the ground opened up and swallowed them.

The Jews remained under the control of the Town Council and still had to pay additional taxes. In 1757, for example, at the outbreak of what would become known as the Seven Years War, the community had to provide the government with 1,000 shirts, 2,000 sheets, one thaler (a coin containing an ounce of silver) of cash per head, and 10 per cent of their personal property. The Jews were confined to a specific part of the town, known as the ghetto.

The Frankfurt Ghetto had been created in 1462 and lasted until 1796. Where it was originally intended for a few hundred inhabitants, it was eventually forced to house nearly 3,000 people in terribly overcrowded and insanitary conditions.

Nevertheless, the Jews were not allowed to leave the ghetto except on business and not at all on Sundays. It was considered that even the sight of them was unacceptable on the Christian Sabbath. The area was, however, relatively safe for its inhabitants, though it was plundered in 1624 and burnt to the ground in 1711. When in 1769 the Jews appealed to the Town Council for permission to live elsewhere, the Council typically called it: 'an example of the unbounded arrogance of the people, who expand every effort to take all opportunities to set themselves up as equals to the Christian citizens'.[1]

They wouldn't be permitted to leave the ghetto for another twenty-seven years. It wasn't surprising that Frankfurt in those days has been described as the 'most oppressive place for Jews to live in Western Europe'.[2] Berlin would have run it a close second, though. Only a small number of rich Jews were allowed to live there. Any Jewish pedlars coming to the city had to use the gate reserved for cattle and Jews: 'Today there passed 6 oxen, 7 swine and a Jew.'[3]

As an example of the blatant anti-Semitism in Frankfurt, as people entered the city they would see a large and disgusting cartoon on the main bridge; the Judensau. It depicted rabbis and a large pig in obscene contact; it had been put there by the city government. In many parts of Germany similar sculptures still exist today in museums and churches and are considered as 'works of art'.

Even so, the chief rabbi in Frankfurt was paid a substantial 600 guilders a year and was also rewarded for the official duties he carried out for individuals – weddings, bar mitzvahs, funerals, etc. He also received free housing. This was in stark contrast with the economic plight of the vast majority of German Jews, who were invariably nearly destitute. As a rabbi in Frankfurt, he wasn't simply a servant of the community but was expected to provide spiritual leadership. In the latter half of the eighteenth century, the Adlers produced a rabbinic leader who was something of a stormy petrel. Rabbi Nathan Adler ('The Pious', 1741–1800) stirred up a lot of controversy in his day and was banned from undertaking rabbinic duties for many years. The Adler family could produce radical as well as conventional rabbis.

Nathan 'The Pious' disagreed with the appointed times of the Sabbath and festivals; he wanted women to wear *tsitsit* (fringed garments); he wanted Ashkenazim to use the Sephardi (Spanish and Portuguese) pronunciation of Hebrew; and more stringent rules for *kashrut* (the dietary laws) to be imposed. He was also a Kabbalist, a follower of the mystic strain of Judaism.

Though he may have attracted few followers for this divisive programme, he was very charismatic and his coterie adored him. Nathan Marcus Adler was named after his rabbinic forebear, even though it was only three weeks before his death that the ban on Nathan 'The Pious' practising as a rabbi was lifted.

The spiritual leaders were closely intertwined. One of Nathan 'The Pious's' pupils was Abraham Bing (1752–1841) who, as a rabbi, would tutor Nathan Marcus Adler and give him his *semichah,* his rabbinical diploma. Nathan 'The Pious' had been a student of David Tevele Schiff (1722–91) who was the chief rabbi in England from 1765–91 and was another member of the Adler family. So Schiff and Nathan Marcus Adler's grandfather were brothers-in-law. Schiff sold his house in the ghetto, no.148, to Mayer Amschel Rothschild and, many years later, the banking family bought 148 Piccadilly as their self-congratulatory London residence.

Over the centuries, the rabbis were constantly faced with the new knowledge which was emerging. They tried to take advantage of new discoveries without altering Jewish law. As, however, society approved of trying to convert the Jews, whatever new knowledge did emerge was likely to be initially suspect to the more pious orthodox members of the Jewish community, simply because of its gentile source. They always feared that it was part of a cunning plan to get the Jews to become baptised. Many rulers, clerics and senior members of society did dangle the possibility of emancipating the Jews, if they made their religion more akin to Christianity. After all, Christianity was an offshoot of Judaism and some of it remained rooted in the Old Testament. If the original Christians could make changes in the tradition, why couldn't the Jews compromise as well? The reward offered was enticing, even if there was no actual intention of delivering it.

If the Jews did convert they might even get a title. As a result, Jonathan Jakob Moses would become Baron Delmar in 1806. It was even possible to get the King of Prussia to become godfather to the child of a Court Jew, often a financial adviser. If the king didn't turn up for the ceremony, it still cost 10 ducats for the honour.

Towards the end of the eighteenth century Rabbi Mordecai Baer Adler (1759–1834), Nathan Marcus' father, went from Frankfurt to Hanover to study at the Michael Davidsche Stifftung. This was a *Beth Hamedrash* (house of learning) founded by Michael David, an eighteenth-century Jewish banker. David invited and supported three Jewish scholars who lived in his house and spent their days studying the Torah. After his death in 1758 his small group continued as a foundation and Mordecai Baer Adler became one of the scholars around 1786. He served as a Rabbinatsverweser (Acting Rabbi) in Hanover and as a Stiftsrabbiner (fund-raiser) in the Michael Davidsche Stifftung from 1802–29.

Hanover's relations with its Jewish community over the years were typical of the oppressive nature of German governments. The incidents may have been different, but the effects were the same. During the Black Death in the fourteenth century the Hanover Jews were driven out of the city because they were suspected of causing the pestilence by poisoning the wells. In 1375 the Duke allowed them back because he needed their banking contacts. To raise some more money, he sold the City Fathers the right to tax the Jews beyond the level demanded of other citizens.

In 1451 it was ordained that all Jews had to wear a circular yellow badge on their clothing. Between 1553 and 1601 there were no less than six Expulsion Orders, though these were either cancelled or not implemented. In 1613 the synagogue was destroyed by a mob. Only twelve Jewish weddings a year were permitted. The De More Judaico oath would continue in force in Hanover until 1850.

Although geographically an integral part of North Germany, Hanover was an anomaly because the King of Hanover was also the King of England. In 1708 the Hanover ruler, George Louis, had been recognized by the Imperial Diet (the Holy Roman Empire general assembly) as an Elector for Hanover. His father, Ernest Augustus, had married Sophia, the granddaughter of James I of England. When eventually George Louis was made King of England in 1715 as George I, Hanover and England became ruled by the same king. George was only 45th in the line of accession to the British throne, but he had the inestimable advantage to the British government in that he was the first Protestant candidate.

Jews had lived in the State for a very long time; the original Hanover cemetery is the oldest in Germany. Opened in 1550, it contains 700 tombstones, a high wall, and a sign telling the public not to destroy or damage any of the graves. The sign is still there. The Jews were only accepted, however, in very small numbers. In about 1700 there were only seventy-two in the state, of whom fifty-one lived in Hanover.

Only rich Jews were allowed to travel through the country and if others were discovered doing so, they would be branded in prison. If they were caught again they would be executed. Traditional Jewish peddling became a dangerous occupation. In 1723 the Judenordnung was passed, placing the Jews under the guardianship of the Duke of Hanover and giving the Duke the right to tax them as a separate entity. This ordinance lasted till 1842. As Mordecai Adler had originally come to Hanover from the Frankfurt Ghetto, he was accustomed to a tight-knit community and long-lasting interfamily friendships which spanned the years. David Tevele Schiff's sister, Jente, married Adler's grandfather, Rabbi Issachar Baer Adler. When Schiff died, he left a legacy to Mordecai Adler.

The Rothschild family also lived in the Frankfurt Ghetto in a red-fronted house. The father, Mayer Amschel Rothschild, was the founder of what would become the greatest banking house of the nineteenth century. So the Adlers and the Rothschilds were neighbours, and connected by marriage, as well as by close bonds of friendship.

Mayer Amschel Rothschild had been orphaned at the age of 12 when his parents died in an epidemic. The lad was sent to be apprenticed to a Jewish court agent in Hanover and stayed there for nearly ten years. He retained an affection for Hanover and, during the Napoleonic Wars on his way through Germany to deal with raising his first government loan, he passed through Hanover and took the opportunity to wake up Mordecai Adler in the small hours of the morning to get his blessing.

That was the depth of the relationship between the Rothschilds and the Adlers. It would come in useful for Nathan Marcus Adler when he applied for the post of chief rabbi in London; the sons and grandsons of Mayer Amschel would still be deeply under their father's influence even after his death in 1812. His word had been law and they would quote him years after his passing. Since Mordecai Adler had been highly regarded by Mayer Amschel Rothschild, his son started as a strong favourite for their vote as chief rabbi in London.

Nathan Mayer Rothschild, the head of Mayer Amschel's London branch, had a grandson in England who would become Lord Rothschild. Mayer Amschel's daughter, Jeanette, married Benedict Worms, and Nathan Marcus Adler's first wife, Henrietta, was from the Worms family. In England the Worms would have an offspring who became Lord Pirbright. So if Adler was going to reach London, he would not be short of very rich and powerful friends in high places.

From 1687–1802 the religious leadership of the Hanover community had been placed in the hands of an official called the Landrabbiner. This appointment was the suggestion of a Hanover court banker, Leffmann Behrens (1630–1714). He was the Elector's financial agent and was admitted to Court in 1673. He was, therefore, one of the Jews who were very welcome to live in the town and his family helped the Elector financially for many years. He proved it was possible to break into the magic circle, as had Jewish army contractors, wholesale merchants, tax gatherers and able administrators. Adler would have learned the lesson.

After Behrens the Jews were given the right in Hanover to vote for and employ a rabbi, who would act as a spokesman for them. In future they were called Protected Jews, to try to ensure their safety from attacks by hooligans. As a tax gatherer for the rulers, though, the Landrabbiner was not always popular within his own community.

He was, however, given authority in spiritual matters and benefited from the substantial salary that the community had to pay. Although he was elected by the community he could only be dismissed by the city authorities. He represented the government in the supervision of synagogues, the teaching in schools and the efforts of Jewish charitable institutions. This level of government-legislated authority would be far greater than that applied to the office of chief rabbi in London when Adler was first appointed.

The Landrabbiner could even fine Jews for not attending synagogue which, with very small communities, was helpful in ensuring there was a *minyan* – a quorum of ten Jews to enable full public worship to be held. He also inspected and appointed all Jewish communal employees throughout the State. His office was, naturally, expensive for the community to maintain though and there were a lot of very poor Jews.

When Nathan Marcus Adler became Landrabbiner of Hanover he undertook these responsibilities, so carrying them out in London would have come naturally to him, even if they weren't in his job specification. He was, if anything, overqualified in London, but then such a wide authority had not been claimed by his predecessors in Britain.

There were five Landrabbiners in Hanover over the 115 years and they were well regarded by the government.[4] However when Behrend Josua Berisch died in 1802 only a few months would elapse before France invaded the State and, indeed, conquered it in the six weeks between May and early July 1803. The window of opportunity had then closed and, with Napoleon's views well known, there would be no Hanover Landrabbiner successor to Rabbi Berisch for decades.

The real importance of Hanover was its key geographical position in relation to transportation on the major German rivers in the days before decent roads and railways. It had a great influence on the trade emanating from Hamburg and Bremen. The main value of Hanover to England, though, was very different. It was normally its ability to provide mercenary troops. When 30,000 French soldiers occupied Hanover in 1803, after the Convention of Artlenburg, the Hanover army was disbanded. Tens of thousands of soldiers then emigrated to England where they were highly regarded by the military. To keep the Hanoverians onside, the British were prepared to provide subventions to the state – £700,000 plus – as they did with many other Continental countries to finance the battles against France. Significantly, a great deal of the money raised in London for this purpose came through the efforts of the Rothschilds.

It wasn't just from a military point of view that Hanover was seriously affected by the Napoleonic Wars. It was also the conflict between different political philosophies. The overthrow of the sixteenth-century House of

Bourbon in France and the success of Napoleon, a ruler who was not born into the aristocracy, put into question all over Europe the absolute right of the established order to rule as they thought fit.

In 1807 Napoleon arranged what he called a Sanhedrin to consider the position of Jews in his new empire. Mordecai Baer Adler went, as part of a German delegation. As a result of the deliberations, and after the delegates agreed to a series of concessions, considerable civil rights were granted to the Jews. It was Napoleon's view that they would be more likely to convert to Christianity if they were treated like other citizens, instead of being persecuted. He was fiercely attacked for his attitude throughout Continental Europe, but refused to budge. Between 1812 and 1819 conversion did, in fact, double, although Jews were still excluded from government posts and from teaching in schools and universities.

Nathan Marcus Adler had been born into a Hanover where, because of the wars, there would be political turmoil for more than ten years. As long ago as 1795 it had been forced to be neutral in the war against France. In 1801 it was occupied by Prussia at the instigation of the Czar. In 1803, by the time of the Convention of Solingen, it had been occupied by the French. Then in 1806 Napoleon allowed Prussia to seize it in exchange for their support, only to defeat them in 1807 at the battle of Jena. So, from 1807–10, Hanover was again ruled by the French, and in 1811 Napoleon incorporated North Hanover into the French Empire.

The British had been able to do little about any of this. While they had remained supreme at sea, they were still not very effective on land, as their performance in losing the American colonies had illustrated. Wellington's victories only really started with the Peninsula War in about 1810.

Mordecai Baer Adler remained a student in Hanover for many years. After Rabbi Berisch died, he, together with his two fellow-scholars, was given the responsibility for the spiritual leadership of the community; they could be described as the town's caretaker rabbis. Within a few years, however, the other rabbis died and when Rabbi Michael Mayer Frensdorff passed away in 1810, only Mordecai Adler was left to lead the flock. This he did from the office of Rabbinatsverweser, combining this with his position as a scholar and teacher in the Michael Davidsche foundation.

Mordecai had married Rebecca Frankel (1767–1861), the daughter of David Frankel, the Chief Rabbi of Hanau, and they had six children. Baer (1784–1866) was the oldest and would become a businessman. Gabriel (1789–1859) would become the Chief Rabbi of Mühringen and Oberdorf. Nathan (1803–90) was the third. He was also brought up to be a Talmudic scholar. Then came a daughter, Hundchen followed by two more boys, Hermann and Benjamin. By the age of 4 Nathan knew the Ten

Commandments, and by the time he was 17 he was making his mark as a Talmudic prodigy, writing *chiddushim*, or novellae, on the Talmudic tractate Chullin.

After Napoleon's defeat, when the Treaty of Vienna was being hammered out in 1814, the delegates intended to retain the equal rights he had granted the Jews in 1807. However, the man who wrote the minutes approved by the delegates was unfortunately anti-Semitic. Johann Smidt, even though he was unauthorised and insignificant in the corridors of power, dealt the Jews a body blow by changing a single word of the covering resolution. Where it had originally been decided that: 'To confessors of the Jewish faith are preserved the rights already conceded to them *in* the confederate States', it now read '...already conceded to them *by* the confederate States.' As a result, it could then be held that if the confederate States had granted the rights – which they hadn't – then they could take them away again – which many did, including Hanover.

At the Congress of Vienna in 1814, George III had been restored as King of Hanover, but England still wanted to keep Britain and Hanover separate. It was the ducal sons of George III who actually carried out the responsibilities of ruling the State, which had been elevated from an Electorate to a Kingdom. The Duke of Cambridge was put in charge as military governor in 1813 and as governor-general in 1816. This was unique. Never before had a member of the British royal family served as governor.

When he appeared before Hanover's Estates General in 1814, he said that the deputies should be the legal council of the nation, but these were really only words. When the Estate asked that the newly formed militia should not be used overseas, George IV rejected the request. The British were held in awe at the time and 'base fear and grovelling respect greeted Englishmen who came to Hanover'.[5]

Another result of the Treaty of Versailles was that Hanover became considerably larger, as part of a new German Confederation. Where it had been slightly bigger than Yorkshire, it now absorbed East Friesland, Hildesheim and Langen which massively expanded the territory. The treaty brought, within Lutheran Hanover, provinces like Hildesheim and Osnabruck which had Catholic majorities, and their claims to equal citizenship should have made it easier to justify the case for similar treatment for the Jews. There was still a fear, though, that emancipating the Jews might undermine the Christian State, though how precisely this result would come about was, inevitably, left very vague.

The Catholics presented the State government with a greater challenge than the Jews, because of their allegiance to the Pope. George IV did extend equal political rights to Hanoverian Catholics in 1824, and this made it difficult for the British government to resist Catholic emancipation in Britain, which took place in 1829. It didn't, however, affect the position of the Jews. In spite of Catholic emancipation in England, there was no similar move for the Jews in Hanover.

Germany in 1815 was an agricultural country without heavy industries or an independent merchant or manufacturing class. There were only handicrafts, with no coal mines or factories. Seventy-five per cent of the population lived in tiny villages. In Hanover the British government did not provide a fund for reconstruction, and it had to recover from the war as best it could. There was a small subvention but it was frittered away and prices collapsed.

The Jews filled some of the gaps where they had friends and business contacts abroad. Financing the Industrial Revolution as it spread involved international bond sales. When they could provide the State with such services, those Jews involved were tolerated and even treated with some respect. Simon Oppenheim, the son of the founder of the Salomon Oppenheim bank, had been elected President of the Cologne Chamber of Commerce as long ago as 1806.

The international fraternity of Jewish bankers stretched over the centuries and would make ideal agents in future for raising the money needed for major projects, like the railways. Those Jews working in the wider world now adopted surnames, rather than the traditional nomenclature of the first name followed by that of the father: Joseph ben Jacob, for example.

In 1819 there was a nominal new constitution in Hanover. The government was, in some ways, similar in form to the British. There were two chambers, and the peasants were included. They had no real power, however: they spent their time on bureaucratic minutiae and on carping at the state of the nation.

Many of the younger generation had no wish to go back to the way things were before the French Revolution. They had fought in the war for the allies and they felt they deserved better than to be placed once more under the rule of the nobles. They formed student societies – Burschenschaften – and each member carried a ceremonial dagger. In March 1819 one of their number used it to murder a minor functionary, and in August 1819 campus disturbances broke out in Wartzburg. They were known as the Hip Hip riots. The protesters wanted more freedom. There were also demonstrations against Jews; the disturbances lasted, primarily at universities, for some time. Hundreds of Jews emigrated to Denmark in fear of their lives. There were, in fact, only two deaths and about twenty wounded, and the riots petered out when the ringleaders eventually left their colleges, though the universities remained centres of liberalism.

The memories of those days and the outbreak of anti-Semitism would, however, have remained with the now adolescent Adler. He would also have noticed that there were no complaints from upper-class Jews about the riots. The divisions between the different Jewish classes and age groups in Germany ensured that concerted communal action was not an option. It was a foretaste of the different viewpoints he would encounter in Britain between the immigrant Jews of the East End of London and the longer established community.

As a result of the student riots, the Carlsbad Decrees were promulgated later in 1819. These banned nationalist fraternities, removed liberal university professors from their posts and expanded press censorship. The decrees would be revived in 1834 when Adler was the Landrabbiner in Hanover. He had always to take the political situation into account in protecting the Jewish communities under his control.

The chopping and changing of rulers made it necessary for the German Jews to be extremely careful about who they supported. Napoleon may have given them emancipation but, after he was beaten, they were once again barred from the professions if they didn't have Letters of Protection. They also remained banned from public office, the army and teaching. Their rights to work, settle and marry were once again restricted. The Registration Certificate for marriage (usually only possible for the oldest son), the Matrikel, could cost 1,000 guilden (about 10,000 grams of silver). If the other children married, they would have to leave the town to enable the government to keep the number of Jews down.

The Jews were again heavily taxed. They were portrayed as upstarts who were trying to take over the financial sector of the economy. There was a fear that they would provide fierce competition for the members of guilds if they were allowed to join them. Not surprisingly, many of the Jews decided to emigrate and a lot finished up in British provincial communities.

Over Germany as a whole, Jewish communities could lose 70 per cent of their members as a result of the discrimination. By contrast, the number of Jews in Hanover itself increased when, in 1830, the new William IV in England endorsed a more liberal regime, agreeing with his brother, the Duke of Cambridge, who was his representative until the king died in 1837.

Napoleon had gathered the 333 German territories he inherited into a much smaller number of large principalities. That new system, effectively, continued after he was gone; it was now called the German Confederation. So, in 1814, the noble families took over in Germany again. The Confederation did provide for constitutional assemblies but these were, basically, talking shops, and real power remained solely in the hands of the rulers. There were no real political movements and only lip service was paid to them after Napoleon's defeat. What the older generation wanted was a quiet life. For the next thirty years this was achieved with only minor problems.

The Confederation was made up of thirty-eight States. Hanover was, geographically, the fourth largest, after Austria, Prussia and Bavaria. The nobility certainly weren't in favour of Germany becoming one country, as this was seen as a potential threat to their local power. The noble families didn't want the masses to have real political rights either; the favoured system was to continue to limit important jobs to the scions of noble families.[6]

The consequence was that largely incompetent aristocrats came to be the heads of administration. Austria and Prussia were the most important voices, with Klemens von Metternich, the Austrian Chancellor, effectively in charge. In his turn, Metternich relied on Salomon Rothschild, who ran the Vienna branch of the bank, to finance reconstruction after Napoleon.

There was, however, a growth in nationalism among the ordinary people and the Jews had to deal with accusations of not being sufficiently patriotic. Although large numbers had fought bravely against Napoleon, the Emperor's emancipation decrees cast doubt on whether the Jews preferred the conditions of his rule. This charge of not being patriotic was further bolstered by traditional Jewish prayers for a return to the promised land of Israel. These had been part of religious services since ancient times. Even so, they invited accusations of chauvinism, resulting in the suggestion that if Jews wanted to live in the Holy Land, then they weren't patriotically inclined towards Germany.

For the Jews there were now two contentious areas; first, the different views on the state of Judaism itself, which led to the Reform movement. Second, the oppression of the local governments. Of course, the Jews could avoid both problems by giving up Judaism and converting to Christianity. By that one action all the discrimination would disappear and often their lives could be saved. They would be able to conform, escape stigma, gain professional rights, bolster their social status and, potentially, gain government and academic posts. Many accepted the opportunity, but those who turned down the offer would devote a substantial part of their lives to maintaining Orthodox Judaism. As far as they were concerned, nothing would begin to rank in importance with that objective.

Nathan Marcus Adler was, of course, an Orthodox Jew and would defend Orthodox Judaism all his life. One noted Jewish historian has said of his ministry in London: 'He created an authoritarian episcopal system that swept away congregational autonomy and rabbinical independence.' As a result: 'The stifling of religious innovation robbed communal life of the intellectual ferment ... in more open pluralistic communities that stimulated the creation of scholarship and religious thought across the denominational spectrum.'[7]

What is not taken into account in this analysis is the prime objective for Nathan Marcus Adler – and all Orthodox Jews – of maintaining the religion in a form which accorded with tradition. No Orthodox Chief Rabbi was going to give a higher priority to intellectual ferment, scholarship or alterations in religious thought, than he did to the maintenance of the *din* (law).

Adler could properly maintain that this was the job specification set out by every community who elected him. If it involved the sacrifice of congregational sovereignty, scholarship or radical religious thought, then so be it. In any case few laymen were learned or interested enough to take Jewish thinking seriously. If they spoke about religious change it was generally in the hope of legislation to emancipate the Jews, since there was a perception that synagogues (and rabbis) were out of date.

The amendment of Jewish religious laws which involved unwelcome discipline for the adherent was another issue, as was the fashionable popularity of the Enlightenment. On the Continent the growth of alternatives to Orthodox Judaism was a more intellectual movement than in England, which was more pragmatic than philosophical or spiritual.

Academics might decry strict adherence to orthodox principles, but it must be recognized that the vast majority of the Jewish communities Adler served in his lifetime did not. On the whole they were respectful of the *din*, and their (even nominal) Orthodoxy was largely a matter of habit.

On the question of sweeping away congregational autonomy in English communities, it is like suggesting that a Magistrates Court should replace the Supreme Court. Only the tiniest of percentages of the lay members of congregations had the necessary Talmudic expertise to lay down the law, and their decisions on religious questions would have carried no weight outside their congregation without the chief rabbi's imprimatur.

The same applied to those holding religious office. When Nathan Marcus Adler arrived in London, he would find the general Talmudic standard of his congregation ministers totally inadequate. The situation was not that much better in Hanover, particularly in rural areas.

Adler's approach could – and can – be criticized by those who don't consider upholding the Written and Oral Laws to be that important. Christianity was an early breakaway movement from Judaism and took that view. Orthodox Jews did not, and they suffered for it grievously over the millennia.

On the Continent the conservative nature of Orthodox Judaism was under attack. One factor was the growth of scientific knowledge and the stirrings of democracy which had led to 'The Era of Enlightenment'; reason rather than tradition became the buzzword. The philosophic outlook of the secular world in much of Europe, which replaced the supremacy of the Almighty by the pre-eminence of man, was continuing to slowly change. This would inevitably be mirrored in Jewish circles.

The advocates of the Enlightenment position embraced change. The thinking was that if something was traditional, it could probably be improved. Therefore, it was proposed that what they considered old shibboleths should be abandoned and scientific thought become the new philosophic role model. Many books emerged concerned with different aspects of Jewish theology, though not so many in England.

It had been the French Revolution which really triggered the great growth in popularity of Enlightenment thinking. After 1789 it showed that it was possible to overthrow a system by which rulers dictated and the ordinary citizen had no say; that it might be possible instead to achieve a fairer distribution of taxation, a fairer legal system, improved parliamentary democracy and a constitution. The belief also grew that it might just be feasible that all men may, in the long term future, be equal. It was a heady prospect and, as Napoleon's armies swept through Europe, there were massive changes, including the emancipation of the Jews.

Of course, the Jews could see the sense of welcoming the Enlightenment. It might even mean that the superstitious accusations against them – blood libels, poisoning wells, spreading plagues – could at last lose credibility. That instead of being treated as pariahs, they might gain equality. No longer would they be confined to the ghetto. They might even be able to work for the state.

That was the pot of gold at the end of the rainbow and European Jewish minds turned to what they could do, for their own part, to bring about this miraculous change. For centuries emancipation had seemed unattainable and its possible achievement had a tremendous attraction. On the other hand the Orthodox were sure that the traditional laws in the Babylonian Talmud needed to be protected, to underpin the sheer existence of traditional Judaism. Change was a double-edged sword.

Of course, not all European Christians were philosophically antagonistic to the Jews. Soon after Adler died, a French historian, A. Leroy Beaulieu, wrote:

> Their children were taught to read from the scrolls of the Torah before our Latin alphabet had reached its final form ... As compared with the Jews, we are young, we are newcomers; in the matter of civilization they are far ahead of us. It was in vain we locked them up for several hundred years behind the walls of the ghetto. No sooner were their prison gates unbarred than they easily caught up with us.'[8]

The Jews themselves were often ambivalent. It is one thing to accept the law; it is another to live by it. Where you might feel that large scale smuggling should be a criminal offence, you might also believe that bringing in an extra bottle of whisky is not the end of the world. So it is with Orthodox Jews. The level of observance varied. There were Jews who could be described as Ultra-orthodox and there were many Orthodox Jews who ate non-kosher meat and were seldom seen in the synagogue.

In Judaism, however, there is no priesthood. Nobody to hand out punishments for non-observance. Dealing with sin is strictly between the individual and the Almighty. So Adler's position, throughout his life, would be that he defended the law in its entirety, but was not going to set out to insist on standards for his congregants that they weren't going to manage. He accepted a middle-of-the-road level of observance, even though he always sought to upgrade the level.

As a consequence he was not considered sufficiently strict to merit the recognition of the Ultra-orthodox communities if and where they existed. At the other end of the scale, his authority was also rejected by those who wanted to break away from Orthodoxy. An additional complication was that, on occasion, there was a wish to wrest authority from him and place it in the hands of the local congregations. A breakaway could possibly be a disguised take-over bid.

There were financial risks involved in attempting to achieve emancipation. When the Jews were initially offered it in Frankfurt, at Napoleon's insistence, there was a hefty charge for their freedom from discrimination. The cost was 400,000 guilders (about £18 million today), half of which was raised by the Rothschilds. When, however, Napoleon was in retreat, in 1811, the money was declared forfeit. It was deeply ironic that Jewish bankers might sometimes be accused of sharp practices, but they were still supposed to accept with equanimity the behaviour of authorities like German governments.

As far as religious change was concerned, most British Jews were genuinely wedded to Orthodoxy. They believed that the traditional laws set down in the Babylonian Talmud were God-given, and fundamental. Any change was suspect and some of the reluctance of many nineteenth-century Orthodox lay leaders in London to endorse the efforts to achieve total emancipation was because it might weaken Jewish practice. The other problem with change was that it was never possible to know where it would stop.

In the seventeenth century, for example, there had been a charismatic rabbi called Sabbatei Zevi who had attracted an enormous following when he was proclaimed to be the Messiah. He finished up making the solemn fast of Tisha b'Av into a festival, because it was his birthday! And he converted to

Islam! Memories of the chaos caused within Jewry by the false messiah did not fade. A couple of hundred years in Jewish history is not a long time. Nevertheless, many Jews in Germany began to wonder if their basic emancipation on the Continent might become a reality sooner if they 'modernised' Judaism.

On the Continent, the idea of trying to 'modernise' the religion, did become more acceptable in the new climate. There was felt to be a widespread opinion among government officials that as long as the Jews did not abandon their ceremonial laws, emancipation could not become an established fact. Conversion was the option governments preferred, as they always had, but now change seemed to less Orthodox Jews to be a more rational way forward. To its opponents, though, it was a decision 'to trade their nationhood for a pottage of illusory emancipation'.

The modernising dam broke when, in Hamburg in 1818, sixty-five heads of Jewish families started a Reform congregation, only 100 miles from Hanover. As a start they produced their own prayer book, which considerably changed the traditional liturgy.

The Hamburg community were following in the footsteps of Israel Jacobson, a Jewish banker, who had started a non-sectarian boarding school in Seesen near Hanover in 1801. Jacobson was the financial agent for the King of Westphalia and he had opened a synagogue in 1810 where the hymns were in German, there was an abbreviated prayer book produced by two laymen, plus a choir and an organ.

The Hamburg reformers were, of course, acting independently and the congregation was immediately denounced by any number of Orthodox rabbis; philosophic arguments between the camps have raged ever since. The perceived weakness of the Reform advocates was that they represented a protest movement, rather than something positive.[9]

Mordecai Adler had long pondered the decision he had to make on where he stood with regard to the world in which he found himself. Should he follow the new Reform programme of changing the religion to have a better chance of the Jews being emancipated? Or should he find a middle road which took advantage of secular learning, but retained all the elements of Jewish law? Or should he stick to the view of the highly traditional Jews that anything German was *trefah* (unclean), including the language? Only the Yiddish, Judendeutsch and Hebrew languages were acceptable to the very pious.[10]

The extreme wing of the Orthodox was always desperately concerned about what they conceived as the possible contamination of Judaism by other cultures. It was well known that it had been a grave threat at the time of the Greek Empire; the rabbis had struggled to ensure the Jews didn't adopt the Greek approach to life. The Greek experience had passed down the centuries as a warning of what could happen if relations became too close. Some Orthodox rabbis even went so far as to ban Maimonides' *Guide to the Perplexed*, one of the greatest Jewish works of the Middle Ages, because it sought to reconcile Aristotle with Jewish philosophy.

Mordecai Adler's final decision would obviously have a major effect on the outlook of his sons. Nathan would be an equally strong influence on his own children. Mordecai Adler had to decide if Nathan would just receive a Talmudic education, or if he would take the unusual step of also sending him to university. He finally opted for college, though he would protect every Jewish tradition throughout his life. For example, when there was a proposal in Hanover to bury Jews after forty-eight hours instead of on the same day, Mordecai opposed it vigorously.

The students at the time were not judged by their record of attendance at lectures. They were simply given their diplomas on the basis of their exam results when they had finished the individual seminars. At Erlangen, though, it was said that: 'diplomas could be obtained by non-residents, without either examination or thesis'.[11] So the standards of academic discipline in some universities might have been somewhat fluid.

Nathan would go to university, learn German as well as Hebrew and Yiddish, and be the first rabbi in Germany to gain a doctorate. Many other rabbis would follow in his footsteps. Jews had, in fact, been allowed to attend the State University of Göttingen before 1800 and the names of over thirty Jewish youngsters who were awarded medical degrees in those early years remain on record. The first Jew to get a law degree was also at Göttingen. The very Orthodox remained averse to secular education; there was a saying among them that when rabbis became doctors, Judaism became sick.

Mordecai Baer Adler recognized that it was too late for him to get the secular knowledge that was now required by Hanover for the position of Landrabbiner. There was, however, no reason to deprive his son, Nathan, of the opportunity. At the Universities of Göttingen, Erlangen, Würzburg and Heidelberg, Nathan eventually had testimonials that he had studied the Bible, logic, theoretical philosophy, political economy, oratory, mathematics and philology. Plus Grecian mythology, practical philosophy and universal history, as well as the Chaldaic and Syrian languages.

University education at the time meant different systems in different localities. Students could be in residence for the period of the seminar, but there wasn't always a residential requirement when studying for a doctorate. The main general requirement was for a professor to act as their supervisor. There was a Jewish association in Heidelberg to help finance poor students which might have helped Mordecai Baer with Nathan's fees, and he may well have stayed with a Jewish family while he studied.

There was a propensity among students for transferring from one university to another. There were two university semesters; one from April to July and the other from October to February. After finishing one semester, it was perfectly acceptable to move to another university.

Göttingen, located within the State of Hanover, was known as the 'university for the elegant world'. This was because of the number of students it attracted from well-to-do families. It had been founded by George II and richly endowed by George III. One of its former students was the Duke of Cambridge; Bismarck was a student there as well. The brothers Grimm (of fairy tales fame) taught there, and the university had a reputation for being the best of the Beamtenuniversitaeten, famous for training German bureaucrats.

The Göttingen atmosphere would have improved Nathan's sophistication. Erlangen was well known for its teaching of philosophic subjects. Nathan's doctoral thesis at Erlangen in March 1828 was on De idea summi numinis – The Concept of a Supreme Being – which neatly married the academic and religious viewpoints. He was awarded the title Doctoris Philosophice et AA. LL. Magistri after having shown 'laudabilis eruditionis specimina'.[12]

In 1828 he received *semichah* from Chief Rabbi Abraham Bing's seminary in Würzburg which was highly regarded throughout the Jewish world. Bing had initially been taught by David Tevele Schiff, and had started his seminary in 1813 after managing to overturn a 250-year-old edict which forbade Jews to even live in Würzburg. At the university Nathan was much influenced by Friedrich Rückert, a professor of Semitic languages and a well-known poet.

In Hanover Mordecai Baer Adler dealt with the aristocrats and officials who ruled the state. Court offices remained lucrative sinecures for the nobility. After they became kings of England, the Georgian monarchs were seldom in Hanover. Indeed George III never visited his German State. George IV went once after the death of his estranged wife, Caroline, in 1821. His brother, William IV, went on only one occasion as well.

Hanover had its own ambassadors and the kings in London still left the running of the country to the local nobles, who advised the monarch. The advice the nobles provided was, of course, likely to reflect well on their actions. The consistent absence of the monarch was the justification for the exercise of ministerial despotism. 'No British law was observed in Hanover. No Briton was employed there. The English parliament never attempted to spread and apply its ordinances to Hanover, let alone trouble itself with Hanover at all.'[13] The State remained arch-conservative, with little innovation or modernity. It simply stagnated socially and economically.

The government did consider appointing Mordecai Baer Adler as Landrabbiner in 1823, but were advised by their officials that the rabbi was not capable of undertaking the role because he was 63 years old, didn't speak German and knew nothing of the laws he would have to administer. The rabbi had correctly anticipated that secular knowledge would be needed if Landrabbiners were reintroduced, and while he had made sure that Nathan received the necessary education, it was now too late for Mordecai himself. One possible solution, of course, was for him to be assisted by Nathan, but the lad was only 20 years old and considered too young. Furthermore he still had two years to study at Göttingen and he had yet to get his *semichah*. The decision was accordingly delayed.

The question of Landrabbiners came up again in 1826 and was put off once more. What was certain, however, was that Nathan was becoming well known as a young man of exceptional promise. The arguments raged on, to the extent that the city official charged with the final decision almost had a nervous breakdown.

A vote on a joint Landrabbinate was held in 1827 all over the State and 486 voted to accept the proposal for father and son to work in concert. They were mostly the young people and there were 156 votes against. The government still wouldn't agree with the majority. They accepted the argument of the dissenters that the community simply couldn't afford the cost and they did so again in 1829.

Notes

1. Wikepedia, 'Frankfurter Judengasse'.
2. Amos Elon, *The Pity of It All: A Portrait of the German-Jewish Epoch, 1743–1933* (Harmondsworth: Penguin Books, 2004), p.25.
3. Ibid., p.23.
4. The Hanover Landrabbiners were Joseph Meschullam Süszel Cohen (1687–1703); Joseph Meyer Friedberg (1704–35); Isaak Selig Karo (1737–58); Levi Josua Liebusch (1761–89); Behrend Josua Berisch (1789–1802).
5. Nick Harding, *Hanover and The British Empire, 1700–1837* (Martlesham: The Boydell Press, 2007), p.245.
6. A.J.P. Taylor, *The Course of German History* (London: Routledge, 2001).
7. Todd M. Endelman, *The Jews of Britain 1656–2000* (Berkeley, CA: University of Californian Press, 2002), p.116.
8. Quoted in Derek Taylor, *Chief Rabbi Hertz. The Wars of the Lord* (London and Portland, OR: Vallentine Mitchell, 2014), p.108.
9. Dow Marmur (ed.), *Reform Judaism* (London: Reform Synagogues of Great Britain, 1973), p.15.
10. Judendeutsch was a kind of German with the words having Hebrew endings.
11. Meir Persoff, *Hats in the Ring: Choosing Britain's Chief Rabbis from Adler to Sacks* (Boston, MA: Academic Studies Press, 2013), p.23.
12. Michael Friedländer, *Jewish Quarterly Review*, July 1890.
13. Harding, *Hanover and The British Empire*.

2

The Hanover Years

Having obtained his *semichah*, Nathan now needed a job. He went back to Frankfurt and became a naturalized citizen in 1829, by decree of the Senate, when he got married to Henrietta Rachel Hitzel Worms. There were still restrictions on the number of permissible Jewish marriages in the town, though, with an annual limit of only thirty.

Henrietta was the sister of Baron Soloman Benedict de Worms, who would become the father of Lord Pirbright in England. She was also related to the Rothschilds and Henrietta's sister married Adler's brother, Baer. Their first-born, Sarah, was safely delivered the following year.

> Dr N.M. Adler, son of a Jewish citizen, having passed the examination which the decree of the 27th of January had ordered, may, as a private teacher of Oriental languages, Jewish theology and philosophy, be admitted to taking the oath of a Jewish citizen on the occasion of his marriage with Henrietta Worms, the daughter of a Jewish citizen, and that this decision be communicated to the Income-tax Commission and the Council of the Jewish Community.[1]

The negotiations to allow his marriage had been delicate:

> Such a decree was not easily obtained. The learned man was asked to serve a term as a soldier, which he did, though the 'term' did not seem to be longer than an academic term. He was also asked to make a material contribution towards the purchase of a fire bucket and a new gun and to pay his gate-closing and other municipal fees.[2]

After unsuccessfully applying for a rabbinical post in Denmark, in 1829 he was chosen by the Jewish community in Oldenburg, near Hanover to be recommended to the Grand Duke as their choice for the position of Landrabbiner. He was interviewed for the position by the Duke and learned at this early age how to behave in the presence of royalty.

The rabbi in Oldenburg would also be under the control of the government. He couldn't appoint teachers or endorse other rabbis without government permission. Any new religious text book had to be approved by the State as well, but he could supervise the synagogue and school and he had to make regular reports to the Oldenburg government.

From the point of view of the aged Duke, a loyal and established ecclesiastical hierarchy was a strong conservative element in a world now heavily influenced by the Napoleonic legacy of equal rights. Such hierarchies existed in the church and the Jewish community was encouraged to follow in their footsteps. The objective, of course, was to ensure support for the State.

When Adler was inducted in Oldenburg, on 6 June 1829, he gave his inaugural sermon to his mixed audience in German. This made a definite statement. It placed him in the ranks of those who believed that the German language should be on a par with Hebrew, Yiddish and Judendeutsch, and could be used for sermons, a belief pioneered by a few rabbis in other parts of the State. It announced that he was not going to be an Orthodox minister in the tradition of rejecting anything in German as unacceptable. In Jewish circles that was still controversial. In Prussia there were Jewish Wardens of the Poor and if a Jew was found with a German book in his possession, it was not unknown for him to be evicted from the town. By speaking in German, Adler also made it clear that, although he had only recently become a rabbi, he was his own man. It was in the spirit of the students he had known at university; a belief that some secular things needed to be changed. It was a courageous stance to declare his views in such a public manner. Accepting German also advanced the possibility of better relations between the Jewish and non-Jewish communities. The Duke of Oldenburg had died in the meantime, but Adler toed the party line and described the new Duke as 'our new father, our new protector'.

The form of his sermon was constructed in the same style that he would adopt throughout his ministry:

> It was couched in a well-chosen language of noble sentiment and devoid of platitudes. It was never scholarly; it never informed; it always preached ... it opened with a short introduction and led on to a main topic that was linked with a passage from the Bible. Then followed a well divided and subdivided main exposition which was finally concluded by a prayer.[3]

He was soon offered a larger pulpit in Cassell but rejected it. He was making progress in Oldenburg where the terms of the De More Judaico oath were ameliorated while he was in office. He did move on to Hanover in August 1830, though, when applications for Landrabbiner were invited. His approval by the new Duke of Oldenburg would have stood him in good stead when he applied for the position. The Hanover government considered him 'the obvious choice for the post'.[4] He was regarded as an, 'educated Jew whose breadth of learning served to enhance rather than diminish his Jewish identity and competence',[5] and he left Oldenburg with a government testimonial which said that he was regular, punctual, and conscientious in the performance of his duties. His own community said he was a trustworthy judge on religious questions, a pillar of Jewish faith, a true guide and excellent preacher, speaking to the heart as well as to the mind.

In Hanover, in spite of its English connection, the laws contained legislation which was horribly anti-Semitic, and would never have been enforced in an English court. It was 'Hanging Judge' Jeffries in Charles II's time who had declared, for example, that the oath of a Jew was as good as that of a Christian. The only argument in Britain on the oath was the phrase, 'On the true word of a Christian' which was required for candidates for public office, though not in court. Jews didn't get that kind of support in Germany. Frederick William IV of Prussia would rail at the, 'despicable clique of Jews who, in their speech, writing and example, daily strike at the root of what is German'.

In spite of all his efforts, Adler failed until the last days of his ministry in Hanover to get much of the anti-Semitic legislation changed. Jews had to pay Stolgebühren which was a tax given to the Church whenever a Jew was born, married or died, and the De More Judaico was not abolished. The Stolgebühren also had to be paid for a letter permitting them to live in the State. The most that could be said in favour of the government was that there was no Judensau image.

England, by contrast, was deservedly regarded as a citadel of democracy, although the London *Evening Standard*, commenting on the growth of radicalism prior to the uprisings of 1848, claimed that 'all the mischief now brooding on the Continent is done by Jews'.

Oldenburg had been a very small Jewish community with only eighty Jews in 1820. Adler was now invited to become the Hanover Landrabbiner and when he departed from Oldenburg there were only fifteen Jewish families left in the town. He recommended as his successor a young 22 year-old rabbi, Samson Raphael Hirsch, who would become a powerful influence on Orthodox Jewry by creating a system known as *Torah im Derech Eretz*, an ancient phrase given a new connotation. It entailed taking advantage of Western culture, but distancing Jewish communities from the Christian practices of their fellow citizens which were considered unacceptable.

It takes a great deal of dedication to become a rabbi and to practice it as a profession. When Adler was in Oldenburg the community was taxed to pay his salary. Only they either didn't have the money or didn't want to pay it. Fortunately for Adler there was one rich Jew in Oldenburg who made up the deficit while he was in office.[6]

In Oldenburg Hirsch lived a poverty stricken life. He appealed to the government which had appointed him. They brusquely replied that they didn't care if the system of Landrabbiners was abandoned and, if he wasn't satisfied, he could always leave. Eventually he did, but in the meantime, his official duties were minimal and he devoted his time to study and writing.

He stayed for eleven years in all but, as he wrote in 1838, 'Jews lived in tiny scattered villages, most of them with no more than five or ten Jewish homes and some with as few as two. Except for Hamburg and Altona there is no community of more than 20 families.'[7]

These were the kinds of communities which Adler led and, when he came to London, he would find a far larger canvas on which to put his mark. To a considerable extent, however, he used the same approaches in London that had stood him in good stead in Hanover. Adler was a man of his time, facing the contemporary challenges and dedicated to upholding Orthodox Judaism in the face of them.

The marriage of Nathan and Henrietta would prove to be a very happy one. Over the next ten years they had five children, Sarah (1830–1907), Jeanette (1832–1920), Minna, (1833–1906), Marcus (1837–1911) and Hermann (1839–1911). Other influential members of the Worms family would also finish up in London.

Sarah married Henry Solomon, a City merchant in London. Jeanette married Rabbi Anschel Stern, the Chief Rabbi of Hamburg. Minna married Jacob Israel, then a linen and general merchant in Berlin. Marcus became an actuary for an insurance company in London, and Hermann followed his father as Chief Rabbi.

After Oldenburg, the Adlers came home to provincial Hanover where Nathan had grown up. Only a quarter of Germans lived in towns, so that the entire urban population of Germany was only half that of Paris. Hanover itself was very quiet, little more than a large village, though it ranked at the time as a small city with its administrative, military, business and cultural elements. There were two main boulevards – Georgstrasse and Friedrichstrasse – and some fine buildings like the Herrenhausen Palace which was the summer residence of the royal family. George II was born there.

There were also a number of splendid gardens. In 1817 George III had bought some eighteenth-century grounds which he renamed the Georgengarten. In the Adlers' time it was laid out as an English landscape garden and the area was also noted for its botanical park, the Berggarten. As a market town, Hanover could boast the huge fourteenth-century Marketkirche which became one of the principal Lutheran churches. Intellectually, they would have one of the first art societies, which was created in 1832. This was the setting in which Adler was to be the rabbinic leader for the next fifteeen years.

It was some time before he took up his new post. Eventually, the Hanover government had to threaten that they would assume he had resigned if he didn't occupy his new office immediately. He was at last installed in August 1830 with the church bells ringing and an inaugural procession. There were friendly articles in the newspapers and royal approval of the appointment. For a 27 year old, it would have been a heady experience.

It was, however, a homecoming which needed sensitive handling as he was going to be the Landrabbiner and therefore senior to his father, who would only live until 1834. This probably accounted for his slowness in taking up the position. He knew his father was vastly more experienced than he was, and had carried out the work for years, even if he lacked the title. He probably needed persuasion by his father to accept the role, though it was the culmination of his father's training and planning for his son. It was certainly an excellent career move.

His preparation for the task had been thorough. From his earliest childhood he had been able to observe his father at work. He had enjoyed the best of tuition in both the secular and religious fields. He understood the pressures of the period and he was committed to following in his father's footsteps.

At the same time he needed the practical experience of being responsible for a sizeable community. He was only the Landrabbiner for Hanover with its 537 Jews. It was the capital of the State, but there were three independently run districts at the time: Hanover, East Frisia and Hildesheim. Rabbi Abraham Lowenstamm in East Frisia was particularly influential, as was Levi Bodenheimer in Hildesheim. Both were strong voices for Orthodoxy.

In Hanover, where the ruler was all-powerful, it was more important to be on good terms with him than to rely on the impartiality of the law. Adler understood this very well and took care to ensure that, almost as soon as he arrived, there was a suitable memorial service for George IV. He could, of course, speak impeccable Hochdeutsch, the superior version of German, which would have made the service even more impressive. There were also special prayers written in English.

The effective ruler of Hanover remained Adolph Frederick, the Duke of Cambridge (1774–1850), who had now been appointed Viceroy by William IV back in London. He was the seventh son of George III and was both Governor-General and a Field Marshal. As a young man he had been described by an English lady visiting Hanover in 1847 as, 'Extremely handsome, tall and finely formed with a fair complexion and regular features, charming manners and a flood of amusing conversation.' In the family he was known as Dolly. It was a good image for a country dominated by the aristocratic families. The Germans remained servile and obedient to their thirty-six despotic rulers.

Unlike most of George III's progeny, the Duke of Cambridge had always lived within his means and there had been no scandals to besmirch his name. He was sympathetic to the Jews – he had attended a service at the Great Synagogue in London in 1809 – but he had been appointed by the court in England to avoid trouble while Hanover settled down after Napoleon, and this was his prime concern.

Like George III and IV before him, William IV was quite content to be advised by his appointees in Hanover, but as one government official pointed out: 'The less the ruler knows his subjects and servants personally, the greater the ministers' influence. Even if the latter are honest, their increasing power cannot help but hurt the constitution.'[8]

This was obvious to those working with the establishment, and Adler would not have failed to learn the lesson. In England, as chief rabbi, he would make strenuous and continuous efforts to get to know his communities and their leaders throughout the country, rather than delegate the task to anybody else.

When Adler took up his post in 1830 a revolution in France had finally ousted the Bourbons. The uprisings spread, and the Treaty of London had to create Belgium to pacify those who didn't want to remain Dutch. There was considerable concern that Europe might be plunged into a new round of Napoleonic-type wars, but since nobody really wanted a major conflict, everything quietened down in a few years.

Nevertheless, it was not the right political atmosphere for Jews to achieve further emancipation. The elders and deacons of the Hanover Jewish community appealed to the government in 1831 for the full rights of citizenship, but their pleas fell on deaf ears. There was a major debate in 1832 in the largest local paper, the *Hannoversche Zeitung*, on whether the Jews should be emancipated, and most of the contributors were clearly against the idea.

The Times in London was particularly scathing about the government of Hanover. It labelled it the worst governed state in Germany, with the absentee monarch akin to an absentee landlord: 'The accountancy of the aristocracy over the people was nowhere asserted with more insolence or exercised with greater oppression.'[9] This was not quite how it appeared in Germany. There were more despotic governments than Hanover, and the Duke of Cambridge had introduced a less autocratic regime. He had even allowed the *Hannoversche Zeitung* to be published without pre-censorship, but Hanover was no democracy.

The Confederation of German States had declined into a farce. In 1834, for example, its leader, Klemens von Metternich, the Austrian Chancellor, got the reactionary Carlsbad Decrees revived. A federal court was created, but it never met. The states paid dues to the Confederation, but these were mostly left on deposit with the Rothschilds in Frankfurt. Every year the financial position of the individual states deteriorated, with the single exception of Prussia. Administration continued to take the place of government.

The attempt to achieve Jewish emancipation led to all kinds of proposals to make the case for the Jews more credible. On many occasions influential Christian officials said that, if Jewish practices became more like those of the Protestant Church, it would help matters. When Reform communities were formed, they did make such changes: ministers adopted conventional clerical garb, and organs were installed in synagogues. Choirs were established, synagogue architecture was modernised and German replaced Hebrew for many of the prayers. As the years went by, many more fundamental elements in Orthodox Judaism would be recommended for abolition or amendment.

Adler had no intention of standing by and letting the *halachah* be undermined by small radical pressure groups, even if they included influential Jewish leaders. The majority of the Jews in the State remained Orthodox. Only two years after his installation, in September 1832, Adler produced a set of regulations for his synagogues: the *Allgemeine Synagogen-Ordnung für die Israeliten des hiesigen Land-Rabbiner-Bezirks* – the rules for his district. They were designed to push forward improvements of synagogues, schools and congregations.

Many of the ordinances were aimed at improving the decorum in synagogue. One complaint by Christians about Jewish services was that they were too noisy. Now, for example, there was to be no banging when the name of Haman was mentioned during the Purim service. No children under the age of 5 could come to synagogue. No unreasonably noisy lamenting would be tolerated on the fast of Tisha b'Av, which commemorated the destruction of both Temples.

Disturbances during the services would lead to fines, as would gathering in front of the synagogue before or after the service. There were detailed rules for attending services; if there wasn't a *minyan* (10 adult male Jews) for a formal service, then anybody over 13 in the congregation could be called from their home to make up the numbers. Refusal could lead to a fine as well. Moreover, if the fines weren't paid, a list would be given to the local government authorities to ensure that they would be collected through that channel. No congregant was to leave before the end of the synagogue service. There could also be no private services without the permission of the head of the community.

The conduct of the services came under scrutiny too. When the weekly portion from the Five Books of Moses is read, there must be no mistakes. The accepted rule was that the reader must be corrected if necessary. It was the custom for any member of the congregation to call out the correction. Adler now ruled that only a member specially appointed by the community should be given this responsibility to avoid a lot of people calling out.

Only the cantor would lead the prayers and the congregation would follow his lead. Noise in the synagogue would be reduced by not allowing congregants to wear wooden shoes. Adler also laid down who had preference to be called to the reading of the Torah. The choice included those who were observing the anniversary of the death of relatives, those becoming engaged or married, or celebrating the birth of children, etc.

There would be sermons in German from time to time, and the prayer for the king and his family would be said weekly. When the opportunity occurred, Adler took care to reiterate the loyalty of the Jews to the State. In 1836, to celebrate William IV's birthday, he preached on the theme of the patriotism of the Israelites. This consisted of, 'loyal obedience to the laws of the country, in a willingness to take their share in the work for the welfare of the state, and in their affection for the father of the Fatherland'.[10]

Where previously the honours had been actually auctioned to raise funds for charitable purposes, this custom would now need the approval of the Landrabbiner. When given an honour, there previously could be a request by a congregant for more than one blessing: for the health of his family, to remember the names of dead relatives, etc. The number of blessings was now restricted to two or, at the most, three. The rules for Barmitzvahs – a boy's confirmation at the age of thirteen – were to be strictly enforced.

The purpose of the regulations was to make clear what the *din*, the law, was. It was also to ensure that no changes could be introduced by individual coteries, as they might be in Reform congregations. The danger for the Orthodox was always that of creeping change. That what might begin as a relatively innocuous alteration to the *din* might develop into something fundamental. That was what had happened before and that was what would happen in the future, wherever the Orthodox traditions were overturned. The favourite description might be as innocuous as 'modern practice', but the result of undermining Talmudic rules would be the same.

There was a general trend at the time for a drop in the numbers attending religious services. This applied to the church as well as the synagogue. A lot of people considered religion out of step with the age, an ally of the established aristocratic order and, therefore, not likely to approve of the growth of the middle classes.

Adler's regulations are surprising at a number of levels. He had only had his *semichah* for four years and he was still under 30 years of age. He had only been Landrabbiner for two years and now he was giving orders to congregants, a number of whom were very prominent in public life. At the same time, he appeared to have had the support of the congregation, because the comments on his work were invariably favourable. He must have been a powerful presence in the pulpit.

The lay leader of the community was Ezechial Simon, who was a court banker and a descendent of Michael David. As such, he was likely to have known Mordecai Adler for many years and Nathan Marcus Adler from his childhood. He would have had first hand knowledge of the young man's Talmudic ability and might well have encouraged him to produce the rabbinical ordinances. If there was a close relationship between Simon and Adler, it would be a good apprenticeship for cultivating the friendships of powerful supporters; Adler would build these in London in the future.

The Duke of Cambridge produced a new constitution for Hanover in 1833 which, effectively, enfranchised the middle classes; but this, too, did little for the position of the Jewish community. Adler, nevertheless, settled down to try to make changes for the 530 Jewish families who now lived in the town.

His primary concern was for better education for the children and, as early as 1831, he persuaded the government to start to reform the school system. The agreement reached was that in Jewish schools the teaching would be in German and attendance would be compulsory. Any form of mandatory universal education was a revolutionary idea in those days. Adler would have to try to ensure that all the teachers were well educated and he would, personally, supervise the religious teaching. He wanted every Jewish child to learn Hebrew from an early age.

The government were so impressed with the results he achieved that eventually they gave him a Christian primary school to run as well. It would irk him in London in the future that he was not invited to accept similar responsibilities for the Jews' Free School. Throughout his life the improvement of Jewish education would be one of Adler's prime concerns.

His success in Hanover was particularly praiseworthy because there were some very substantial difficulties to be overcome. Teaching ability was just one of the skills the individual small communities ideally wanted. They also needed a *mohel* to circumcise male babies and a *shochet* to kill animals for meat. Paying for these officials was a financial strain on the community. There was also the running of the cemetery to be considered and the administration of the synagogue. Adler had to balance the needs of the communities with their ability to pay for them.

If the congregation was setting priorities, then the shochet was the most important official, ensuring there was kosher meat, but if he doubled up as the Jewish teacher, his academic qualifications could well be totally inadequate. In selecting candidates Adler had different standards to apply. There were no extensive examinations or massive texts which the successful candidate would have mastered in order to become a school teacher. Carrying out circumcisions, the *mohelim*, on the other hand, had to be highly professional, but they would not be needed on a day-to-day basis. They could travel to a location where a new baby boy had been born.

Administrators needed no official qualifications either, but *shochtim* certainly did. The *din* was punctilious about the method of killing animals for food. They couldn't, of course, be killed for sport. The rules concerning the knife alone were extensive. The skill of a *shochet* was regularly checked, and those who failed the tests had their licences revoked. The regulations for the humane slaughter of animals were far more complicated than the requirements for teaching children. With those newspapers who leant towards Reform principles, this would be exactly the opposite of what they wanted. Good teachers would have been their predominant requirement in the attempt to create a more educated society.

Where the *din* was not affected, Adler did introduce changes. He, too, wanted regular sermons in the vernacular and he established a proper choir. He reorganized the Jewish school system. He didn't move, though, where the *din* was involved. The traditional prayers were in Hebrew, as the *din* required, but the sermon could be in German.

Adler never missed opportunities to advertise the loyalty of the community: in 1836 he gave a sermon to celebrate the birthday of William IV, but this time in excellent Hebrew. That year also marked the opening of a new synagogue in Emden after the old one had been destroyed in a flood. It was the largest synagogue in Hanover and tickets were sold for the opening ceremony. After the accusations that synagogue services were too noisy, it was a relief to find local papers referring to the Cantor's 'most melodious voice'. The service was composed and translated by the Emden Rabbi, Abraham Löwenstamm, who always preached in German. The construction of the synagogue also improved the relations with the townsfolk because Christian tradesmen were employed to build it, not just Jewish contractors.

The reports of the excellence of Adler's educational work made Hanover a welcoming centre for academic publications. In 1836 Salomo Ephraim Blogg produced a new edition of the Passover Haggadah. In 1838 Jacob ben Asher's commentary on the Pentateuch was published and Adler himself contributed a translation of part of Judah Halevi's *Kuzari*.

The Landrabbiner chaired the rabbinate in his area and was also responsible for keeping the government informed of all the items of income and expenditure within the community. He had to authorize rabbinical appointments, and here Adler had to decide if the candidate was likely to try to influence the congregation towards Reform. This led to many arguments about candidates' suitability.

The cost of maintaining the community was high, but Hanover was one of the few States in the Confederacy where the Landrabbiner held a semi-State authority similar to the Lutheran clergy. In 1836 the government made small concessions to its Jews by passing some improvements to their conditions in the Standeversamlung, the legislature, but still not granting equal rights.

In 1834, however, a situation had arisen which led the Duke of Cambridge to feel himself hugely indebted to Adler. The Duchess was having a very difficult pregnancy and had fallen seriously ill. Her doctors told him there was little hope of her surviving. When Adler heard the news, on his own initiative he held services in the synagogue to pray for the Duchess's recovery. The congregation's prayers were answered and the Duchess got better. The Duke was overjoyed and sent Adler a very handsome gift of 100 Friedrichs d'Or; the coin was 21 carat gold and 6 grammes in weight. In today's money, the gift was worth about £15,000.

The largesse would have been very welcome, but in Judaism praying for the sick is taken for granted and no reward is needed for carrying it out. So Adler sent the gift back to the Duke with the request that the money should be given to help the poor. From that time until his death, the Duke of Cambridge was a very warm supporter of his local rabbi. Back in London, when he learned that Adler was a candidate for chief rabbi in 1843, Cambridge drove to the home of Baron Lionel de Rothschild, who was an elder (warden) of the foremost Ashkenazi synagogue, the Great, in order to recommend his old Landrabbiner.

Adler also had the support of the recognized lay leader of the Jewish community in Britain, Sir Moses Montefiore. Their association was based on a £20 contribution (at least £1,500 today), which Adler had raised from the Hanover community some years earlier to support an appeal from Montefiore for the Smyrna Jewish community. In 1840, they had been caught up in an outpouring of anti-Semitism. In acknowledging the receipt of the gift, Montefiore said that: 'I feel most anxious to obtain a copy of your sermons. It would be presumptuous in me to express how greatly they would prove serviceable to our brethren in England.' So close did the two become that, after Adler moved to England, Montefiore would make a point of always calling on the rabbi's mother, Rebecca, when he was in Hanover where one of his companies installed the street lighting in the town.

Montefiore was always an internationalist. He had been born abroad, in Leghorn in Italy, where his paternal ancestors had lived since the seventeenth century. The rulers, the Medicis, had transformed the fortunes of the town by granting religious freedom, and the Jews had been happy to set up a community there, together with a famous yeshiva, which produced two Sephardi Hahamim in Britain: David Nieto and Raphael Meldola. .

Montefiore came to London as a young man and made a fortune as a Jewish broker on the Stock Exchange. He retired at 40 and devoted himself to looking after Jewish interests at home in Britain and overseas. He was elected to office in the City, and as Sheriff of London in 1837, the year Princess Victoria became Queen, he was knighted.

The Duke of Cambridge was in Hanover to protect British as well as Hanoverian interests. When the Prussian government, which with Austria dominated the German Confederation, wanted to create a customs union, Hanover opted out. They wouldn't even agree to common weights and measures. The customs union was the Zollverein, which was designed to produce common tariffs and to lessen the forces of nationalism which aimed for a single German state. The Zollverein actually had the opposite effect and became the mechanism for the creation of Germany. The Dukes still resisted the Zollverein. Instead, with Hamburg to the North, they looked for more trade with England.

It had been realised for years, however, that Hanover might soon not have the same ruler as Britain. When William IV died in 1837, Victoria became Queen, but this severed the Hanover connection. There, the semi-Salic law which ruled on successions, stated that the throne would go to the nearest male descendant, if one still lived. Ernest Augustus (1771–1851), the Duke of Cumberland, the oldest surviving son of George III, had the necessary qualification, and it was the Duke who succeeded as Ernest Augustus I. He promoted his Hanoverian credentials at an early stage by reminding everybody that, from the age of 14, he had been educated in Hanover and considered it his native land. Cumberland was also a philosemite but, like his brother, was more concerned with the state of the kingdom than with the emancipation of the Jewish community. The Duke of Cambridge now returned to London.

Although the new King of Hanover introduced gas lighting, better sanitation and a residential area, he was no democrat. Cambridge's new constitution in 1833 had deprived the ruler of the crown lands and Cumberland recovered them as early as November 1837, simply by revoking the constitution and restoring the 1819 version.

He also dismissed a number of university professors – known as the Göttingen Seven – whose liberal thinking did not meet with his approval. What was even less democratic, he stopped Saloman Gans, the Jewish lawyer who had defended them, from practising afterwards for months. Those seeking a more liberal approach to the constitution pulled in their horns. The *Hannoversche Zeitung* now became a government paper when its liberal editor resigned in 1837.

Articles in local newspapers, written by Jews, advocating emancipation, disappeared after that time.[11] Hanover became a harsher state. Adler kept his head firmly below the parapet; he didn't consider it any part of his responsibility to make political statements about the new absolutism; in his list of priorities the image of the Jewish community, as totally loyal to the state, would be the ongoing prime objective.

When the English prison reformer, Elizabeth Fry, visited the town in 1840 she was appalled that 400 of the prisoners were kept in chains. She wasn't that impressed with the whole administration, finding Lord Bligh, the British ambassador 'very haughty and grand'.[11]

The overall economic situation in Hanover deteriorated during Adler's last years in office. The continuing complaint was that 'administration took the place of government',[12] though the town was now to become a major rail junction, supported by Ernest Augustus who also approved a new opera house.

Concerns to never again see the like of the Napoleonic Wars left the German Confederation on tenterhooks, and in 1840 there was another war scare when the French demanded a revision of the borders of the Rhine. It blew over though, and in 1842, the Chamber of the States reverted to more parochial matters and held a debate on a proposal to ameliorate those laws which only applied to Jews.

There was still considerable support for the view that Jews were not like other citizens. It was suggested that the duties of the state to Jews were not equal to its duties to others.[13]. They pointed to the Judenordnung, which, since 1723, had restricted the number of Jews allowed to live in Hanover and was still in existence. Petty trading, to which many Jews were confined, was denounced as immoral and degrading. As a way of keeping the number of Jews down, Jewish teachers and servants were still not going to be admitted from outside the state. In London the *Voice of Jacob*, wrote: 'We present this exhibition of Hanoverian intolerance in all its deformity, not deeming it necessary to offer a single comment.'[14] The Jewish population was increasing naturally though and it was now decided to have four Landrabbiners in the State.

In 1842, as the possibility of Adler succeeding Solomon Hirschell as chief rabbi in London became more likely, the Duke of Cumberland finally granted a larger degree of legal equality for Jewish citizens in Hanover. The Judenordnung was abolished, though Jews still couldn't hold State posts. Jewish professionals and tradesman would henceforth be relieved of the domicimal tax. This was an annual payment for permission to live in the State. There was still the problem for younger sons that their father's permission to live in the State didn't cover them if they got married. They would have to find another State to allow them residence. Jewish factory owners could still only employ Jews but not as servants if they came from foreign States. The move towards equality did, however, get one additional boost in early 1845, when it was finally agreed that Jews could serve in the army.

One consideration which influenced the government was the importance of the Rothschilds as bankers to the State. As Hanover's economic strength declined, so the Rothschilds became ever more important as the source of loans, and the Rothschilds could always be relied on to appeal for better conditions for their coreligionists. In 1843, when Cumberland held a Grand Assembly, no less than seven Rothschilds received an invitation.

Adler was still not neglecting the value of religious services to mark events outside the community. In July 1844 he conducted one on the death of the Queen of Hanover, a gesture which was much appreciated by the rulers. Whenever possible, the orthodox position of the community would be promoted.

In January 1843 new laws had been promulgated in Hanover whereby all rabbis, cantors and teachers in the State had to be examined as to their competence by the Landrabbiner. Adler also had to deal with the problems arising from the new law that all children had to go to school from age 5–13 and if there was no Jewish school available, then they had to go to a Christian school. They were excused the classes in Christian instruction, but Adler wanted them to be taught Judaism.

Every Jew now had to belong to a congregation and a sermon had to be given every Sabbath and festival. With membership now compulsory, the number of congregations increased markedly, and in later years it was reported to have reached a hundred. It remained difficult to control such small communities dotted all over an area similar to that from London to Birmingham, and Adler had to decide whether to approve local initiatives. One district, for example, decided to demand that the community always provide two *minyan* men; Jews who could make up the ten needed for a quorum for public worship.

In such delicate decisions, Adler could exercise his veto, but only by aggravating the community; this was good training for the questions he would have to resolve in England where he would always strive for a peaceful solution, as had been important with his far-flung communities in Hanover.

He was also faced with the growing problem of the Reform movement. In the beginning, the ideas of the Hamburg Reform community had only spread slowly, but it did gather adherents. One of its advantages was that most Hanover papers remained Reform-leaning. There were also a lot of powerful Reform voices. The conflicting arguments were often voiced in the newspaper columns, and the Reform rabbis grew in influence.

The general theological approach of the reform rabbis was to question the Divine authorship of the Torah. It was suggested that only ethical laws were binding and that the rest of the *halachah* could no longer be viewed as normative. In 1844 a rabbinical conference was called at Brunswick to discuss the future of Judaism. What changes might be made? There were many minor and many fundamental proposals, because there were so many different viewpoints. One proposal, for instance, was to abolish Kol Nidre, the initial section of the Yom Kippur evening service. Other suggestions were to allow instrumental music in religious services and to translate the prayer book from Hebrew into German.

Some delegates wanted to accept any marriage as legitimately Jewish where both partners belonged to monotheistic faiths. The only proviso they added was that the children of the marriage should be brought up as Jews. They were also anxious to have legislation enacted that swearing an oath on God's name was sufficient, which meant abandoning the hated De More Judaico. This latter proposal was one of the few things on which all the delegates could agree.

Many recommendations struck at the heart of Orthodox practice, and when seventy-eight Orthodox rabbis – later 116 – produced a document protesting against all the Brunswick decisions, Adler's signature was among them.

In the same year as the Brunswick conference, there was a movement among reformers in Frankfurt to abandon circumcision. Very few of the old ways appeared to be sacred. The conference reconvened in Frankfurt in 1845, even adopting resolutions to cease praying for a return to the Holy Land. Even after 1,800 years, that return was still central to Orthodox thinking. There is a shell of a synagogue building in Spain today where the only sign that it was once Jewish is a few Hebrew words still visible, scrawled on a wrecked wall. They read 'Next Year in Jerusalem', which is also a plea in the Passover *Seder* service. The writing would date from the fifteenth century.

Another Frankfurt conference recommendation was that, instead of the usual cycle where portions of the first five books of the Bible were read in synagogue every Sabbath over the course of the year, the so-called 'triennial cycle' should be adopted, by which the reading of the Torah would take three years. This would shorten the Sabbath service by reducing the normal reading time by two thirds.

There was another contentious proposal. At the end of the weekly reading there is a portion recited on an analogous subject, from the books of the Prophets. This is known as the *haftarah* and in Orthodox synagogues it is generally read in Hebrew. The Frankfurt conference wanted it read in German. In addition the reformers turned their attention to a congregation's ritual bath, the *mikveh*, used by married women after their monthly period. The Frankfurt conference wanted a city's public baths to be acceptable as an alternative. They were also in favour of allowing an organ to be used at the Sabbath service.

The Orthodox rabbis were deeply concerned with these new proposals, but in Breslau, in 1846, the delegates went even further. Now they wanted non-Jews to be allowed to carry on a Jew's business on the Sabbath. The Fourth Commandment, however, clearly states that servants have to have the day off. The conference also held that Jewish soldiers should be able to work on the Sabbath, and it wanted to abolish the second day of all the festivals except the New Year.

It also advocated bread being eaten on the eighth day of Passover and only three days observed instead of seven for mourning the dead. It was felt that mourners shouldn't have to tear a garment to illustrate their grief, and they should be able to shave during the mourning period. They said the ram's horn, the *shofar*, could be blown when the New Year festival fell on the Sabbath. This was considered unacceptable in Orthodox communities and, therefore, forbidden. Similarly the waving of the *lulav* (four species of plants), on the Festival of Sukkot was to be allowed on the Sabbath. Though these resolutions were not all adopted, the fact that they were approved by differing groups of rabbis horrified the Orthodox, who saw it as the beginning of a wholesale undermining of Orthodoxy.

The Reform movement also faced opposition from the governments of a number of German States. Prussia forbade Reform because it considered any change in religion to be a direct threat to the state's hegemony. They took the same attitude towards dissident Christian sects. Bavaria even stopped its rabbis from attending the Reform conferences, though other states, like Baden, encouraged Reform.

The ambition to convert the Jews was still paramount and it still carried commercial advantages for those who succumbed. In 1846, however, the Upper Tribunal decided that the baptism of a parent should not mean that the children could be baptised as well. They would remain Jewish until they were old enough to decide for themselves.

The reformers themselves were by no means of one mind. They encouraged Orthodox rabbis to discuss their views with them but, from the Orthodox point of view, there was little room for discussion. Fundamentally, they believed in the *din* and didn't intend to alter it. The recommendations of the Reform movement were considered unmitigated heresy, to be opposed at all costs. As Samson Raphael Hirsch, Adler's successor in Oldenberg, said:

> The old Jewish religious legislation, which forms the fundamental statute of every Jewish community, has given the Israelitish congregation also the fundamental rules for its religious guidance, and nothing could nor can obtain validity in it which is not in accord with this religious legislation, as it has been handed down to us in Torah, Talmud and the rabbinical codes of the Shulchan Aruch.[15]

The overriding importance of the Talmud to the Orthodox rabbis is also illustrated by the fact that while the Orthodox rabbis had *semichah*, the Reform rabbis were likely to also have university doctorates. Of the 106 Brunswick delegates, sixty-three had doctorates, though in many instances the continental doctorate was more or less the equivalent of a British Bachelor's degree. To most Orthodox rabbis only the study of the Talmud was relevant.

Adler's plan to create a seminary for training Hebrew teachers moved closer to fruition when the Hanover government gave it their support in 1845. They even made vague promises of a grant. The mere fact that the seminary was now likely drew effusive praise from the Jewish press in London: 'Would to God that a similar successful result may attend Dr. Adler's efforts for establishing a seminary for Jewish teachers in this country.'[16]

His success in Hanover came at the same time as he was chosen to succeed Solomon Hirschell as Chief Rabbi in London. The government in Hanover gave him a glowing accolade to present to support his candidacy.

> We are commissioned to bear testimony to the especial satisfaction of the Minister of the Interior with Dr. Adler's conduct in his distinguished office. Much as we regret to be deprived of his services here, it nevertheless rejoices us that so exemplary and praiseworthy an official should have been recognized in his call to the post of Chief Rabbi of the Jews in Great Britain, a distinction for which his many years experience of a laborious and difficult service have eminently qualified him.[17]

At his final service, the farewell sermon was reported to have left the congregation in tears. It was significant that a number of state officials came to the synagogue as well. As there was no longer a need to be diplomatic, Adler finally told the congregation what he thought about the state's treatment of the Jews: 'We know not whether we are citizens of this country or foreigners, for we must beg even for the smallest piece of land we wish to acquire.'[18] He said that the reformers were wrong to arbitrarily change the Torah and the Oral Law because, in trying to please the government, what was left was tantamount to State worship.

Even after he had left, Adler's influence remained. When the resolutions of the Reform rabbis at the Brunswick Conference were published, the Hanover congregation confirmed: 'their entire satisfaction with the step taken by Dr. Adler, their former rabbi, in signing the protest against the proceedings at Brunswick.'[19]

The opposition to the proposals of the reform rabbis was led by Haham Isaac Bernays, the rabbi of Hamburg, Jacob Ettlinger, the rabbi of Altona and Dr S. Enoch, the headmaster of the Jewish Secondary School. They looked to Adler in London as a major supporter of their position, together with Moses Montefiore. When Adler came to Hanover in 1847 to celebrate his mother's 80th birthday, an emissary had a two hour discussion with him. Adler was reported as 'according to their opinion, the very centre and headstone in this matter.'[20] When reporting back to his friends, the emissary said: 'I find him to be a wise man, of exceedingly great deliberation in his words ... his advice was not to rush.'[21]

At the time it was difficult to predict what the Reform rabbis would adopt and what they would drop. As they were considering moving towards the customs of the Christian church in Germany, they were becoming conformist in official ecclesiastical eyes.

In Britain, by contrast, the breakaway group which would move away from the Orthodox Jewish approach would make the traditionalists the natural ally of the established Church of England; it was the breakaway group who would behave like the nonconformists. Changing the traditional approach in Britain would also not be more likely to lead to full emancipation. When this was realised, it made the evangelical efforts of what would come to be called the Secessionists, more difficult.

Adler was ambitious and the possibility of being chief rabbi in a great Britain, despite his claims of reluctance, would be a dream come true. He would not, however, be carried away. He was a realist. He knew the praise of the Hanoverian State had to be set against their continued failure to remove the discriminatory measures they had imposed on the Jews over the centuries.

Yet all was not ideal in Britain either. The far more tolerant, democratic approach of British governments could not disguise the fact that Jews could still not be members of the House of Commons unless they took an unacceptable oath. Adler would always look for the hidden agenda. As it is said 'fair words butter no parsnips.'

Notes

1. Michael Friedländer, *Jewish Quarterly Review*, July 1890.
2. H.D. Schmidt, 'Chief Rabbi Nathan Marcus Adler (1803–1890): Jewish Educator from Germany', *Leo Baeck Institute Yearbook*, 7, 1 (1962), p.292.
3. Ibid., p.293.
4. Meir Persoff, *Hats in the Ring: Choosing Britain's Chief Rabbis from Adler to Sacks* (Boston, MA: Academic Studies Press, 2013), p.23.
5. Dr Peter Schulze, current archivist of the Hanover Jewish community today.
6. Derek Taylor, *British Chief Rabbis, 1664–2006* (London and Portland, OR: Vallentine Mitchell, 2007), p.239.
7. *Occident and American Jewish Advocate*, March 1845.
8. Nick Harding, *Hanover and The British Empire, 1700–1837* (Martlesham: The Boydell Press, 2007), p.244.
9. *The Times*, 21 January 1831, p.2.
10. Ibid.
11. A.J.P. Taylor, *The Course of German History* (London: Routledge, 2001).
12. David Meola, 'Jews in Hanover and their Role in the German Press, 1815–1848' (PhD dissertation, University of Alabama, 2012), p.367.
13. *Voice of Jacob*, 20 January 1842.
14. Ibid., p.71.
15. Dr Peter Schulze, archivist of the Hannover Jewish community today.
16. *Jewish Chronicle*, 6 February 1846, p.75.
17. *Voice of Jacob*, 14 March 1845, p.118.
18. H.A. Schmidt, 'Chief Rabbi Nathan Marcus Adler (1803–1890): Jewish Educator from Germany', *Leo Baeck Institute Yearbook*, 7, 1 (1962).
19. *Voice of Jacob*, 1 August 1845, p.212.
20. *Transactions of the Jewish Historical Society of England*, Miscellanies, Vol.5, p.143.
21. Ibid.

3

A Pause for the *Herem*

While it is possible to write about Adler's life in relatively chronological order, there was one problem area in London which started while he was still in Hanover and would only come to a long-term conclusion when he had been in office for some years. It was the promulgation by his predecessor, Solomon Hirschell, of a *herem*, a sanction for offending against the community. It was a complicated story, with those involved well stocked with hidden agendas.

Solomon Hirschell, the previous chief rabbi, had died in 1842 at the age of 80. He had broken his hip in 1840 which, effectively, restricted him to his house. His formerly powerful frame had also been wasted by continuous fasting. His public image was naturally diminished by his absence from community occasions, though he remained a highly respected figure. His opposite number among the Sephardim, Haham Raphael Meldola, had died in 1828 and had not been replaced. Meldola and the Sephardi lay leaders, the Mahamad, had not seen eye to eye on several occasions and had quarrelled very publicly. When he died, the lay executive was in no hurry to replace him. Indeed, it would take thirty-eight years to appoint a successor. Normally the chief rabbi and the haham worked in harmony but in Hirschell's later years there was no haham.

The Jewish religious authorities were not, therefore, at their best in 1840 when a small mixed breakaway group of both senior Sephardi and Ashkenazi congregants, about twenty in total, decided to leave Bevis Marks and the Great Synagogue and set up a new congregation. It fell to Hirschell to deal with the problem because there were some Ashkenazim involved and no Sephardi of equal rank to himself to determine the correct response. Meldola's son, David, however, also signed the *herem* as the Sephardi's *Av Beth Din* (head of the ecclesiastical court).

The secessionists, as they were called, wanted a synagogue in the West End where so many of the community now lived. Moses Montefiore, the Sephardim's most senior member, was nearly 60 and would walk from Park Lane to the City every Sabbath, but for those with less energy or determination, it was a struggle. Montefiore would stay with friends in the City until after Shabbat. The group also wanted services at more convenient times, better decorum, some minor changes to the ritual and more religious instruction. The Mahamad had no liking for these suggestions and wishes. They considered that they had been selected to be the lay authority and they had no intention of allowing others to change the congregation's traditions.

Although the breakaway group was categorized at the time as secessionist, they are often described today as Reform. Compared to German Reform communities, however, they were only a pale imitation of the far more extreme approaches on the Continent. Most of their motivation had little to do with theology or the *din*. Nevertheless, their intention to start a new congregation created an unholy row.

Some background is needed. Over the centuries, when Jews committed offences of a religious nature, they could be condemned by a decision of the *dayanim* (judges) of the Beth Din. What the Beth Din couldn't do was punish the offenders for serious offences by putting them in prison, because the Jews had no prisons.

On the other hand there was a strong case for unity. The Jews had no say in the way that governments behaved towards them, in terms of discrimination and worse. So the best chance of a peaceful existence for any community was for the members to stick together. The Jews also inherited a tradition that they had a responsibility for all their coreligionists which bound them together. It's one of the reasons for the Jewish emphasis on giving charity to the poor and accounts for the success of international appeals to help communities in trouble in different parts of the world; for instance, for rebuilding synagogues destroyed by mobs in pogroms.

As a consequence of a diaspora court's limited power, the most severe penalty that could be handed down by the Beth Din was to withdraw the support of their fellows. To use an English phrase, to send them to Coventry. To throw them out of the community. This was called a *herem*, a caution, but it was not, in Christian terms, excommunication.

The original decision to issue a *herem* in response to the decision to form a separate congregation, was made at a meeting at Hirschell's home on 9 September 1841, with Sir Moses Montefiore in the chair. The decision was not made public in the hope that negotiations with the secessionists would be successful, as a result of which it would be unnecessary to invoke the proposed penalty. Everybody knew how disruptive it would be. It would have far reaching effects, including splitting families. Montefiore was particularly annoyed that his brother, Horatio, was involved on the secessionist side.

In March 1840 the Mahamad did promise to consider the creation of a branch synagogue, despite *hascamah* (rule) No. 1 of their congregational laws. They were insistent, however, that any new synagogue must still be governed by Bevis Marks. The subsequent arguments had become so bitter, though, that the seceders refused to alter their stance.

The rules of the Sephardi community in London had been laid down since the congregation was authorised in the time of Charles II. The very first of these forbade the creation of any other place of worship than the synagogue. No new synagogue could be created within six miles of what was now the Bevis Marks *shul*. Congregants were forbidden to set up an alternative congregation, or even to hold services in their own homes, unless it was for mourners, and the ultimate penalty was the *herem*.

The reason given for the *herem* to be issued was, however, broader; not just geographical but religious. It was because the new congregation was going to observe 'a ritual which has been proscribed by authority'.[1] That was a very serious offence in Orthodox eyes. Setting out to make any changes was not just against the rules of Bevis Marks. It was a fundamental principle of Orthodox Judaism to abide by the Oral Law created over the centuries, though most Orthodox Jews found it impossible to discipline their lives sufficiently to obey the hundreds of dictates it contains.

As a result of their decision, and after protracted negotiations with both Bevis Marks and the Great Synagogue, on 22 January 1842, a communication from the Chief Rabbi was read out in most British synagogues. It said that a *herem* had by then been issued against the proposed new community, which had acquired a former Dissenters' chapel they had refurbished in Burton Street near Euston Station.

It didn't change the minds of the breakaway group. The secessionists were members of distinguished Jewish families – mostly the Goldsmids, Henriques, Montefiores and Mocattas – and they took the *herem* in their stride and held their inaugural service five days later. What they couldn't do was appoint a marriage secretary. For that they had to be confirmed as a body of Jews by the Board of Deputies, and there was no way that was going to happen under the circumstances.

One criterion for being confirmed as a Jewish community by the Board of Deputies, the body recognized by the government as representing the Jews in Britain, was acceptance of the Oral Law, and as members of the new congregation were intent on denying parts of it, they were, effectively, voting themselves out of the established community.

The *herem* split the higher echelons of British Jews and the community. Congregations like the Western Synagogue in London and the Manchester and Liverpool congregations in the provinces refused to publish it. Plymouth went further and burned it. The situation was further complicated when Hirschell died some months later, in October 1842, leaving the resulting problems to be sorted out by Adler when he succeeded him.

The breach might well have been avoided if there had been less personal animosity to exacerbate the situation. The origins of the animosity within the Sephardi community went back a long way. In 1840 the Mahamad was controlled by the descendants of Jews who had been evacuated from Gibraltar when Spain was shelling it in 1782. Over the years the Spanish fired 250,000 shells at the Rock and the entire civilian population had to be relocated.

In London, after they arrived and joined Bevis Marks, some Gibraltarians had held a service, after saying mourning prayers, in a private house one evening. It was on the festival of Shavuot and there are special prayers to be recited, so it was natural for those present to continue from one service to another. They didn't think twice about doing so, but to hold such a service was held to be against the laws governing the Sephardi community. The Mahamad condemned the house as a competing synagogue, and declared that those taking part in the Shavuot service had therefore failed to abide by *hascamah* 1. It was close to Lord Acton's aphorism that power corrupts and absolute power corrupts absolutely.

The Mahamad had the authority to take this action and the worshippers were roundly condemned by them. It was very embarrassing for the alleged offenders even after the *herem* was lifted. It so happened, though, that some of those who castigated them went on to become forebears of the families who wanted change in 1840. The Gibraltarians and their descendants had long memories and were now equally intent on applying the letter of the law to the seceders instead of compromising. As a correspondent wrote in 1845:

> It is well known that when three members of our congregation several years ago separated from us ... and had prayers read at their houses, a *herem* was read against them in the Bevis Marks synagogue ... one of those most determined to see the pain and penalties carried out against these three gentlemen, is now one of the seceders to Burton Street.[2]

The seceders were considered out of order by the Orthodox on many other counts; in particular, they had agreed upon their own form of prayers, which differed in minor ways from the traditional services. There was support for a proposal to abolish the second day of festivals which would certainly be proscribed by any Orthodox authority. The second day of festivals was part of the Oral Law and anybody who didn't accept the authority of the Oral Law was not going to be welcomed into an Orthodox community.

The 1840 *herem* was not the first to be issued by the Sephardim, and its predecessors had also been contentious. There had been concerns about issuing a caution at the time of Haham David Nieto in 1705. The Mahamad had then asked the advice of the Attorney General on whether they had the right to issue it. Sir Edward Northey had held that:

> I am doubtful that the pronouncing excommunication, being an act of ecclesiastical Jurisdiction, the Synagogue of the Jewes are not allowable by the Lawes of England to exercise the pronouncing of same, and for assuming the exercise of ye power in England.[3]

Sir Edward thought that those who were considered culprits could be denied burial in the cemetery, but that was about all. Nobody, however, would have dreamt of testing Hirschell's *herem* in the civil courts because it would have reflected badly on the Jewish community as a whole. After all, the advice received from the Attorney General in 1705 was highly likely either to have been forgotten or deliberately overlooked.

There were two justifiable reasons why the creation of another place of worship appeared to the original Sephardi authorities to merit such a draconian reaction. The first, which came up in Stuart times, was that the senior members of the congregation were afraid of upsetting the King and his advisers. They wanted to control the lines of communication with the government in order to make sure that nothing untoward was said. Their permission to live in England was not so assured that any risks of adverse results from a word out of place could be ignored.

There was opposition to allowing the Jews to remain in Britain. In 1661 a delegation from the City of London had asked Charles II to revoke the permission, but the King had decided that there were definite benefits to the country if they were allowed to stay. That permission, however, would have to be confirmed by his successor as well. The Sephardim didn't want to take any chances. This was most easily achieved if control was centralised in the synagogue Mahamad.

When that concern disappeared over the years, there remained the problem of trying to look after the whole congregation, much of which was poverty stricken or in need. If there were two communities, there would be two sets of overheads. Charitable donations would be split between the two congregations. To avoid this, the Mahamad wanted everything concentrated in just one body.

Yet there could have been a pragmatic reason for flexibility in negotiating with the secessionists. Many of the breakaway group were leading lights in Jewish charities. When the secessionists had moved from Burton Street to the nearby Margaret Street, with the *herem* in force, Sir David Salomons (1797–1873) warned the Board of Deputies that they were: 'running the risk of losing the heads of your schools, the patrons of your benevolent institutions and the supporters of your charities, for many of such honourable positions were held by members of the Margaret Street congregation.'[4] That eventuality was, in fact, quite feasible. Isaac Lyon Goldsmid was just one member who left the Great Synagogue in a huff and took his promised legacy of £3,000 (a quarter of a million pounds today) to the new synagogue with him.

The elephant in the room, however, was the emotions aroused, ranging from irritation to fury, among those seceders who were simply unaccustomed to having their decisions questioned. In their own fields, many of the Margaret Street leaders were rich and powerful and normally surrounded by acolytes. They now found themselves in the highly unusual position of being contradicted by men who, apart from their religious authority, did not measure up to them in material means or positions of influence in the wider community. Salomons, who for years was a pillar of the upmarket Hambro Synagogue in London, recognized the possible reaction.

This rejection of their views by the majority of Jews would be an ongoing aggravation for the seceders as long as they lived. That in spite of their eminence, they were never to be able to persuade more than a small percentage of the Jewish community to follow their lead. Intellectual argument, scientific discoveries, their version of common sense and their claim to be more in line with modern times, would all prove to be of little avail in their attempt to win their argument.

Moses Mocatta became the warden of the secessionist synagogue and warned his congregation: 'For any least deviation, unqualified censure will be heaped upon us and the self-styled Orthodox of our co-religionists will gladly seize on the minutest point to vilify our minister and cast obloquy on our congregation.'[5] This was not an experience they wished to suffer.

The vast majority of the Jewish community in Britain would remain in the Orthodox fold, including David Salomons, and the seceders found this a very hard pill to swallow. They would look to augment their numbers with defectors from the Orthodox, but the paucity of their membership, a tiny proportion of the whole community, could not be denied.

The chief rabbi in the future was going to have his own powerful lay supporters. His most crucial support, which fortunately lasted throughout almost all his long ministry, would be Sir Moses Montefiore; very Orthodox himself, very powerful in Jewish and national circles and a man who approved highly of Adler's work and approach.

The relationship between Adler and David Salomons was complicated. Adler was the spiritual leader of the community and devoted to the protection of the *din*. Salomons was equally devoted to the cause of obtaining the total emancipation of the Jews in England, whatever that took. Where in the future the two causes might clash, Salomons was going to follow his own agenda and he was a very determined individual.

Salomons was a banker and the son of a banker. He was a stockbroker, a lawyer and one of the most important figures in the creation of Britain's high street banks. He was the first Jewish magistrate, the first Jewish Sheriff of the City of London, having successfully lobbied Parliament to pass the Sheriff's Declaration Act, and would become Lord Mayor in 1855. Two of his aunts were married to Nathan Mayer Rothschild and Sir Moses Montefiore, respectively, and his brother was married to a relation of Montefiore. He would serve as a warden at the Hambro Synagogue and become a member of the new Central Synagogue, the forthcoming outpost of the Great Synagogue in the West End of London.

Elected a Liberal MP for Greenwich in 1851, Salomons would be removed from the House of Commons when he attempted to take his seat and make his maiden speech without swearing the Christian oath. On a motion to decide on the matter, he lost by a margin of 192 votes. He was also fined £500 (£50,000 today), for his trouble. Adler actually went to the House of Commons on the day Salomon tried to take his seat to show his support, but he could only be a spectator and watch the unhappy events.

Salomons was a hero to the Jewish community and deserved to be. At the same time, his views on the future shape of Victorian Jewry were often at variance with those of Adler. When, for example, Adler was trying to raise money to start a school whose pupils would go on to a college to train as ministers, Salomons wrote to him:

> Although I feel confirmed in the opinion first expressed to you that your proposed educational scheme as a whole was open to grave objections, I fulfil my promise of sending you a contribution. I must, however, make special conditions in respect of it. I wish to promote the education in this country of such of our Jewish fellow subjects as are destined for the Ministry of Her Majesty's Dominions and I offer my donation with that sole object in view. I wholly disapprove of the proposed day school as inadvisable and unnecessary. I also desire that my contribution be left distinct from the funds of the Beth Hamedrash.[6]

Salomons was himself a governor of the Jews' Free School, and David Woolf Marks, the secessionist minister, was one of the school's keenest supporters. The relationship of Adler with the Free School would always be very cordial. His attendance at their Examination Day just a few months after his inauguration was greeted with enthusiasm. Over the years, however, having been given no more than a ceremonial role in the governance of the school, he turned his attention to his new Jews' College. Salomons and Adler would have their differences on a number of subjects in the future, and the Chief Rabbi would be grateful for Montefiore's support on those occasions, though even that didn't always swing the balance in his favour.

Another major lay figure was Sir Francis Goldsmid. He would become a QC in 1858. In tracts and speeches he urged the community to tone down their reliance on the Talmud if they wanted and expected political emancipation. There was a strong secessionist group among those who sought emancipation. Sir Moses Montefiore was having none of it, though. As he wrote in his diary: 'I am most firmly determined not to give up the smallest part of our religious forms and privileges to obtain civil rights.'[7]

The secessionist minister, David Woolf Marks (1811–1909), had been a pupil of Solomon Hirschell and had read the Mishnah to the rabbi's wife when her sight failed. His advocacy of changes to Orthodox practice had been a great disappointment to the old chief rabbi. Marks had given himself the dual task of persuading many of his senior members, as well as the Jewish community, to his point of view. When the inaugural service took place in 1842 at the new Burton Street Synagogue, he had questioned the Oral Law:

> We solemnly deny that a belief in the divinity of those traditions written in the Mishnah and the Jerusalem and Babylonian Talmuds is of equal obligation to the Israelite with the faith in the divinity of the Laws of Moses ... these books are human compositions; and though we are content to accept with reverence, advice and instruction from our post-biblical ancestors, we cannot unconditionally accept their laws. For Israelites there is but One immutable Law – the sacred volume of the Scriptures commanded by God to be written down for the unerring guidance of the people until the end of time.[8]

In other words, he accepted the Written Law – contained in the first five books of the Bible – but not the Oral Law. Within the secessionist movement, this approach would remain a source of contention for many years. There was no unanimity. It was even opposed by a number of the founders who were determined not to give up the Oral Law and did all they could to ensure that their new congregation fell into line.

In 1844 Hyman Hurwitz needed to be replaced as Professor of Hebrew at University College London. Dr Louis Loewe, a protégé of Montefiore, was better qualified than Marks, but Montefiore had fallen out with his relative,

Sir Isaac Lyon Goldsmid, who was very influential at University College. Marks was appointed. It gave him additional standing in the community.

Questioning the Oral Law covered a vast area of Jewish theology and the religious agenda of Marks turned out to be far more radical than that of the original secessionists. There were many reasons, therefore, why Marks encountered difficulties in winning over members of the community to the changes he proposed. For example, the familiar prayers enjoyed the popularity of long-standing.

When Marks revised the Passover Haggadah and removed the rabbinic passages – part of the Oral Law – the changes in a ceremony which could trace its origins back over thousands of years were unpopular and the new Haggadah was abandoned. Similarly he could assure his community that lighting candles on Shabbat eve by the woman of the house was not ordained in the Pentateuch, but the ceremony had been part of the family gathering over the generations; its theological justification was unimportant to most people in the light of its honoured place in family life.

Some of Marks' proposed changes were too esoteric for the vast majority of the community; for example, he wanted the memorial prayer to be said in Hebrew rather than Aramaic. He argued that the procedures for the laying of *tefillin* (phylacteries) had been developed by rabbis and was, therefore, incorrect. Nevertheless, he chose to wear them himself on the fast of Tisha b'Av.

Marks was also trying to bring together the two strands of Judaism – Sephardim and Ashkenazim – which had developed separately in minor ways over the centuries. He produced a new prayer book which attempted to combine the two liturgies to enable: 'the house of prayer [to] exercise that salutary influence over the minds and hearts of congregants which it is capable and intended to exist.'[9]

A lot of it was above the heads of ordinary people and Adler was quite clear on the subject. Speaking at the Hambro in 1847 he defended the Oral Law: 'If human laws require interpretation, how much more must divine laws.'[10] It was a catchall justification, but the truth was that there had been any amount of interpretation over the centuries, as Adler pointed out. In their time, the greatest Talmudists – Rashi, Maimonides, Caro – had been questioned by their rabbinic contemporaries. Holding the brethren together had always been a monumental task.

There were also plenty of examples of disastrous consequences for breakaway factions in other religions; Albigensians, Hussites, the purges of Sunnis and Shiites. The arguments for change could be potentially lethal.

As the *herem* affected and split some of the most important families in the community, it gave rise to a great deal of disaffection. To try to improve matters, *hascamah* 1 was repealed in January 1843 by a majority of 3:1, but that didn't affect the existing *herem*. It was even agreed, after the horse had bolted, that any future chief rabbi – whoever he was – should have no power to declare a *herem*. That did not alter the fact that Adler would have to inherit the one in existence. In January 1845, the Beth Din confirmed that this was the case.

Adler's own view was that stringent action had to be taken in order to prevent the spread of Reform in Britain. He was, after all, appointed to defend the Orthodox laws, would have the authority to do so, and was a lifetime advocate of Orthodoxy.

The alterations to Judaism considered at the German reform conferences were not, in fact, of any immediate relevance in Britain. The community was perfectly content to remain Orthodox, even if the majority of the members were dilatory in carrying out most of the *mitzvoth* (commandments) in their personal and family lives. The wardens at Burton Street also had no intention of giving Marks carte blanche to make his proposed alterations. They even denied that they were making changes which warranted the *herem*. In March 1846 they stated: 'not that the slightest idea is entertained by the congregation abandoning the opinions respecting the Traditional, or Oral Law, or any other of the views expounded by their ministers in the consecration service.'[11]

Adler, however, was in no position to declare the *herem* invalid because there was definitely a case for its issuance and it hadn't been lifted. It was certainly necessary to try to find a solution, but in the meantime the *herem* would remain in place and Adler would start his ministry with few people happy about it. There would soon be uncomfortable individual situations to be resolved, even if these were few in total. They did, however, affect a number of important families in the community.

It was decreed, for example, that members of the new congregation would not be allowed to be given honours in an Orthodox synagogue. They would not be allowed to be buried in an Orthodox cemetery, or be married in an Orthodox synagogue. Their charitable donations to Orthodox causes would not be accepted. They would be ostracized in all those areas. It naturally raised hackles to a high level; *The Voice of Jacob* reported that one meeting to discuss it in 1846 was adjourned: 'amidst a sense of confusion which beggars description'.

During the next few years situations would arise which involved all the prohibitions, and Adler fully accepted that he was there to uphold the law and must do so. The question came up again of whether the new synagogue minister could be recognized as a Secretary for Marriages, approved by the Board of Deputies. It was Adler who said 'no' and the Board of Deputies acquiesced; it was clearly set down in their rules that they left spiritual decisions to the chief rabbi.

In 1846 an Orthodox bride-to-be was made to promise Adler not to attend Burton Street in the future. When this became known, the two Jewish newspapers, the *Jewish Chronicle* and *The Voice of Jacob*, took sides. The *Jewish Chronicle* published the views of secessionists and anti-secessionists but *The Voice of Jacob*, for the most part, supported the chief rabbi. They compared him to a magistrate who had to carry out the law, whether he approved of it or not:

> When called to assess the chief ecclesiastical functions of the uniting synagogues of the Empire, he found the law existing and he naturally feels himself constrained to abide by it as long as it shall be unrepealed. Before it can be assumed that he is responsible for the spirit of the law, it is proper to ask ... has he been memorialized by his flock to revise and alter the law?[12]

That neatly summed up Adler's position but there were some exceptions made if the families involved were rich and powerful enough in the community. Adler did not want to alienate them if it could be avoided; he was primarily concerned to get his feet under the table for as long as his honeymoon period could be extended. As he told Rabbi Solomon Eger, back home in Germany in 1847, he was: 'afraid to fight publicly with the wealthy to publicize such a decision about the reformers'.[13] So he did allow such marriages, but he always ensured that both parties had been born to Orthodox parents. That remained a sine qua non.

There were also a number of exceptions, though, to the policy of not upsetting the rich and famous. In February 1848, when Benjamin Elkin, a member of Burton Street, died, the question arose of whether the *herem* prohibited his burial in the cemetery of the Great Synagogue. The wardens were happy to approve the interment and Elkin had paid 10 guineas (£10.50) a year for the grave. The Chief Rabbi, however, in conjunction with the Sephardi Beth Din, refused to allow the burial. There was uproar in the community, but Adler still had little option. The *herem* had been proclaimed, it still existed, and his duty was to carry out its ordinances until it was repealed.

It was interesting that Mrs Elkin had been cremated and her husband wished to be cremated as well. Cremation is not allowed in Orthodox communities, though this was obviously condoned in Mrs Elkin's case. Adler was making it clear that he was not prepared to go against the *din*, even if he was under considerable pressure to do so. Elkin was, therefore, buried in the Burton Street cemetery, with Marks officiating.

When Adler put his foot down there was further adverse publicity by those affected and their friends. Mrs Horatio Montefiore, one of the illustrious family, had to be buried in the Ashkenazi Maiden Lane cemetery, rather than that of the Sephardim. Fortunately for the family, Maiden Lane had decided not to apply the veto and was not subject to Adler's authority.

The new congregation continued to be referred to as 'The Seceders', and actually was little more than that, but any breakaway was going to be considered Reform by Adler at the outset of his ministry, deeply influenced by his German experiences.

In January 1847 the *yehidim* (members) of Bevis Marks would ask the congregational Elders to work out how to abrogate the *herem*. The head of the Sephardi Beth Din took advice from eminent rabbis on the Continent. The customary way for a *herem* to be lifted was for the culprits to apologise. This the leaders of the secessionists refused to do in April 1847, as they felt it would be a humiliation. The Elders, for their part, agreed to cancel the *herem*, but only subject to the approval of the Sephardi Beth Din. Discussions dragged on. It was finally agreed in the November of that year that a nominee could apologise for the seceders and this was effected. There were then three meetings in January 1848 at Bevis Marks to try to finally resolve the problem. It wasn't until two months later in March, after further meetings, that it was at last agreed to abolish the *herem*.

Even then the agreement to do so was by no means unanimous; the resolutions were agreed or turned down by single-figure majorities. These proposals included several attempts to draw in the chief rabbi to make a decision, but this was unacceptable to a small majority of the Sephardim, probably because of their commitment to the community's independence from the Ashkenazim.

It would eventually take until March 1849 for the *herem* on the individual secessionists to be removed. Even then the *herem* on the secessionist congregation as a whole remained in place. Most charitable donations from the community could still not be accepted, which remained the case until 1865.

The Burton Street congregation still grew and needed to move to larger premises in Margaret Street in 1849. Even so, the secessionists were laying their foundations in unpromising soil. Three quarters of the seceders had come from three rich families: the Mocattas, Montefiores and Henriques. They did their case no favours by approving the formation of a Council of Founders and then self-electing themselves for life.

The committee that subsequently decided on their form of prayers had Marks as a member, but it also included Francis Goldsmid, and Abraham and Moses Mocatta. The Jewish literacy of these lay members could be said to have hardly fitted them for the role, though Marks would have done most of the work. Arthur Cohen QC, an eminent jurist and President of the Board of Deputies towards the end of the century, expressed himself bluntly. His opinion was that: 'I don't believe in reforms being brought about by merchants and city men.'[14] Most of the community were of the same opinion.

As against the Reform movement in Germany, which had already had twenty-five years to grow and develop its philosophy, the secessionists in London had more practical objectives:

> The foundation of the West London Synagogue of British Jews had, in fact, represented as much an attempt by its founding fathers to have a neighbourhood synagogue as to alter the ritual. Many of its members were strict Sabbath observers.[15]

It was readily recognized that the Reform rabbis in Germany had programmes of change which were far more radical than those of the secessionists. Nevertheless, the possibility remained in Britain that the position might alter if determined action were not taken to ensure that it didn't. In the future, placing the chief rabbi on a religious pedestal was one element in counteracting defections towards a version of German Reform.

It didn't take long for Adler to realize that he wasn't faced with the same challenge to Orthodoxy in Britain that the Reform posed in Germany. For a long time he would indeed try to mend the fences between the two sides and it is significant that a number of the members of the breakaway synagogue were strong supporters of his efforts to create a school and college to train future ministers and teachers for the community.

There were a few elements of the new congregation's plans – the new prayer book for example – which mirrored the Hamburg community's original thinking. In 1851 it was decided that an organ could be used in the synagogue on Sabbaths and Festivals because there was precedent that instrumental music had been used in the Biblical Temple service.

To many, however, the changes, overall, didn't seem too radical. The German Jewish newspaper, the *Allgemeine Zeitung des Judenthums*, couldn't understand the fuss. This was a popular magazine aimed at the intelligent Jewish laity in Germany, and it held that the secessionists' form of prayers involved no theological reforms whatever.

Adler's insistence on the din certainly did not prevent him seeking some modus vivendi with the secessionists. If he was not successful in achieving this, he did try. Marks recalled the discussions when reminiscing after Adler's death.

> When the late Chief Rabbi entered on his office he sought to put ecclesiastical pressure on the congregation in order to bring about

> union. When he found he did not succeed he tried a more conciliatory attitude. He requested the late Sir Francis Goldsmid to call on him, and at the interview between them, the Chief Rabbi said, 'I am so desirous of bringing about union with your congregation that I would go out of my way and am ready to give up my whole body, if you will give up the paring of a nail.' 'What do you regard as the paring of a nail?' asked Sir Francis. 'Tonight is Chanukah', replied Dr. Adler, 'and I would wish to say the blessing – Blessed are thou O Lord who hath commanded us to light the Chanukah lamp.' 'But', answered Sir Francis, 'you know that is not true. Chanukah was instituted long after prophecy ceased. Is it not enough for you to know that we so far obey tradition as to keep up Chanukah? But we cannot utter a lie.' 'Not so', rejoined the Chief Rabbi, 'because it is a maxim that when the rabbis command, God commands.'[16]

If the maxim was accepted, it was the end of the argument and the secessionists would have to comply. In fairness though, getting all the rabbis to approve the same command over the centuries had not always been possible.

Justification for change, as against the immutability of the *din*, were arguments for which each side had its own powerful advocates. Goldsmid was a major influence among the secessionists, not just because of his own eminence, but because of his deeply felt conviction that the insistence on the Talmud adversely affected the case for political emancipation. This viewpoint he expounded in meetings, tracts and speeches, but he knew very well that he would have gained more followers if he had propounded the same views in Germany.

The new secessionist minister would have found it ironic that Adler was possessed of an authority that his secessionist honorary officers were not granting Marks himself:

> The West London Synagogue of British Jews was run by its Council of Founders and their committees, not by the clergy. The minister had to refer to the governing body on nearly all synagogue matters, taking instruction as to when and where to preach.[17]

One result of the breakaway was that it concentrated the minds of the City synagogues on the problem of their increasingly unsatisfactory locations. In November 1848 the Committee of the Great Synagogue came to the conclusion that: 'it being considered of the utmost importance that a place of worship in connection with this synagogue be established in the West End of the Metropolis, this committee do take the subject into consideration at the next meeting.'[18]

Eventually the Hambro and the New would decide that they didn't want to be involved, but the Great would go ahead and, seven years later, there would be a new Central Synagogue. Its membership would be restricted, however, to existing members of the Great.

Notes

1. *The Voice of Jacob*, 3 February 1842, p.76.
2. *The Voice of Jacob*, 28 February 1845, p.111.
3. Derek Taylor, *British Chief Rabbis, 1664-2006* (London and Portland, OR: Vallentine Mitchell, 2007), p.90.
4. *Jewish Chronicle*, 16 September 1853, p.400. The Secessionist synagogue was first in Burton Street, then in Margaret Street, and then in Upper Berkeley Street.
5. Taylor, *British Chief Rabbis, 1664–2006*, p.224.
6. Lecture by Rabbi Raymond Apple.
7. Ibid.
8. Ibid.
9. Ibid.
10. Ibid.
11. *Jewish Chronicle*, 27 March 1846, p.103.
12. *The Voice of Jacob*, 2 January1846, p.59.
13. Steven Singer, *Orthodox Judaism in Early Victorian London, 1840–1858* (New York: Yeshiva University, 1981), p.68.
14. Ibid.
15. Taylor, *British Chief Rabbis, 1664–2006*, p.224.
16. *Jewish Chronicle*, 27 June 1890, p.16.
17. Taylor, *British Chief Rabbis, 1664–2006*, p.223.
18. Aubrey Newman, *The United Synagogue, 1870–1970* (London: Routledge & Kegan Paul, 1976), p.3.

4

Election – 1844

When Solomon Hirschell died at 81 in 1842 it was generally agreed that, because of his advanced years, he would not be a terribly hard act to follow. Hirschell had been more effective in his early years and had cemented the authority of the chief rabbi during his ministry. As *The Voice of Jacob* commented when he died:

> though independent minded enough sometimes, they have found reference and subordination indispensable in Shechita, marriage, divorce, etc. etc. and hence, not from design or system, but from inevitable necessity, the late Rabbi was recognized as the spiritual head of most Jews claiming British origin.

In fact Hirschell was considerably underrated, as just one of his important achievements was to create the first English Ashkenazi Beth Din.

The Selection Committee charged with the responsibility for vetting candidates drew up the job specification. The process was led by the Great Synagogue, which circulated the Jewish communities in both Britain and throughout the Empire after the chief rabbi's death. The impression they gave was that this time the election would be totally democratic, involving all the Jewish communities, instead of just being an appointment by the major London synagogues, as was the case with Hirschell forty years before. The reality was that the election was carefully fixed in favour of Adler, though it took over two years to get the desired result.

To begin with, the committee laid down that the successful candidate would have to be more than 30 years old and not more than 42. The significance of 42, rather than a round 40 or 45, was surely that Adler just qualified; he would be 42 in 1845. There were a number of other specifications agreed in February 1843, which also fitted in with Adler's curriculum vitae. An example was that the candidate had to have been a chief rabbi somewhere for at least six months prior to Hirschell's death. The successful candidate also needed 'to be well acquainted with Ancient Classical and Modern General Literature'.[1]

These qualifications had to benefit Adler, with his record in Hanover and his university diplomas in precisely such studies. There was, of course, justification for the criteria. As British Jews were about to play their part in local politics, the professions and the academic world, their leaders felt that their spiritual head should be secularly, as well as religiously, educated. Though the qualifications were reasonable enough, most of the other applicants were unlikely to have them.

The successful candidate would be given two years to learn English, which would be ample for Adler, who had seen to it that there were prayers in English for the memorial service for George IV in Hanover over ten years before. Adler would, indeed, have little difficulty in acquiring a working knowledge of the new language in twelve months, for he was an excellent linguist.

The rules were also aimed at ensuring that the new chief rabbi would be the sole authority, responsible for 'the general religious direction and superintendence' of the congregations, for shechitah, marriages, Jewish education and responding to religious queries from provincial and overseas congregations. It was readily conceded that there were enough internal arguments within the communities without allowing for lay intervention on spiritual matters.

Many of the great and the good had concerns about the image a new chief rabbi might project to the wider world. Sir David Salomons wrote:

> I hope the presiding depository of the conscience of all the Jews in the British Empire will be a person who shall command the respect of all persons quite as much by his appearance as by his learning ... Of the two I would prefer a commanding person to great talent. Not that I mean that I do not value talent, but there are other qualities besides this essential to the position of so important a functionary.[2]

Salomons was, effectively, saying that the new chief rabbi should not be too Jewish, and should be regarded as a functionary, serving lay masters, rather than a competitor for leadership of the community. Adler, as a former government appointee, might not see the lay leaders in such a superior light. He would also be averse to the image of a commanding personality. He would expect there to be quite enough quasi-megalomaniacs in the community without adding to their number or fighting with them for supremacy. Adler would offer an appealing rather than a commanding personality.

The only thing the new chief rabbi was not going to be allowed to do, according to the job specification, was to issue a *herem*. Apart from that constraint, though, most of the other leaders of the community wanted to ensure that the man chosen as chief rabbi would at least have far greater authority than anybody else in religious matters. For example, in cases involving provincial congregations, even the Beth Din would not be allowed to intervene; only the chief rabbi. Adler wouldn't have to battle for spiritual supremacy; the community was looking for a qualified volunteer.

The next move for the Adler camp was to rig the electoral roll. This was done by means of a proviso that if a community wanted a vote, it would have to commit itself to supporting the cost of the chief rabbi's office by paying an annual fee of £5. If the congregation gave that much a year they got one vote. If, however, the congregation couldn't afford £5, then they couldn't have a vote. £5 in 1844 is about £500 today. Most of the British communities were very small and even the large ones, like Birmingham, were only prepared to promise £20. They got their four votes. By contrast, the Great Synagogue in London promised £500 and then, voluntarily, restricted itself to an apparently magnanimous fifty votes, rather than the 100 to which it would have been entitled in the circumstances. However, as the New Synagogue bought twenty-five and the Hambro Synagogue twenty, the three major London synagogues had a comfortable majority of 95 votes out of an eventual total, including the provincial communities and the rest of the London synagogues, of 141.

The three main London synagogues had their differences. These were often concerned with the retention of members who provided their income. There would be complaints of poaching, like apples off a tree. There had, however, been a treaty agreed in 1834 to split their joint expenses in the ratio of 50 per cent for the Great and 25 per cent for the Hambro and the New. They agreed to work more closely together and, of course, the election would be one of the occasions when this could happen.

The next hurdle for Adler's supporters was to see that the three synagogues voted in support of their candidate. The system was that members of each synagogue could individually cast their votes, so long as they were Free Members. The congregation was divided up into Free Members – effectively, the founders or their coterie – and Seat Holders who paid the same subscriptions but had no vote. This applied in almost all the important congregations around the country.

Obviously the way the Great was going to vote was crucial. There was illustrious lobbying. The Duke of Cambridge called on Lionel de Rothschild, who had been elected a warden of the synagogue in 1840, to recommend Adler. He still felt himself deeply in debt to the rabbi for the prayers for the recovery of the Duchess in 1834.

Lionel de Rothschild would stay in office until 1876 and would have needed little persuading. He was the grandson of Mayer Amschel

Rothschild and knew the affection the founder of the firm had for Adler's father. What was more, the Rothschilds were very religious. They had been horrified when Hannah Mayer Rothschild married the non-Jewish Henry Fitzroy in 1839. Unlike Salomons they would want a Talmudic talent, first and foremost. They were quite capable of providing the commanding personalities themselves.

So the task of lobbying the Great's Free Members behind the scenes would have been in the hands of Rothschild, one of the most important men in the community.

There was one other very senior figure whose support would help Adler a great deal; Sir Moses Montefiore, the first Jewish knight since Sir Solomon de Medina in 1700, president of the Board of Deputies and head of the very prestigious Sephardi community. The Sephardim had decided not to take part in the election because they had their own chief rabbi, the Haham and even though the Haham's position was vacant at the time, they still did not want a joint chief rabbinate with the Ashkenazim. They took their independence as a matter of pride and eventually – and it would not be until more than twenty years later in 1866 – they did get round to appointing a supreme spiritual leader of their own.

Even without participating, though, Sir Moses was a predominant power in the Jewish land. As president of the Deputies, who had represented Jewish interests with the government since 1760, he was acknowledged as the leading Jew in the country. Sir Moses crossed all Orthodox religious boundaries and advocated a vote for Adler. This was the rabbi who had so generously supported the Smyrna appeal when in Hanover, and whose sermons Sir Moses so much admired.

Montefiore and Lionel de Rothschild made a formidable team. Montefiore had worked with the Rothschilds during the Napoleonic Wars and he had one other qualification for Lionel de Rothschild's support; he was his uncle. He had married the sister of Nathaniel Rothschild.

The Great Synagogue vestry was the moving spirit in the election process and everything was done according to the book. Testimonials were required from the candidates and, as all were in German, Dr Abraham Benisch, a linguist and a scholar, was given the title Foreign Secretary, and appointed to translate the documents.

There was plenty of discussion, both in public and in smoke-filled rooms behind closed doors. The thirteen initial candidates were reduced to four; nine were rejected as not meeting the advertised criteria. The short list that remained was Adler, Rabbi Samson Raphael Hirsch, Rabbi Hirsch Hirschfeld, the Chief Rabbi of Wollstein, and Rabbi Benjamin Auerbach, the Chief Rabbi of Darmstadt.

Each of the remaining four had their supporters, but Adler now had by far the most influential backers. The testimonials he received from his professors in Germany were also enthusiastic and carried weight. Count Kielmanseger wrote to the Rothschilds on his behalf, as well as Professors Eisenfasser and Herling, and Dr Weischnier paid tribute to the depth of his knowledge.

The infant Anglo-Jewish press, *The Voice of Jacob* and the *Jewish Chronicle*, made editorial comments which gave all the candidates a fair appraisal and went so far as to question the academic rigour of Adler's doctorate:

> No one at all acquainted with the rank of foreign universities will for an instant pretend to compare Giesen or Erlangen, respectable as they both are, with the high fame and illustrious pre-eminence of Berlin. At this last-named university, no student can obtain his Doctor's degree unless he has been resident there during his course of studies, has submitted to a rigid examination, and maintained a thesis or public disputation; whereas, both at Giesen and Erlangen, diplomas can be obtained by non-residents, without either examination or thesis.[3]

The newspapers, however, had no votes and could twist no arms. The Duke of Cambridge, together with Montefiore and Rothschild, were in a far stronger position, both in their social contacts and in the money they could bring to bear to get the result they wanted.

The non-Jewish press took an interest in the election as well. The popular *Illustrated London News* reported of Adler:

> Each one would of course have had his own man elected, but yet everyone spoke of Dr. Adler in terms of kindness. He was said to be a learned man, strongly given to philosophical enquiry, and more deeply affected with the spirituality of religious observances than is usual with the Jews.[4]

Eventually the votes were cast on 4 December 1844. A substantial majority of the Free Members at the three London synagogues voted for Adler. The congregations' combined ninety-five votes, therefore, went to him. The total scores were 121 for Adler and thirteen for his nearest rival, Rabbi Hirschfeld. Initially, Samson Raphael Hirsch had been tipped as the favourite candidate, but in the event he only got two votes; Glasgow and Penzance.

The only major opposition to Adler came from the very independent Western Synagogue in London, though the Birmingham, Bristol and

Newcastle communities refused to vote as they objected to the way the election had been conducted. On the other hand, smaller congregations, like Falmouth, voted for Adler and its President, Moses Jacob, would always call on the chief rabbi in future when in London. Adler noted that he never had to settle any problems with Falmouth.

Meanwhile, the fourth candidate, Rabbi Benjamin Auerbach, had decided to withdraw as he felt that a community should invite a rabbi to accept the post, rather than have a contested election; it was a diplomatic withdrawal in the face of certain defeat. All the defeated candidates went on to have distinguished careers.

Adler wrote to 'The Council of the United Congregations assembled in London' that he hoped, with the help of the Almighty:

> to take up the stumbling block out of the highways, to remove thorns out of the fields, to lead back those whose souls were diseased, from the shadow of death to the shadow of the Almighty; for, in accepting this responsible post, he had only one ambition; to exalt the horn of the Torah and to keep the way of the trees of life.[5]

Adler was inducted on 18 July 1845. The agreed salary included the payment of a secretary, £100 for life insurance and £120 as relocation expenses. In addition to his salary, he would receive marriage fees where appropriate and there were occasions when, as chief rabbi, he might officiate at a dozen weddings on a single Sunday. The costs of his home and office expenses would be taken into consideration as well.

Unlike its synagogue ministers, the community looked after the financial welfare of its chief rabbi. His predecessor, Solomon Hirschell, had left £14,000 (about £700,000 today). A minister might be paid £100–£200 a year, although they might also get an income from tutoring children, acting as *shochtim*, taking in boarders and even by running their own businesses.

The installation took place six months after Adler's election, because it was necessary for him to give that much notice to the Hanover government before leaving, and neither the estate of Hanover nor the community wanted to lose him: 'They confess how much the prosperity of their institutions owes to his superintendence. They recall the edifying effects of his powerful appeals from the pulpit.'[6]

It would have been more convenient at the British end if Nathan and Henrietta had come to London without the children and it was suggested that they do so for the time being. In those days it was quite acceptable for Victorian children from wealthy families to see little of their parents. The Adlers were not similarly minded:

> I regret sincerely not to be able to meet your wish to leaving my children here and first coming over without them, but my wife and I are so very attached to them, as they are yet of a tender age, that we could not part with them even for a time.[7]

At his final service in Hanover it was significant that a number of state officials came to the service as well. The Adler family left Hanover at 11 o'clock at night but there was still a crowd to see him off, 'to implore a final blessing on their way'.[8] The state population of 500 Jews when he took office had risen to 10,000.[9] In his obituary in 1890, the *Jewish Chronicle* said that there had been 100 synagogues in the state of Hanover when he left, which showed remarkable progress.

When Adler was appointed in London, there was a move to replace him in Hanover with his brother, Gabriel, but the position eventually went to Rabbi Samuel Mayer in October 1845. He had been a pupil of Adler and was to become a very successful incumbent.

It was a long journey from Hanover, which Adler's 6-year-old son, Hermann, found particularly boring, but the family were very impressed by the row of carriages drawn up to greet them as they disembarked in Dover. These included those of Montefiore, as head of the Board of Deputies, and Rothschild, on behalf of the Great Synagogue. In reply to the address of welcome, Adler responded in English and tactfully promised an improvement progressing by degrees, rather than by a sudden spurt.

The illustrious committee waiting to greet Adler knew exactly what they wanted from their new chief rabbi. The community had many problems. There was the highly contentious breakaway secessionist movement. Then again, many of the Jewish leaders were deeply involved in the campaign to win full political emancipation for the Jews, particularly as members of parliament. The very Orthodox were concerned at the possible effect this might have on Jewish observance; what would a Jewish MP do, for example, if there was a vote on a festival?

Outside London, most of the congregations struggled to maintain their Judaism without the infrastructure, the money, or the necessary numbers to do so without considerable difficulty. To make matters worse, the large communities in Liverpool, Birmingham and Manchester were often riven by power struggles over who should run their affairs.

What was needed, in reality, was what would be called in business terms today, a Company Doctor. Somebody who could sort out the mess. Who would also be a spiritual CEO, to ensure that the community grew and thrived, instead of splintering or even disappearing through indifference and intermarriage. The electoral board also wanted peace in the community. The problem of the secessionists would remain outstanding and, eventually, insoluble.

The man the electors had chosen was little known to the general community in England. *The Voice of Jacob* tried to sum him up:

> He is not above the middle stature but his bearing is self-possessed and well calculated to produce respect. His garb is that of a German ecclesiastic, and his head covering a species of cap made of black velvet, having somewhat the shape of a Scottish bonnet.[10]

Adler entered a Britain which had been affected by Enlightenment thinking, but probably had less need of it than in most of Europe. Parliamentary democracy was already the law of the land and the constituencies had been made fairer as a result of the 1832 Reform Act, which reflected the demographic changes in population. There was also a growth in the numbers of the middle class who were gaining public office. Sir Robert Peel, the Prime Minister, had been the spearhead of the movement, and the traditional power of the aristocracy was being more extensively criticized.

Jewish emancipation had been progressing steadily. Before Adler arrived Jews were given the right to vote in 1835 and the first Jewish juryman took the oath on the Old Testament in that year. The Sheriff's Declaration Act was also passed at the same time and that historic office was now opened to Jews as well. As a result, in 1837 Montefiore had become a Sheriff in London and Middlesex. The year before, in 1836, the Marriage Registration Act had qualified the Board of Deputies to approve marriages and in 1841 Francis Goldsmid, who had been called to the Bar at Lincolns Inn in 1833, became the first Jewish barrister and the first Baron.

There was more good news. The week after Adler was installed, the Royal Assent was given to the Municipal Disabilities Removal Act which made Jews eligible for all public offices except Parliament, granting them the right to take the oath on the Old Testament. In 1847 Salomons would become the first Jewish Alderman in London and Lionel de Rothschild would be elected to Parliament though, as he wouldn't take the oath in the prescribed manner, he couldn't take his seat.

By this time Jews had been able to attend University College in London, if no other university, for the past twenty years. There were no ghettos, no discriminatory taxation and they could live where they liked. They could follow any occupation and, in 1846, an ordinance of 1271 preventing them from owning land was also abrogated. In the same year the Religious Opinions Relief Bill repealed an Act of Queen Elizabeth which laid down that everybody had to go to church.

One of the strong planks in the philosophy of the Hamburg reform congregation was, therefore, not relevant to the British secessionists. Judaism in Britain didn't have to change in order for Jews to be emancipated. Only the unacceptable parliamentary oath remained in force, preventing believing Jews from becoming MPs. If they were still denied parliamentary seats because they wouldn't swear the oath of allegiance 'on the true faith of a Christian', this only bothered a comparatively small percentage of the community. Those who fought for that further element of full emancipation were still disappointed, however, at the lukewarm support they received from Sir Moses Montefiore, to whom the prospect of emancipation did not seem to lack its downside.

He was concerned, exactly like Adler, that the price of full emancipation might be a weakening of adherence to the Orthodox laws. That was the basis of the bargain the German reformers had tried to reach with their Christian authorities. It hadn't worked completely by the time Adler left for London, but there had been progress. It could have been put down to the attempt to compromise, even if it had been more due to the residue of the emancipating measures under Napoleon. There is no doubt that the approach of German Jewry towards the new conditions was a warning and a guiding light for Adler during his ministry.

There was, however, political turmoil on the horizon within a year of the new chief rabbi's installation. On 15 May 1846 Peel, as Prime Minister, repealed the Corn Laws and split the Conservative party. Aristocratic farmers had benefited from high tariffs on imported corn. This commercial advantage was destroyed by the repeal. As a direct consequence, on 21 June 1846, Peel's government was defeated on a relatively minor bill and he resigned.

The battle for control of the country between the aristocrats and the new middle classes would now continue for the whole of Adler's ministry. The struggle was to prevent a small minority running the country, as had happened again in Germany after the Napoleonic Wars. An indication of the ongoing battle is that the Liberal Party would be elected sixty years later with a Commons majority of over 300, and almost all its legislation would be thrown out by the House of Lords.

It is not possible to divorce Adler's hidden agenda from what was going on in the wider world. Adler wanted unfettered, unilateral control over any question which affected the Jewish community in religious matters. His objective was to protect Orthodoxy from its critics. His lay opponents, like Sir David Salomons, had their separate agenda, which was to achieve the final mark of equality by fighting for Jews to be able to take their seats in parliament.

The problem Salomons and others perceived was that, if it was desirable for everything else to be decided democratically, what was the case for the chief rabbi making decisions on his own? In the future, Salomons and others would work to ensure that the chief rabbi was not given unfettered power where it affected the state, notably in the forthcoming marriage legislation.

In setting down the formula for the chief rabbinic office in 1843, there had indeed been an effort to curtail his authority. It was suggested that the representatives of London and provincial synagogues, plus the honorary officers of the Great, with three committee members and representatives of other London synagogues, should constitute: 'a permanent committee with which the Chief Rabbi may communicate when necessary on any subject relative to the exercise of the duties of his office, through the medium of the President of the Great Synagogue'.[11]

The wording was vague; who would decide when communication was 'necessary'? The chief rabbi or the committee? The idea was criticized in the press and not taken further. A hundred years later, Chief Rabbi Israel Brodie was told by the president of the United Synagogue that there would be such a committee as a condition of his appointment. Brodie accepted its existence but didn't consult it.

The error in Salomons' thinking was in putting Adler's approach into a political context. Adler was not a dictator. His task, as chief rabbi, was to lay down the law on what was the law – not to make it, but to see it was accepted and, as much as possible, observed. There was no legislative body with powers to make Jewish law; nothing equivalent to the European Commission or the United Nations. As far as the Orthodox were concerned, the law had been laid down in the Talmud, and although it could be interpreted, it could not, basically, be altered.

Many Anglo-Jewish historians continue to have some difficulty with this. One distinguished academic sums up the general view of such writers about Orthodox services: 'Disorder was commonplace, a point to which repeated, ineffective legislation on decorum bears sad testimony'.[12] Orthodox services are in Hebrew and the Sabbath service lasts more than two hours. Even today, few of the congregation can speak or understand Hebrew, but it has only been by continuing to use Hebrew, that the language has survived 2,000 years. The decorum at the shorter weekday morning and evening services is normally impeccable.

On the other hand, going to synagogue on the Sabbath is, to some extent, a social occasion. Traditional congregations dressed for synagogue as the public dressed for church. It might not be like a church service, but then a synagogue is not a church. It is three things; a place of prayer, a place of meeting and a place of study. To say most prayers, a Jew doesn't even have to go to synagogue, but can pray at home. If there are ten male adult Jews present, public worship can be held without leaving the lounge.

On the Sabbath there is a tendency to chat to those on adjoining seats and to exchange comments on current events. There are parts of the service where only the *chazan* says the prayers aloud and often in an undertone. Talking then disrupts praying less. If the noise becomes overloud, the rabbi will call for quiet. 'Disorder' is described in the Oxford English Dictionary as a commotion or confusion. Neither applies to an Orthodox service. Each individual prays as he feels inclined, some seemingly to themselves and some more loudly. It is a personal decision, not laid down by a rabbi, because a rabbi is a teacher, not a priest.

The secessionists, who a century later became the Reform movement, saw the service as far more like that in a church; as the clergyman led the congregation, so they felt their minister should lead his flock. Everybody should pay attention and follow the service, which many felt should contain prayers in English. That was not the Orthodox way and while Adler also wanted a high degree of decorum, he knew very well that the congregants' more laid-back approach had been a complaint of rabbis for hundreds of years, but without much practical result.

It was also true in Britain that the Church of England was the official religion and Orthodoxy was the official choice of the majority of British Jews. By contrast, the Lutherans in Germany were the radicals who had turned away from Catholicism, as Reform had turned away from traditional Judaism. The philosophical approach of the Lutherans and the reform in North Germany would, therefore, contrast with the natural partnership of the Tudor Church of England and the Jewish Orthodox. Reform would have less appeal in the United Kingdom.

Prayer, at the time, was an integral and crucial part of daily life. For example, in large hotels today, it is customary for the General Manager to have a meeting of the senior staff early in the morning. Throughout the industry, this conference is still called Morning Prayers. This is because, in Victorian times, the staff – and the guests – would assemble in the morning to pray together.

What really mattered to Adler was that Jews attended synagogue and remained within the faith. In 1855 there would be approximately 25,000 Jews in the country but under 4,000 seats for them in a synagogue. Apart from Yom Kippur, when 3,000 could attend an overflow service at the Jews' Free School alone, this was adequate. By way of contrast, Reform services failed to inspire greater observance. The new secessionist congregation soon had to abandon daily evening services because hardly anybody came. They would only hold morning services on Mondays and Thursdays for the same reason.

The decorum might be improved, but without a congregation there could be no service.

Similar criticisms of Orthodoxy like 'People wandered in and out of services as they pleased'[13] were equally inaccurate. The very pious would be present for the whole two hours plus. Others would come for the central part of the service and might arrive half an hour or so after the service began. They might also need to go out for a few minutes over such a long period. Synagogue and church services are different.

On another occasion the atmosphere in the synagogue on the festival of Simchat Torah was described as like 'a bear garden'. The Stuart diarist, Samuel Pepys, had been equally critical 200 years earlier. He went to the Sephardi synagogue in 1663 and it happened to be on that day. He wrote of the atmosphere in his diary: 'But, Lord! To see the disorder, laughing, sporting, and no attention, but confusion in all their service.' Rabbi Kopul Kahana, later a lecturer at Jews' College, was a Talmudic genius who escaped certain death in a gas chamber by fleeing to England before the Second World War. He took a Masters' degree at Cambridge, but in the congregation at the university synagogue one Simchat Torah, he went onto the dais in front of the Ark and danced, taking swigs from a bottle of brandy as he did so.

While the critical comments are understandable, they tend to stem from ignorance. On Simchat Torah, at the end of the reading of the Book of Deuteronomy, the congregation moves straight on to Genesis, the first book of the Bible. The yearly cycle begins again and the Orthodox congregations are told to rejoice that they have been spared to carry on the millennial tradition.

There are at least two occasions when synagogue services are a mixture of devotional prayer and a lot of fun; the other is Purim with its derisive knocking when the name of the archenemy, Haman, is invoked. The emphasis on these occasions is not on decorum but on involvement in celebrating survival; from the Persian vizier, Haman, at Purim, and from every country that set out to destroy the Jews at Simchat Torah.

In Adler the election committee got what they considered the perfect candidate, but, of course, they were a long way from Hanover and could know little of the man himself. Certainly, he was highly recommended and well connected with some of the best Jewish families in the country. On the other hand, he came from a very different milieu than that which existed in England.

All his life, Adler had been buffeted – as were all German congregations – by the discriminatory treatment from which German Jews suffered. He had seen them treated disgracefully by the authorities in so many ways. He knew the futility of open resistance, because despotic governments held all the cards. Adler learned to win battles for his congregations by personal charisma, deference to authority, flattery, long term planning and careful manipulation. The situation in Britain, by contrast, would have seemed like paradise because he had been forced to deal with far worse for well over a decade. In such a democratic country, his diplomatic arts were almost unnecessary. Adler was almost overqualified if problems arose, highly educated as a diplomat by the world in which he had lived.

He had also learned how to polish his image in the outside world. He had dealt with royalty, like the Duke of Oldenburg and the Dukes of Cambridge and Cumberland. He had been appointed in Hanover, not by the Jewish community, but by the government. In Britain he would sometimes refer to his father as Marcus Cohen Adler in order to anglicize his background.

A leader needs self-confidence and Adler had been tutored to have that quality too. He had been a Landrabbiner, representing the Jews with the authorities. This was the designated role of the spiritual leader in Germany and not that of the lay heads. So Adler was not accustomed to knowing his place, as a bad second to the senior laymen. This, of course, would not be true of many ministers of small British communities. Their president could well be a public figure, serve on the local council and support local charities, with the spiritual leader well in the background.

The minister was, invariably, a badly paid employee, though Adler's basic salary was about £1,000 of which the Great provided £500. As in the small Hanover communities, the minister was often initially employed as a *shochet*, to provide kosher meat. As described, he could also be a teacher, a *mohel* to perform circumcisions and he might take in boarders. As far as his status was concerned, he did not acquire the same respect as was afforded the major lay figures. On the other hand it was also highly unlikely in Britain that he would be a Talmudic expert, capable of laying down Jewish law in difficult cases.

In the future Adler would be accused of developing a too tight system of control over his congregations and communities, which would later become known as Adlerism. It wasn't so different in its scope, however, from the situation in Hanover. Adler would leave the administrative detail of synagogue finance and internal arguments to the individual lay leaders to sort out, unless they developed into a crisis. His concern was the defence of the Orthodox practices of the communities he led.

Sometimes, though, this would involve him in turning a blind eye, for Adler inherited a British community which cut a lot of religious corners. When Sir David Salomons presided at his inaugural banquet, when he became the first Jewish Lord Mayor of London in 1855, there were tables with kosher food. It would be eaten, however, from plates which had been used before for non-kosher food. This was not a minor consideration, but Adler saw there was a need for pragmatism; where he must draw the line and where he could be in danger of overstepping the mark. As he had promised at his inauguration, he'd take it slowly.

The installation ceremony at the Great Synagogue was attended by a full complement of the great and the good. Even the Aldgate Church rang its bells in celebration. The *Jewish Chronicle* called it: 'the most important event in Anglo-Jewish annals, from the days when our fathers first landed on these hospitable shores, even to the present hour'.[14] A canopy of blue damask embroidered with gold was placed over Adler's head. The assembly was a lot more impressive than in Oldenburg fifteen years before. The congregation said *minchah*, the afternoon service, and settled down to hear Adler address them in German. Those who spoke Yiddish would have understood perfectly well.

He was anxious to buy time. He knew every inch of his bailiwick in Hanover, but this was a great foreign capital where he didn't yet even speak the language. He said in his installation address that where previously he had worked among friends, he was now a stranger. He hoped his listeners would 'meet his timidity with love'.

That sermon was a masterpiece of tact and determination. It is reprinted in this volume as Appendix C. On the one hand he was addressing some of the most powerful men, in a Jewish community far larger and more powerful than he had in his charge in Hanover. On the other, he had a list of objectives he intended to achieve. These were not subject in his own mind to any form of change that might please the laymen, some of whom were prepared to compromise Jewish practice to achieve total emancipation. This all mirrored the situation in Hanover when he became Landrabbiner.

So he laid out his programme, sugar-coated with a high degree of deference to his audience. He told them he was going to observe the din like the biblical high priest. He talked of the high priest's responsibility for excluding 'strange fire' from the Temple. It was possible to read between the lines that anything like the programme of the Reform movement in Germany would never be introduced into one of his synagogues while he remained in office. He intended to control his schools and synagogues, and he brought in quotations from the Biblical books of Jeremiah, Zechariah and Joshua to support the case he was making.

All these objectives, he told the congregation, were only attainable with their full-hearted support. Indeed he praised the congregation to such an extent that the impression must have been given that he wouldn't make a move without their approval, which would have reassured them. While it was true, however, that he would always try to get agreement from his flock, it would be clear soon enough that this was not a necessity in his mind. He could always remind them that he had said in his address that, as far as the *din* was concerned, it was:

> extremely difficult to guard it at a time in which one party seeks its glory in pulling down existing structures of religious theory and practice; the other in preserving everything hallowed by age, though opposed to the foundations of the law; in which one minister worships progress and the other adores conservatism.[20]

At the same time there remained leaders in the community, like David Salomons, whose primary focus was elsewhere. They wanted the same relations with the established church as other dissenting groups enjoyed. Ironically, there was the one great difference; that the government accepted Jewish divorce as the equivalent of a church divorce, where dissenters needed the approval of the Church of England. This anomaly did not worry the government, but it worried the Jews who wanted emancipation. They wanted exactly equal treatment, even if the result was detrimental to traditional practices. This attitude would cause dissension in the future.

Adler had shown his support for emancipation in his sermon when, at the conclusion, he included an invocation for the 'Royal Family and the Parliament' with a special reference to the removal of 'ancient barriers between citizen and citizen'. Now he would go to work.

The general movement in Britain, for greater general participation in making important decisions, also had its equivalent in synagogue communities. The founders of provincial synagogues were often intent on remaining in control; they formed the Free Members. Those who were not in the magic circle were allowed to pay for their seats, but were usually given no say in the running of the synagogue.

This often led to unrest. Disaffected members formed – or threatened to form – breakaway communities. The autocratic behaviour of the controllers of the Bevis Marks Synagogue – the Mahamad – was one of the complaints of those who had broken away from the synagogue in 1840.

Burton Street had David Woolf Marks, who was an excellent preacher with a good enough intellect to be Professor of Hebrew at University College, London from 1848–98. Years later, the Rev. A.A. Green, no mean speaker himself, said that Marks had: 'The most glorious voice I have ever heard. He never failed to sweep a meeting off its feet.'[16] Marks was appointed to be the first minister at Burton Street in 1841, but it was typical of Jewish congregations at the time that his room for manoeuvre was restricted by the control of the Council of Founders.

Besides the *dayanim* there would be other Talmudic experts in Britain during Adler's ministry, but they did not usually serve congregations. Samuel Gollancz was employed at the British Museum, Joseph Zedner was the Hebrew Librarian there, and Emanuel Deutsch the Assistant Librarian. Adolph Neubauer catalogued the Hebrew manuscripts at the Bodleian in Oxford and, of course, there was, eventually, the able leader of the forthcoming Jews' College, Michael Friedländer. To such men, however, the challenge of becoming a synagogue minister was always going to be less attractive, less academically prestigious and less rewarding.

Adler could see from the make-up of the Burton Street congregation that their appeal was to middle-class Jews and those of an intellectual bent. It was, basically, a lay movement with its main objective to have a synagogue nearer their homes, as well as to help the cause of Jewish emancipation by creating a public image closer to the norm of the established church, with more use of English and a higher level of decorum.

They wanted to emphasise their Englishness. This was illustrated when two Jewish deputations called on the Prime Minister, Sir Robert Peel, in 1845. One, led by Sir Moses Montefiore, asked that the emancipatory measures of recent years should be extended to every other area of public life. The other deputation, led by Sir Francis Goldsmid, demanded total emancipation as the right of all Englishmen.

Adler had arrived in London in July 1845. In March of that year the Duke of Cambridge had warmly endorsed Adler's work in Hanover in a speech in the House of Lords on the remaining Jewish disabilities. Talking of Adler's educational work, the Duke said: 'I can speak to the care which these persons evince in bringing up their orphans belonging to their persuasion in useful trades, so as to make them worthy members of society.'[17]

As early as April 1846 Adler was telling the governors of the Western Jewish Boys School that there also needed to be a girls' school, which was a major innovation for the time. The Duke of Cambridge agreed to be the patron and Baroness de Rothschild and Lady Montefiore agreed to take it under their wing. It opened in October and Adler's English was now good enough for him to give his opening address in the vernacular. He emphasized that girls should be educated exactly like boys and took the opportunity of praising the importance of Jewish mothers. Within a month the Jewish press were: 'highly delighted with the humility and fatherly conduct of our splendid Chief'.[18]

There was no dissension in the Welcoming Committee about their own religious position, vis-à-vis Adler. They said very clearly at the installation that they spoke, 'on behalf of all those who have invited you to preside over them'.[19] They said they wanted a commanding spiritual leader. Like so many other public statements, a lot of the lay leaders liked the principle, but weren't so happy when it was spelt out in detail.

The position of chief rabbi was not well understood by the general public. The correspondent of the *Illustrated London News* wrote of the appointment:

> An event has just occurred of great importance to the Jewish nation. In the absence of a High Priest, the post of Chief Rabbi of the English Jews is regarded as one of the greatest sacerdotal importance. The religious destinies of 'the scattered people' may be influenced, or even consummated by his councils; he is their mediator with heaven, the shadow of their former priests and kings and may one day 'lead them forth as sheep' to reoccupy the now desolate land of their fathers. His principles are as important as his position. A Christian bias, or even a liberal tendency in favour of a due regard to our 'evidences' would expose both himself and his flocks to the displeasure of foreign synagogues and to the certain abhorrence of the lower and less educated orders.[20]

Adler was not, of course, the Jewish mediator with heaven, but the question of the reaction of Jewish communities around the world to his decisions was a point well taken. The Jewish joke that two Jews will come up with three opinions is met with a wry smile. It was very necessary for the chief rabbi of Britain to merit a good reputation.

Notes

1. Meir Persoff,, *Hats in the Ring: Choosing Britain's Chief Rabbis from Adler to Sacks* (Boston, MA: Academic Studies Press, 2013), p.9.
2. Chaim Bermant, *The Cousinhood: The Anglo-Jewish Gentry* (London: Eyre & Spottiswoode, 1971), p.177.
3. *The Voice of Jacob*, 30 August 1844, p.210.
4. www.geni.com/people/Chief-Rabbi-Dr-Nathan-Marcus-Adler/6000000008939854310
5. Michael Friedländer, *Jewish Quarterly*, July 1890.
6. *The Voice of Jacob*, 1 August 1845, p.212.
7. Letter from Adler in Hanover to Samuel Ellis received 14 January 1845.
8. Ibid.
9. Dr. Peter Schulze, Archivist of the Hanover Jewish Community.
10. *The Voice of Jacob*, 18 July 1845, p.194.
11. Ibid., 3 March 1843, p.121.
12. Eugene C. Black, 'The Anglicization of Orthodoxy: The Adlers, Father and Son', in Frances Malino and David Sorkin (eds), *Profiles in Diversity: Jews in a Changing Europe* (Detroit, MI: Wayne State University Press, 1998), p.305.

13. Rabbi Raymond Apple, address to the Jewish Historical Society of England, Israel Branch, 30 May 2010, p.1.
14. *Jewish Chronicle*, July 1845.
15. *Jewish Chronicle*, 8 August 1845, p.217.
16. *Jewish Chronicle*, 22 January 1912, p.18.
17. Derek Taylor, *British Chief Rabbis, 1664–2006* (London and Portland, OR: Vallentine Mitchell, 2007), p.224.
18. Ibid.
19. *The Voice of Jacob*, 28 March 1845.
20. *Illustrated London News*, 1845, p.389.

5

Taking up the Reins

As they settled down, the Adlers found a home in South Street, in the City near the Great Synagogue. Within a year the new chief rabbi could speak good English, having been taught by the successful actor, Alfred Wigan. This tuition would not only have improved his vocabulary, but would have addressed the techniques of public speaking, beyond those that Adler already possessed.

As minister of the Great he performed regular ecclesiastical duties, including reading the prayer for the royal family on the Sabbath, guiding the sounding of the *shofar* on the New Year, and reading the dirges on Tisha b'Av. The Great Synagogue was the most powerful community in the country and Adler looked after it very carefully. The synagogue was very traditional and for years Adler had a *meshores*, a personal attendant, who always accompanied him. He would be the last *meshores*, though.

On the one hand he had greater responsibilities because there were far more Jews, albeit fewer congregations, than in Hanover. Membership of a synagogue was not mandatory, as it had been at home. On the other hand, Adler was not responsible to any government body. If the government wanted to discuss matters affecting the Jewish community they did so informally with individuals, or they would officially consult the Jewish Board of Deputies whose origins dated back to the reign of George III.

In London Adler took stock of his new office. He would enjoy a long honeymoon period as the community took pleasure in having an active chief rabbi after the declining years of Solomon Hirschell. Adler gave well received sermons in all the main London synagogues. He had the advantage that his predecessor never learned to speak good English, and listening to sermons in the vernacular was a novel experience for almost all the congregation.

As rabbi of the Great he was only committed to preaching on *Shabbat Hagadol* before Pesach, and at the New Year, but he soon announced that he would give a sermon every month to mark *Rosh Chodesh*, the coming of the new month. One sermon in 1846 marked the birth of Queen Victoria's third daughter. He always set out to reflect the loyalty of the British community to the Crown, as with his similar sermons in Hanover. Adler always played the long game: he planned his actions in advance meticulously.

While he was improving his English he hardly ventured outside London, and suggestions that he might visit the main provincial centres during the High Holy days were discreetly put on the back burner. He took a particular interest, though, in bar mitzvah boys and would have them come to his house on the Sunday after the ceremony to test their knowledge of the religion. There was much weighing up of the new spiritual leader, to see whether he would be an ally or an opponent of the emancipation agenda. Both sides were going to take each other's measure.

It would all have been very challenging. He was in a city far larger than he had ever known before, with a responsibility immensely greater than he had previously undertaken. He was working in a foreign language and a lot of the lay leaders of the community were not particularly observant or committed, as he was, to carrying out all the *mitzvoth*.

When, however, in his inaugural address, Adler had said that he was now among strangers, this wasn't entirely true. Besides his residence, there was one building in the City where he was entirely at home. That was the Beth Hamedrash in nearby 1, South Building, where the very Orthodox would gather to study the rabbinic texts. Such an opportunity for learning was a traditional part of every Orthodox community and the Beth Hamedrash in London had been in existence since at least 1782, when it received a legacy from Samuel Falk, known as the Baal Shem of London (a man with a fine reputation), and an important rabbinic figure.

Most of those who came to learn were immigrants from Eastern Europe. They would talk in Yiddish, redolent of their childhood and without the stigma of being considered 'a bastard language', which led so many of the British lay leaders to wish it could be forgotten.

Within the Beth Hamedrash building was the Ashkenazi Beth Din, the ecclesiastical court, which had been founded by Solomon Hirschell in 1805. There the *dayanim* (judges) would consider the cases brought before them, under Adler's chairmanship as the *Av Beth Din*. It wasn't an ideal setting. The building was dilapidated, there was little room to wait in comfort, and the atmosphere outside the court was crowded and frenetic. Nevertheless, it was the only Ashkenazi Beth Din in the English speaking world at the time. If decisions were needed by the British communities or those within the Empire, it was to London that they had to turn.

One of the court's most important functions was to deal with weddings. Throughout the country this was the normal responsibility of the church, which required a vicar to be present at the ceremony and the banns to be read. The law setting down the procedure dated from 1753, but it had been decided that the Quakers and the Jews should be excluded and left to deal with their own marriages. Even in 1836, when the concept of civil marriages was introduced, the Jews were still allowed to be independent. It wasn't, in fact, legal for Jews to father non-Jews with Christian mothers. Such partnerships were forbidden by the 1698 Blasphemy Act, but its implementation had fallen into disuse.

Solomon Hirschell had created the Beth Din to deal with this responsibility, because the authenticity of a marriage was of prime importance to the legitimacy of Jews as Jews. If there was any question of a child's mother not having been Jewish, the offspring could not be part of an Orthodox community. There were detailed procedures which had to be followed to confirm her status, though the qualifications to be a member of a Beth Din were rather more elastic.

Many Beth Din procedures such as divorces (*gittin*) can be carried out if the presiding judge is a fully qualified rabbi, in which case the two assistant judges need not be ordained rabbis, so long as they are Orthodox with a basic understanding of Jewish law. As a divorce document (*get*) must comply with the detailed rules of Jewish law, the scribe must be a trained, learned expert. There could not be a single error in the wording of a scribe's document. The witnesses must be Orthodox and able to sign their names in Hebrew, but they need not be rabbis. In Solomon Hirschell's time there were very few people qualified to carry out these functions, which explains why Hirschell relied on men from the Continent.

Once a member of the Beth Din (a *dayan*) became a permanent part of the court, he normally remained in office for life. In the years before Hirschell's death, two *dayanim* had passed away and were replaced by Azriel ben David Ha Levi Segal and Aaron Levi (Reb Oran). They would serve until 1861 and 1876 respectively. Another *dayan* would be Arieh Leib ben Rabbi Issachar Ber, known as the Rev. A.L. Barnett. His *semichah* (ordination) came from the famous Akiva Eiger of Posen.

All these *dayanim* were from the Continent and had *semichah*. Hirschell, himself, was one of the only three chief rabbis to have been born in England – he was the son of the former chief rabbi, Hart Lyon – but his roots were firmly in the Continent. His brother-in-law was from Lissa in Poland which had a famous yeshivah and three of the six *dayanim* whom Hirschell appointed were from Lissa. When Hirschell died, Aaron Levi, the scribe, took over as acting head of the Beth Din, until Adler was elected; the necessary, though temporary, replacement scribe was also from Lissa.

Levi was born in Poland in 1794 but had come to England when he was 16 during the height of the Napoleonic Wars. He was a great scholar and highly regarded by Hirschell, who had made him a *dayan* after he had returned from a seven-month trip to Australia to effect a divorce. He was a much loved character in the East End and, apparently, felt no resentment in surrendering his position as *Av Beth Din* to the new incumbent.

When, therefore, Adler took up his post as head of the court, he had colleagues who spoke Yiddish, had *semichah* and were Talmudically expert. They were about his age and they all got on very well for many years. From the beginning, therefore, he was among friends. It was also significant that the official title of the Beth Hamedrash was the Beth Hamedrash of the Holy Congregation of the German Jews in London.

Its links to the continental tradition were far stronger than those to the Great Synagogue. The immigrant community was very observant of Jewish practice, even if they preferred small groups of worshippers to the establishment synagogues. If there was ever any difficulty in getting a *minyan* for services at one of the major synagogues, there would always be one available at the Beth Hamedrash.

South Street could be considered the clubhouse of the very Orthodox. Its 4,000-book library had been Hirschell's collection, bought for them by a kindly benefactor. In 1849 Adler would also persuade Abraham Moses to give the institution £2,000 in gilt-edged stock, the interest on which would pay for a librarian who lived in the building. Aaron Levi held the post till 1872.

The community of the Beth Hamedrash formed a second segment of English Jews, with its own criteria. As a consequence where, in the future, British ministers with overseas *semichahs* would cavil at the ruling that they should be addressed as reverend rather than rabbi, this would hardly affect the *dayanim*. The Holy Congregation of German Jews in London could see the nomenclature ruling as just another strange quirk of the British community. The city neighbours of the *dayanim* would know very well their qualifications. Even Adler didn't use his rabbinic title in public and was referred to as Rev. Dr N.M. Adler.

The problem remained that the wider community could be led to water but couldn't be made to drink. Few books were borrowed from the library: 'The reading room proper, however, was fairly well attended and the Rev. Aaron Levy, the resident Dayan, was frequently in attendance during the summer months, at three or four in the morning, to admit persons for the purpose of study'.[1] The Orthodox community took Talmudic study very seriously. Though they had to work all day, at night they were perfectly prepared to give up their sleep, and Levi was ready to do the same.

The Beth Din also dealt with a wide range of other legal matters, notably conversions and divorces. While it was up to the couple divorcing to settle their own terms of separation, the interest of their children was the responsibility of the Beth Din and would need to be approved before a divorce could be granted. The chief rabbi was, however, the only authority for cases brought from outside London, though, at Adler's request, the *dayanim* could act for him.

By tradition, the Beth Din met on Mondays and Thursdays. Adler presided and chose the same days to teach at his newly created Society for Talmudical Study. The meetings took place every evening, from 8.00 to 9.00. He paid the *dayanim* out of his own pocket, though they had other sources of income from teaching to taking in boarders. Aaron Levi was responsible for the cheder (Hebrew school) which educated the children.

The reputation of the Beth Din was more paternal than authoritarian, as this was Adler's style: 'He was perhaps seen at his best when presiding as Av Beth Din at the sittings of the Beth Din ... his exhortation, admonition and efforts at peacemaking, were weighted with a remarkable power of persuasiveness which few could resist.'[2] The chief rabbi's experience in Hanover would have been good training for the Beth Din in London. Adler would normally start the discussion by asking 'What can I do in the matter?' The court would never disregard the *din*, but if there were mitigating circumstances, or the opportunity to give the litigant the benefit of the doubt, the court would try to do so. As a consequence it was highly regarded and very popular.

Levi, himself, was an iconic figure and when he eventually died, it was reported that 2,000 people attended the funeral. For his part Adler would always treat his colleagues with great respect, even though they were not ministers of major congregations.

Between 1845 and 1850, sixty conversions were approved, of which thirty-six were the children of mixed marriages. There were seventy between 1851 and 1855, of which forty-one were minors. There were half a dozen divorces a year, but this small number was not surprising. For the general public, divorce was rare and stigmatized. It was normally pretty well out of the question, anyway, as it needed an Act of Parliament to be approved.

The number of conversions of formerly Christian brides would not appear to have been very great. The best records are those of the Great Synagogue where about 4 per cent of the weddings during the reign of George III were of a convert bride, noted in the records as a Daughter of Abraham. When it was agreed to convert a non-Jew, ritual immersion was the final step, though Adler never attended this procedure himself.

As the London Beth Din was the only one in the Empire, requests for its help came from many parts of the world; Aaron Levy travelling to Australia was an example. The Beth Din also had to decide on the married status of women who had lost touch with their husbands, through convict transportation abroad, death in battle or simple disappearance. There is no presumption of death in Judaism and if it could not be proved that the husband had died, the wife would not be pronounced a widow and free to marry again. An extreme case was of a soldier who had not been heard of since 1793 and whose wife asked for him to be declared dead in 1816. It had taken the Beth Din three years to complete their enquiries and agree with her.

Of course, it was always possible for litigants to ignore the Beth Din and apply to the British civil courts. On the other hand, some of the cases brought to the police by immigrant Jews were so difficult for the authorities to understand – particularly if they involved aspects of the *din* – that, on occasions, they directed them to the Beth Din in order to avoid having to become involved.

Sometimes the London Beth Din could be asked by rabbis on the Continent to confirm that a divorce document was valid. Validating a divorce was particularly important for the children of a second marriage who would be considered illegitimate if there was something wrong with the first divorce. Adler validated at least one divorce granted in New York. In 1864 there would be a divorce (*get*) granted in Australia, following a request from a Polish woman who had asked London to write to Australia to confirm her status.

Although, officially, he was the Ashkenazi Chief Rabbi, Adler was held in high respect by the Sephardim. His friendship with Sir Moses Montefiore was the rock on which the community's religious and communal policies would depend for the next forty years. There was a clear division of labour; Montefiore would support Adler's religious decisions, and Adler left communal matters to Montefiore. Montefiore always referred to Adler as 'our excellent chief rabbi' and never left on a journey overseas without getting Adler's blessing. Their teamwork was an essential factor in the way the growing community would develop.

The relationship of the Sephardi and the Ashkenazi communities had seldom been without its problems. Both communities wanted to be the senior: the Sephardim claimed pre-eminence as the forerunners of the Jewish return to England, while the Ashkenazim based their claim to seniority on their greater numbers. Their relationship was so fraught that there were even occasions when a Sephardi married an Ashkenazi that the Sephardi family sat *shiva* (mourning) as if their offspring had died. It was a distasteful measure of contempt for the other side.

Montefiore and Adler came from very different strata of society. They were born in different countries, one was Sephardi and one Ashkenazi, and where Montefiore was already a public figure, Adler was a newcomer. Nevertheless, they gelled, and worked together for the good of the community in perfect harmony. Their mutual commitment to the *din* was the crucial factor.

When Montefiore returned from his travels, the two families would get together for the Sabbath dinner. As Marcus Adler recalled many years later:

> It was a treat to be a guest at his [Montefiore's] table. The Sabbath meal often lasted until nearly midnight, and he told us of his many experiences and the incidents connected with his missions. He quivered when telling us of the horrible treatment the Jews had to endure in the days of Nicholas I and how the Cossacks used to surround many villages and snatch from their mother's arms the most robust and best looking of the children in order to devote them to military service.[3]

The new chief rabbi found himself in an illustrious position. Besides being welcomed by the leaders of the Jewish community at home and abroad, within a few months there was a formal visit by the Hanoverian ambassador to London, who called to pay his respects. In his turn the chief rabbi called on the Duke of Cambridge, who had no hesitation in making it clear that he had been instrumental in having Adler appointed.[4] They had become good friends. The Duke attended Jewish functions, at one of which Adler apologized for the length of the Grace after Meals. The Duke replied that he didn't mind how long it was after the meal, so long as it was short before they started eating!

The system of centralised control, soon to be created by the new chief rabbi and based on his Hanover experience, came to be known in some circles as Adlerism. In the minds of some of the lay leaders, though, this was not meant as a compliment. Until the nineteenth century there had been little need for centralization. Most British Jews lived in London until that time. When Adler collected information about the provincial communities after he arrived, it was typical of the minute size of communities that there were thirty-five Jewish families recorded in Sunderland, six in Nottingham, twenty in Oxford, nine in Ipswich and forty-one in Glasgow.

Such small congregations needed some central system to help them with their problems and this was very similar to the position in Hanover. Adler dealt with the complexities in the same way, by providing them with expert and authoritative decisions on their queries. It was a far better service than they had enjoyed in the past. Rather than some new invention of Adler, it was a variation of the Landrabbiner set-up in Hanover. It did have the effect, however, of introducing another layer of authority besides the lay leaders, and this was not always welcomed when the laymen had contrary views.

Nevertheless, a centralized body needed to be put in place. The alternative was *halachic* decisions made by unqualified synagogue functionaries, and these would never have been automatically accepted by other communities outside the United Kingdom. Rulings made by Adler would be. That was the crucial point. Jews worldwide relied on the validity of his decisions.

It therefore needed to be clearly stated by the Chief Rabbi that if the personal preferences of honorary officers of synagogues were not in accordance with Jewish law, they would not have his approval. Of course, if there were also conflicts within British congregations, an umpire would be highly desirable. When Adler mediated and/or applied the *din*, the warring parties normally accepted his decisions without question.

The community was very ready to accept Adler as the ultimate authority. At the outset of his ministry in 1846, when Dr Kreuger was appointed in Manchester, *The Voice of Jacob* reported: 'His election to be preacher to an English congregation was very properly made subject to his obtaining a letter of licence from the Revd Dr Adler. This we think is the first election of this kind since the accession of our Chief Rabbi.'[5] In 1847 when the Dublin community advertised for a *hazan*, they spelt out the same requirement: 'It will be indispensable that moral character and qualifications be certified by the Revd the Chief Rabbi.'

Adler's rulings were requested on a whole range of subjects affecting individuals. Could a member with doubtful morals be given a synagogue honour? If a couple were living together, but not married, did the *din* allow them to get married in synagogue? If a child ran away from home, did the parents have to take it back? If a father died owing money to the synagogue could the honorary officers refuse to allow his son to put up a tombstone for him, unless the debt was paid? Adler and the Beth Din dealt with all the questions. For example, he wrote about the debt: 'Our law demands that the father should not suffer for the son, therefore we are not justified to do such an open insult to an innocent man.'

End of discussion, and Adler would spread his net very wide. He exchanged correspondence with *rabbanim* and lay figures in other lands, in a variety of languages. In addition there were a great many long-standing local problems to overcome. Even before he arrived, Adler had been told that the situation he had inherited in many of the provincial communities was unsatisfactory. In Falmouth, for instance, Joseph Rintel was the *shochet*, *mohel* (for circumcisions), secretary, prayer leader, occasional preacher and teacher. He was paid £1 a week for carrying out all these duties and this was quite typical. Adler tried to ameliorate such situations.

He would also act as an employment agency. The provincial communities were often poor and could not pay decent salaries. Often the only possible candidates for vacant posts were refugees and immigrants, and the culture of their upbringing might well clash with that of the community they were going to serve. On the other hand, with such difficulty in filling posts, every effort had to be made to keep the officials in place.

When another Falmouth *shochet* accepted a better job, the community withheld his salary. Adler had to write to them: 'Mr. Herrman is leaving for Sheffield and complains that you object to him leaving. I think you have no right to form an impediment to the man's promotion in life.' Adler would not avoid confrontation if he felt synagogue officials were badly treated. In 1851 after a row in Exeter, Adler wrote: 'I cannot suppress stating that no respectable reader will now go to Exeter to be exposed to such insults.'

Because the standard of education was poor, the level of religious observance was lax and the congregations lacked guidance. The original election committee hoped that their new chief rabbi would make substantial improvements in all these areas. When he addressed the objectives, though, some would label his efforts Adlerism and impugn less creditable intentions. It was usually sour grapes.

There was one other major difference between the spiritual organization of German Jews and those in England. There were hardly any Talmudic experts in the ranks of Anglo-Jewish ministers. There was no equivalent in England to the German rabbinic families. Where Oldenburg, with hardly any Jews in the state, had Adler followed by Samson Raphael Hirsch, as their spiritual leaders, there was as yet no minister with *semichah* in a similar congregation in England.

In addition, the ministers would always be appointed by laymen, rather than the state and: 'Few would be able to preach at any level or in any language.'[6] Adler even composed an address in English for marriage services, in case the local minister was unable to do so. As a result the British ministers were not given the status they deserved. They would find themselves at the beck and call of the synagogue founders, who were often accustomed to running the synagogues as almost private fiefdoms.

So in setting out to build up a cadre of qualified ministers, Adler was, effectively, starting from scratch. He also had the constraint, not perhaps surprisingly, that a ministerial career for their sons did not appeal to most well-to-do Jewish families. It lacked authority, income, time for study and time to teach. When the ministers became too old to officiate, they were often abandoned to a poverty-stricken old age. If they died young, there was no formal provision for their families. It was not surprising that the typical minister Adler inherited in England could never approach the Chief Rabbi's all-round ability.

There were a very few reasonably knowledgeable exceptions in Adler's early days: Morris Raphall, the Birmingham minister, was an able and popular preacher, but he would accept a call to America in 1850; Henry A. Henry, who had been educated at the Jews' Free School and became its headmaster for a time, was another who was a competent, if not outstanding, preacher. He was then also lost to a pulpit in the United States.

David Aaron de Sola was a pillar of the Sephardi community. He was born in Holland and was officially only a reader but, in fact, he was also a preacher and a composer. Aaron Levy Green was another fine minister but, like many of his colleagues, he was self-taught; he became the first minister at the new Ashkenazi Central Synagogue in the West End of London, but he died relatively young. .

At the Hambro, with the title of reader, was Herman Hoelzel, who possibly had *semichah* from his time in Germany where he had served under Adler in Hanover. He certainly had ambitions for higher posts and was recruited for Hobart in Tasmania. In Australia he attempted to establish himself as the chief rabbi for the country, but when he went on to Sydney, his self-proclaimed grandiose title, Presiding Rabbi of the Australian Colonies, proved to lack substance. Falling out with the congregations, Hoelzel left Australia and disappeared from historical view. Knowledge was one thing, but diplomacy, a quality Adler had in abundance, was also very important.

Once he had mastered the English language Adler could fairly claim to have created the English-speaking pulpit. He didn't lose his Hanoverian accent, according to the *Manchester Guardian*, but the paper admired the distinction of his delivery and the excellence of his thought.[7] In the provinces when he gave a sermon, it was a revelation.

He had, however, left Hanover for London with one important task yet to be achieved. He had wanted to start a seminary there for training Jewish teachers. A commission had been set up in 1841 to implement this and the project was eventually supported by the government. The Minister of the Interior, I.C. von Wisch, even went so far as to recommend it in the press. Everything, however, took time and money and, in 1844, Adler was still appealing for financial support for the cause.

In England there was a similar agenda. It was an embarrassment to the lay leaders that the Jewish community was part of the greatest nation of the nineteenth century but, in 1842, they couldn't produce even one native born candidate for the office of their spiritual leader. All four of the shortlisted nominees were German. This was considered demeaning to the community and, in principle, they wanted to be able to train their own ministers and teachers. Adler found it ironic that: 'hardly one post was occupied by an

English-born Jew',[8] which explains why a knowledge of English was increasingly demanded of candidates. The same applied to teachers.

The future creation of Jews' College by Adler was approved as an attempt to produce British ministers. Initially he didn't set out to try to have them trained to *semichah* standards. That would have been running before they could walk. Equally, however, the hidden agenda of the congregational lay leaders remained to maintain and improve their own status, rather than preside over a community steeped in Talmudic knowledge. When even Adler's limited religious curriculum started to be an educational priority, the leaders lost interest. Although they would sing the praises of the future Jews' College, they did so in a very minor key.

Adler was just as anxious to encourage general adult education. In August 1845 a Literary Institute had been opened at Sussex Hall in the City. This offered lectures on a wide variety of subjects. In the first three years 118 papers were delivered and 40,000 books were borrowed. Adler gave the Institute a set of the works of Moses Mendelssohn. He often attended the lectures and took his wife, Henrietta, with him. As time went by, though, attendances dropped, as other attractions emerged, and the Institute would close in 1859. In retrospect it was considered likely that it would have been more successful if it had confined its studies solely to Jewish subjects.

It wasn't surprising that, faced with all the problems, the newly installed chief rabbi first set out to do a survey to find out exactly what he had got and what was missing. As early as August 1845 he sent out a detailed questionnaire to The Presidents and Wardens of the Jewish Congregations in the British Empire; forty-four of them responded, including the congregation in Jamaica.[9] From this would come his religious regulations for their communities.

Adler's first year mirrored many in the future. In 1846 he spoke at the Great Synagogue, at the New in Crosby Square and the Hambro in Fenchurch Street. At the Hambro he spoke on behalf of Russian Jewry. The aim of the Russian government was to convert its citizens to the Russo-Greek church. To encourage this, the Jews were persecuted. Among other disabilities, they were only allowed to live in a few towns and were expelled from others. They were taxed on such items as Sabbath candles and kosher meat, and their children were conscripted for periods of service, as long as twenty-five years, in the army.

Many Jewish leaders outside Russia, like Adler, protested and Moses Montefiore left for Russia in March 1846 to intercede with the Czar. Adler supported his endeavours by writing a special prayer to be read in all the synagogues beforehand. At Montefiore's urgings, the Czar did agree to abrogate the law which had been passed to prevent Jews living within fifty miles of the German and Austrian borders. There was little more progress. When Montefiore came home, though, his efforts were recognized by the government and he was made a Baronet by Queen Victoria.

There were many problems closer at hand. In February 1846 it was reported that the Whitechapel Union Workhouse had seven Jewish inhabitants. It was discovered that one old lady there, to widely felt shame, was a relative of the former reader at the New Synagogue. Here the whole community was of one mind; the whole concept of the workhouse was anathema to them, and Adler had no hesitation in instructing the Great's honorary officers to have the Jewish inmates removed and looked after. While his authority was officially restricted to religious matters, Adler would always defy anybody to object when he addressed moral issues. The honorary officers took the necessary action.

It was less easy to deal with the financial problems of the majority of the community who suffered from unremitting poverty. Its relief, such as it was and could be, was largely due to the generosity of the few wealthy Jewish families, though many others made whatever contribution they could afford. It could never be anything like enough. Many synagogues increased their income by fining members for shortcomings related to synagogue matters; among them for not accepting offices, for not attending services and for chewing tobacco in *shul*. Slowly these were abandoned over the years, with the Great raising seat prices in 1843 to make up for the loss of revenue.

The Chief Rabbi's reputation was soon acknowledged outside his own community. In the same winter month he was asked to attend court as an expert witness. There was a case involving corrections to the Hebrew version of the Bible and the magistrates wanted Adler's opinion on their authenticity. He was treated with great respect and invited to sit on the bench with the judges.

Later he was invited to attend Queen Victoria's levee where he was presented to the Queen by Montefiore. He would have had much in common with Prince Albert, and this time his German would have come in useful: 'Because of his German origin and upbringing, the Prince Consort found him congenial company.'[10]

Adler's involvement with the court behind the scenes was, naturally, confidential and can be overstated. There is a story in the family that Victoria went into labour with her first child when on holiday in Hanover, and that Adler suggested the baby could be born on a British battleship in international waters to maintain its British nationality. The court circular in London at the time, however, says that the baby was born at Buckingham Palace and lists all the worthies who attended. Furthermore an author who attempted to confirm the story recently referred to the child as a boy who would become Edward VII.[11] The problem with this is that Victoria's first child was a girl, also named Victoria, who would become the Princess Royal. Although it would link Adler with the Queen, there seems little reason to accept the folklore.

Individual organizations were not slow to seek Adler's support, but the *herem* he had inherited on the Burton Street congregation continued to be very divisive. At the Western Synagogue in February 1846 the discussion on the subject deteriorated into 'a scene of uproar and confusion'.[12] *The Voice of Jacob* and the *Jewish Chronicle* were divided on the subject; *The Voice of Jacob* accused the *Chronicle* of being on the secessionist side and later in the year, the *Chronicle* had to make clear on its front page its position regarding Adler's rulings:

> It is enough that he has authorised them [the Beth Din], and our duty is to obey. No committee of surveillance should be tolerated ... he is our judge and by his decision we must abide; he is our teacher and his instruction we must adopt; he is our spiritual guide and we must follow him.[13]

That needed saying because Adler was not intending to be, in any way, a mere figurehead. He knew from past experience that there would be opposition to whatever he said, from right or left, and when he authorised minor changes to the Friday evening service he was immediately accused, in letters to the Editor, of putting 'the synagogue in danger'.[14] He wasn't deterred.

That year the Sheerness community started an appeal to buy their building and Adler sent a guinea (£1.05p). In June it was the community in Canterbury who were in difficulties, as their building was commandeered for the development of the railways. That was another guinea. For the next fifty years he would always be found on the published list of supporters for charitable endeavours, to emphasize their credibility. Those guineas must have mounted up. In today's money we're talking about more like £100 a time. The funds of the Chief Rabbi's Office or the support of wealthy friends might well have been called on. Fortunately, the financial support of Moses Montefiore was always available, though it would have been discreetly provided.

The public, naturally, knew very little about the Chief Rabbi's own finances. A letter has survived, however, from December 1869 which probably raises more questions than it answers. It is from a stockbroker called Joseph Sebag. It reads:

> My dear and respected Sir,
> I have, by desire of Messrs Louis Cohen and Sons, applied on your behalf for an allocation of £8,000 of the Ottoman Loan.
> I return the Bankers Receipt for the amount of deposit fixed. I have, at Messrs Cohen's suggestion sold £6,000 stock at 5/8 per cent for the settlement. I enclose contract and remain,
> Yours respectfully, Joseph Sebag.[15]

Now the minimum current value of £8,000 is over £650,000. The attraction of the Ottoman Loan is easy to see; where the rock-solid British Consols paid 3 per cent interest, the Ottoman Empire in 1869 was offering 6 per cent. The only problem with overseas investment, as is well known today, is that foreign countries can have difficulty keeping solvent. The Ottoman Empire borrowed vast sums after the Crimean War and in 1876 it would be unable to pay the interest on its loans. It didn't manage to start again until 1879.

When a government cannot service its loans, their capital value declines very sharply and that is what would have happened to the Ottoman Loans. It might well have been very embarrassing for Joseph Sebag, who would serve as President of the Board of Deputies.

There is one possible explanation but it's very much supposition. It does, however, fit the facts. Joseph Sebag was the stockbroker acting for the Chief Rabbi. He was also Moses Montefiore's nephew and so was, most likely, his uncle's stockbroker as well. Throughout his ministry, Adler, as Chief Rabbi, was always at the top of the list of contributors to good causes, but he was, obviously, not a rich man. Where was the money to come from? Well, if Montefiore had lent him the £8,000, the 6 per cent annual interest would amount to nearly £500, which would help support a lot of charities.

It was not unknown for a chief rabbi to take financial advice from members of his flock. Solomon Hirschell, Adler's predecessor, died a rich man, but then one of the wardens at the Great in his time was Nathan Meyer Rothschild, and the Chief Rabbi's estate included substantial quantities of valuable railway stock. The richer members of the community would also usually be supportive if approached individually.

One way in which Adler's standing in the provinces outside London was soon superior to the lay leaders, rested on his readiness to try to raise funds for them They may have felt themselves neglected and ignored by the synagogues in the capital, but the support of the chief rabbi was always forthcoming. There were occasions when, by contrast, the provinces neglected the appeals of Adler: support for his new Jews' College was one example, but there was never a reciprocal lack of concern by the Chief Rabbi on their behalf. He was repaid in the loyalty and regard he received in return.

Adler also didn't distinguish between the law-abiding and the criminal in his efforts to improve matters. He wrote to the governor of Dartmoor prison asking him not to insist on Jewish convicts being made to work on the Sabbath. He sent the prisoners money to enable them to buy *matzot* for Passover and he kept in touch with many of them individually.

It was also important for the community that Adler was welcome in the higher ranks of the establishment. It lent lustre to the office and, by association, to all the Jews in Britain. If, however, the Establishment was involved, he would be perfectly happy to take his place in the ranks. He would, for example, accept the lesser role of vice-patron of the Jewish Orphan Asylum, but then the patrons were the Dowager Queen Adelaide, wife of William IV, the Duchess of Kent, Queen Victoria's mother, the Duke of Cambridge, George III's son, and the Duke of Buccleugh, whose first ducal ancestor was the illegitimate son of Charles II.

When it came to less illustrious appeals for support, the pleas for help often came from Jews who were considerably in awe of the Chief Rabbi. One such came from the Society for Relieving the Poor in Confined Mourning, a charity trying to help the poverty-stricken pay the bills for a death in the family. Adler declined to become a patron, in what was for him a rare refusal, citing the number of similar requests he received. He, nevertheless, answered the letter with the graciousness which marked his ministry:

> I appreciate your charity the more highly as it was called into existence by youths, whose imagination generally gilds every state of life and whose pleasures could allure on every side. You nevertheless have directed your attention towards the afflicted and those who are heavy of heart, in order that they may forget their poverty.[16]

That was approbation indeed and the endorsement of their Chief Rabbi was keenly sought by all kinds of community organizations. In September the Jewish National Friendly Association for the Manufacture of Passover Bread was delighted to receive his approval. He was a patron of everything from the Hand-in-Hand Asylum 'for the support of aged and decayed tradesmen' to the Soup Kitchen for the Jewish Poor.

During his ministry he would write many prayers for his congregations to read out on special occasions. They ranged from comments on good (or bad) harvests to military victories in the Crimea and India. There was always a prayer for the success of Montefiore's journeys. There would be another to mark the death of the Prince Consort and there would be supplications on behalf of the Jews facing difficulties in many parts of the world, particularly in Russia. It didn't matter to Adler where in the world a Jewish community was in difficulties; he would always try to help.

In 1850 Protestant missionaries had reported on the parlous situation of the Chinese Jewish community in Kaifeng-fu. They had been in existence since Biblical times and were known in London, but their location was so remote that communication was very difficult. Adler immediately asked the Board of Deputies to try to help, and they would have done so if civil war hadn't broken out in China at that time.

When the community looked for religious leadership, the Chief Rabbi would never be found wanting. Of particular importance were the prayers of thanksgiving he wrote when attempts made on the life of the Queen were unsuccessful; there were no less than five of these during his ministry (two in 1842, 1849, 1850, 1872 and 1882). Victoria lived a charmed life.

In April 1846 Adler wrote a new prayer for the Royal Family,[17] spoke in German at the New Synagogue and attended the anniversary dinner of the Jews' Free School. He had by now managed to get the Duke of Cambridge to agree to be the patron of a proposed new girls' school, though the Duke insisted that he would only do so if Adler took charge of it. It was a very busy life.

Notes

1. Philip Ornstein, *Historical Sketch of the Beth Hamedrash* (London: United Synagogue, 1905), p.6.
2. *Jewish Chronicle*, 24 January 1890, p.1.
3. Marcus Levy, lecture at the Jewish Institute, 6 June 1909.
4. *The Voice of Jacob*, 18 July 1845, p.194.
5. Aubrey Newman, 'The Chief Rabbinate and the Provinces', in Jonathan Sacks (ed.), *Tradition and Transition: Essays Presented to Chief Rabbi Sir Immanuel Jakobovits to Celebrate Twenty Year in Office* (London: Jews College Publications, 1986), p.219.
6. Derek Taylor, *British Chief Rabbis, 1664–2006* (London and Portland, OR: Vallentine Mitchell, 2007), p.239.
7. H.D. Schmidt, 'Chief Rabbi Nathan Marcus Adler (1803–1890): Jewish Educator from Germany', *Leo Baeck Institute Year Book*, 7, 1 (1962), pp.289–311.
8. For example, in a speech in 1850 when distributing the prizes at the Western Jewish Girls Free School.
9. M.L. Mashinsky, *Chance Encounters: Stories that are Hardly by Chance* (New York: ArtScroll Mesorah Publications, 2000).
10. Newman, 'The Chief Rabbinate and the Provinces', p.221.
11. Presentation by Rabbi Raymond Apple to the Jewish Historical Society of England, Israel Branch, 30 May 2010, p.1.
12. *The Voice of Jacob*, 27 February 1846, p.87.
13. *Jewish Chronicle*, 13 November 1846, p.1.
14. Ibid.
15. Letter in the Adler archive at the Jewish Theological Seminary in New York.
16. Ibid.

17. For Pesach 1846 a new prayer for the Royal Family:

Thou art great in counsel and mighty in work. Thy righteousness is as the great mountains and Thy judgements are everlasting. Thou givest strength to the hero and inspirest the brave with courage. Thou guidest their arm to victory if they practice justice and mercy on earth, and causest the mighty to tremble before them. Though hosts encamp against them, their heart faileth them not; and though war rise against them, they scorn danger and dread it not; for Thy rod and Thy staff accompany them; in safety they encamp and march.

Thou art powerful in saving. Thou hast achieved repeated and signal victories for the British troops in India; lion-like they faced the enemy and conquered; they repelled his iniquitous aggression and totally discomfited him. What now shall we offer to Thee for all these great benefits? Thy condescending kindness alone encourages us to approach Thy presence with our thanks and to acknowledge that from Thee we derive every thing, and that to Thee belongs victory and triumph. O King of kings, continue to bestow Thy blessing on Our Sovereign Lady, Queen Victoria, Adelaide, the Queen Dowager, The Prince Albert, Albert Edward, Prince of Wales, and all the Royal Family. Grant her peace and exalt her glory; let no weapon that is formed against her prosper, and may the nations that lift up the sword against her people be converted into allies, and never again break the covenant of friendship, so that peace may be established on earth, that swords may be beaten into plough-shares and that every man may dwell beneath his vine and fear not. Even as Thou didst show us extraordinary mercy in the days of our departure from Egypt, so may Judah and Israel be saved in our own days, and may the redeemer come to Zion and let us say, Amen.

6

Settling In

The new chief rabbi needed a plan for a far larger and more geographically diverse office than he had ever had responsibility for before. Congregations all over the world would now be looking to him for spiritual guidance. Where they were part of the British Empire, they would not be experiencing persecution, but there were problems with communities elsewhere who suffered every kind of discrimination, and British intervention might help. The persecution of Jews in Damascus, after a totally fallacious accusation of complicity in the murder of a priest, was only one recent example. Montefiore had returned from Russia with more promises from the Czar of better treatment for the downtrodden Jews, most of which would not materialize. There was an old joke – 'May the Almighty keep the Czar – well away from me!'

Adler concerned himself with a number of external problems but found his Anglo-Jewish responsibilities more than heavy enough to occupy most of his time. This was quickly appreciated and, as early as 1846, he would have been pleased that it was reported that his health had been drunk at the Jews' Hospital dinner with 'the most hearty cheers we ever witnessed'.[1]

Adler turned his attention almost immediately to Jewish schools. He personally attended the examination day at the Jews' Free School to hear the headmaster, Moses Angel, examine the children in Hebrew and English. Not yet fully aware of the misery of conditions in the East End, he spoke to the assembled parents, encouraging them to send their children to school regularly. He was soon to recognize, however, that many youngsters would have to go to work, instead of school, at a ridiculously early age, if they were to avoid malnutrition and even death by starvation. Only the Irish were likely to have a larger proportion of paupers than the Jews.

It was no surprise, under the circumstances, that half the population were illiterate and that getting children a good education meant private and costly schooling. Many of the richer people were suspicious of the alternative concept of compulsory state education anyway because they had the idea that educating the poor might lead to revolution.

Where Adler was at first half inclined to blame truancy at the Jews' Free School on a lack of interest on the part of the parents, he was soon to be thoroughly disabused, when, in January 1847, he went into the East End to see for himself. As the *Jewish Chronicle* reported:

> Rev. Dr Adler paid a visit to some of the poorer classes residing in the neighbourhood of Middlesex Street, Bell Lane, Stoney Grove, Gravel Lane, Angel Court etc., whose children had absented themselves from the Free School. Although the weather was very unfavourable, the Rev. Dr did not object to grope through the dark, narrow courts and alleys, nor to ascend the miserable attics, in seeking the parents of young deserters, with whom he pathetically remonstrated for neglecting the education of their children, and pointed out the evil consequences of keeping the children away from an institution which, if properly attended, might be the means of making them respectable members of society, and of perhaps one day cherishing their humble parents in old age.
>
> The general reply to the Rev. Doctor's remonstrances was that poverty prevented them from regularly sending their children to school, oftentimes not having any food to give them, previous to their arrival there, and momentarily awaiting the arrival of some member of the family, who would bring a trifle for purchasing a bit of bread and providing a drop of warm drink before they went to school; but this providential benefactor came often too late for school hours. The parents promised they would endeavour to do the utmost in their power to secure the better attendance of their children in future. The Reverend Dr did not depart in any instance without leaving at least so much as would provide a breakfast for the family on the following day.[2]

Without the dole, which would only be introduced more than fifty years later, it was a disastrous time for the poor, and Adler was deeply affected. He became well known for his readiness to be involved, and much admired for it. Financially, though, his contribution was, inevitably, very limited. A breakfast for the following day was a kindly gesture, but no more than that. The possibility existed, however, of inspiring the richer members of the community to do more for the disadvantaged, and new initiatives to this effect came regularly from Adler during his ministry.

In January 1854 the Soup Kitchen for the Jewish Poor was established in the East End in Spitalfields. Its purpose was to provide soup, bread and meat twice a week during the winter. Twenty years later, with Adler as its patron, it was distributing 78,000 rations to 600 families. It was a very positive effort, but far more of the destitute needed to benefit.

It is, perhaps, difficult in these more affluent days of the Welfare State to appreciate the full horror of the conditions of the underclass in Victorian times. It wasn't just the poverty wages in the sweat shops. It was also the wide range of industrial diseases which cut down the workers as early as their 20s and 30s; for example, lung and chest diseases in the textile industry, phossy jaw in match workers, and a wide range of industrial accidents manning dangerous machinery.

The alternative to such occupations, however, was literally starvation, and children as well as adults were put to work in appalling conditions for daily working hours of twelve and more. Factory Acts regularly emerged to improve matters a little, but trade unions would be treated with hostility for many years to come and the workers would continue to suffer until long after Adler's time.

Workers organizations and religious bodies should have worked together to better the condition of the poor, but the clergy were often concerned that the growth of socialism among the deprived might be mirrored by a growth in secularization. Adler, himself, was not in favour of socialism for this reason.

Whatever historical distinctions might exist, both Montefiore and Adler were anxious to ensure that relations, as a whole, between the Sephardi and Ashkenazi communities were warm and friendly. There was rivalry between the two communities about who represented the community with the authorities. For example, the Sephardim had sent delegates to court to congratulate George III on his accession. The Ashkenazim had immediately protested that they hadn't been invited to join the representatives. The Sephardim had accepted this and agreed that in future both communities would be involved. They created a new body called the Board of Deputies of British Jews, but for many years it seldom met. The Sephardim had recently rejected the opportunity to vote in the elections for a new Ashkenazi chief rabbi after Solomon Hirschell, but their undisputed leader, Moses Montefiore, didn't want their independence to become a barrier between the two communities. The Sephardim were proud of Montefiore and he had strong support. He was an imposing figure, considerably taller than Adler, but always deferential to the chief rabbi.

As a gesture of cooperation, the Sephardim invited Adler to be a life governor of the Beth Holim Sephardi Hospital and he inspected it with Montefiore in July 1846. Yet it took until 1849 before he was at last invited to preach at Bevis Marks, the illustrious Sephardi Synagogue. In his sermon he emphasized the 'Bonds of Brotherhood' that bound all the Jews together which he characterized as a common religious belief, a common language and a common history. That message went down well.

In Europe, August 1846 saw the report of the conference of Reform rabbis in Breslau. Adler was no longer involved in the religious fracas, but his brother, Baer, attended an alternative conference of Orthodox theologians in Dresden. The Breslau recommendations were very radical and a timely warning to the Chief Rabbi that he had always to keep in mind the possible influence of continental reform on his own community.

A far more immediate national problem in Britain was the failure of the Irish potato crop which led to widespread famine. The government's policy of trying to make the Irish more independent of British financial support led to horrific numbers of deaths from starvation. Adler did what he could by composing a famine prayer to be read in his synagogues, but what the Irish peasants needed was a proper programme of famine relief and the provision of very cheap food, which was not forthcoming.

Where necessary, the Jewish community in Ireland were supported by their brethren elsewhere but vast numbers of the general population emigrated to America. Where the Irish constituted 30 per cent of the total British population in 1820, they only comprise, North and South, less than 10 per cent today.

The seminary for teachers in Hanover had finally been opened. The *Jewish Chronicle* offered the hope that a similar theological centre would be forthcoming in England. The efforts to raise sufficient funds for a new girls' school had also been successful. This was particularly commendable, as little attention was normally given to educating girls. A few beat the system in later life and became successful in their own right – Jane Austen, Mrs Beaton, Harriet Samuel (H. Samuel – the jewellers) – but they were rare. Adler went on record:

> Those who believed that the destiny of a girl was poverty – that her destiny was an inferior one – might entertain such an erroneous opinion; but those who knew that she was fashioned for a higher life – for a better life – could not doubt that schools for girls were of the greatest moment.[3]

He asserted that if Jewish girls were not educated about Judaism, 'it would not be in accordance with the spirit of the Torah'. Jewish mothers were vital role models. In 1853 the boys and girls would be combined in one school with nearly 300 pupils. The Jews' Free School now had 600 boys and 360 girls, but was still always seen as a school for poor East End children, rather than for middle-class girls who were catered for by the new establishment.

Additional problems came thick and fast. In December 1846 it was the congregations in Adrianople in Turkey, which needed help after a disastrous fire. Adler instructed his synagogues to appeal for funds to support rebuilding.

The results of Adler's audit of the current situation in the synagogues which acknowledged his authority had come through, providing the information he needed. The audit was based on his similar investigation in Hanover. The picture that emerged this time was that the communities around the country, outside London, had about 5,000 members. The largest had synagogues, but a city as big as Leeds could only muster seventeen members in all. Jamaica was one of the largest communities in the return, with 450 members. Some communities only had services in private homes; indeed, weddings were often held by choice in the open air and not in a synagogue. It was true that twelve of the provincial communities had over 100 members and seven more had over fifty, but half of the latter were struggling to get started or survive. Among those which would more or less disappear in time were Canterbury with over 100, Falmouth with fifty, Dover with thirty-one and Sheerness with twenty-six. Among those which later grew were Brighton (150 then) and Cardiff (only nine at the time). There are over 2,000 Jews in Wales today, so it is necessary to recognize the likelihood of demographic shifts in population.

The core requirement was always the basic ten males over 13 years of age, and not a building. If ten males were not likely to be regularly available, a few would often be paid by the synagogue to attend all the services. They were known as *Minyan* Men. Congregations were always envious of the magnificence of Christian cathedrals, often partially financed originally by a tax on the Jewish communities in pre-expulsion times. The synagogue does not, however, have the same status in Judaism. When creating a congregation, the historic priorities start with a burial ground, a *sefer torah* (a scroll of the first five books of the bible) and a *mikvah* (a ritual bath.) Not a synagogue and not a minister.

It transpired that twenty-one of the congregations had a *mikvah* which had been constructed to the *halachic* specifications (specified in the Written and Oral Law.) The rest used public baths or sea immersion. The *mikvah* was recognized as an important part of a congregation's facilities. The report from Exeter regretted that their *mikvah* was two inches short of the size laid down in Jewish law. The importance given to cleanliness in Judaism was one reason why, when the plague broke out, it was less prevalent in their localities, but as this led to accusations that they were spreading it, this could become a mixed blessing.

Half the congregations employed just one officer, though the two Liverpool communities had eight in total; Manchester had seven and Birmingham had four. By far the largest provincial community was

Liverpool, but they had internal leadership problems at the time, and had split into two. As with the congregations in Liverpool and Manchester, if there were two congregations there could be two sets of honorary officers, which helped to bolster the self-importance of many laymen but was not, necessarily, good for Judaism.

The question of status continued to be highly contentious. In the provinces, the authority for running the synagogue rested normally with the Free Members. They were listed in the responses to Adler's questionnaire as *baalei batim* (householders). In Birmingham, for instance, there were thirty-eight *baalei batim*, but ninety-nine seat holders who had no say in the running of the shul. The total membership of nearly 700, including non-seat holders, were subject to the rulings of the thirty-eight.

This was an area of discord which the Chief Rabbi avoided whenever he could. However, he was still the nominated umpire if one was needed. To suggest that the local minister could fulfil that role if rows got out of hand was not considered an option. A typical example would occur within the Portsmouth community in 1855. They asked Adler to help and later at a Special General meeting they passed a resolution, thanking him: 'for the sympathy and zeal he had shown for the interests of the congregation by travelling to Portsmouth for the purpose of restoring unanimity and good feeling amongst them'.[4]

It was this kind of support which would ensure that the various communities did what the chief rabbi asked. In 1874 Adler would advise Portsmouth to reintroduce the prayers for the community which are said by the *Cohanim* on Festivals. There was considerable opposition to this because Portsmouth hadn't followed this procedure for twenty-six years. The resolution to approve the chief rabbi's request was, however, passed by a comfortable majority.

If the first priority for a congregation was to have a cemetery, five of the congregations couldn't even achieve that: Cardiff, Dover, Exeter, Oxford and Southampton had nowhere sanctified to bury their dead. Another cause for argument was the donations offered by members of the congregation who received honours during the service; this is known as *shnodering*. These honours were auctioned in 70 per cent of the communities. They helped fund the synagogue charities, but hardly enhanced the dignity of the service. The receipts from the cry of 'One penny to open the door of the Ark' might help the synagogue to remain solvent, but it grated as part of a religious service. Adler was torn between communal spirituality and financial reality.

Learning about the provision of education for Jewish children was, naturally, of prime concern to Adler, and the questionnaire went into this area as well. The number of pupils was identified, together with the hours of instruction, the subjects studied, the books used, the names of the teachers, and the fees charged. The picture that emerged was of relative inadequacy, and Adler would set out to correct that situation too.

The time was right. The mood in the country was for the liberalization of education; Prince Albert in 1849 persuaded Cambridge to accept Jewish undergraduates and in 1854 Oxford would allow them to take degrees.

The Jews' Free School was not involved in the questionnaire process. The headmaster and the governors kept the East End education behemoth strictly under their own control. They were committed educationalists but, in fact the school had been founded about thirty years before as a defence measure. It was created to offer an alternative to the schools of Christian Conversionist Societies. The mission statement of these evangelical institutions was to endeavour to convert Jewish children to Christianity. They offered such inducements to the poor parents as a meal a day for the pupils and a suit of clothes. These should have been powerful attractions. Alternative support was needed and it came from the Rothschilds. They were among the benefactors of the Jewish school and their generosity was based on the highly commendable belief that they should offer thanks to the Almighty for their good fortune by helping their less fortunate brethren.

The Rothschilds kept the Jews' Free School in existence, providing about £10,000 a year in direct support and as much again in special donations for refurbishment and new buildings as the school grew. In today's money that is about £2 million a year. The generosity of the Rothschilds is still an example for every wealthy Jewish family. In their honour, the JFS house colours of blue and gold are still those of the Rothschilds.

When Adler was first appointed, his Rothschild support was soon enrolled in the creation of his Western Jewish School for Girls. That was his own initiative, however, and his efforts to become involved in the JFS curriculum were gently rebuffed. Apart from the governors' wish to remain independent – the Rothschilds provided the chairman of the governors for the next 100 years – the headmaster throughout Adler's ministry felt the same way. This was Moses Angel (1819–98), who was the highly esteemed headmaster from 1842–97. As he drew his pupils from the poorest families in the East End, he realized that the best education he could give them was one which would enable them to earn a living when they grew up.

He didn't consider his first objective was to teach them Judaism, though it certainly figured prominently in the curriculum. Adler's viewpoint could not be expected to be the same. Angel also had to convey an image of massive personal integrity, faultless work, immense application and total devotion to the school. All this was true of his nature, but Angel had a greater need for an unblemished record than most.

The truth was that he wasn't born Moses Angel. He was born Angel Moses. His father, Emanuel 'Money' Moses (1781–1841) was, of all occupations, a very successful dealer in stolen goods, notorious in the West End of London. He was a fence. His luck ran out in 1839 when gold dust to the value of £6,700 was stolen (in today's money at least half a million) and Moses handled some of it. He was caught, tried, and sentenced to seventeen years transportation to Australia. He did manage to survive the journey, in spite of being nearly 60, and arrived in Tasmania in 1841, but he died a few months later.

As a consequence, Angel Moses changed his name to Moses Angel. Throughout his life he would have to avoid being contaminated with the record of his father. Angel had been educated at University College School and University College, though he gained no degree at UCL because it didn't have the right to grant them until 1839. At both institutions, though, he would have met many Jews who would be prominent members of the community in future years. UCS and UCL were among the very few who accepted Jews.

When interviewed in later life, Angel gave the credit for the financing of his education to a rich benefactor, but he probably didn't need one in his youth as his father was not just a criminal, but a very successful one. It has been suggested that 'Money' Moses was unable to provide for his family, but his nickname seems to suggest a much happier financial position.

Angel had left UCL at 17 – in 1836 – and got a job in an Irish bank. In spite, however, of his lowly clerical position he was soon appointed editor of the *Jewish Chronicle* and assistant editor of *The Voice of Jacob*, which were temporarily combined in 1842. He had admittedly done well at both school and college but, at 23, he must have had some powerful friends to get the posts. He also started teaching at JFS, which involved the Rothschilds. The owners of the papers and the governors of the school must have been very impressed by the young man.

Did Adler know the background? The robbery happened before he arrived. There was no reason to connect Emanuel Moses and Moses Angel but a lot of people must have known the truth. From Angel's point of view, he would have wanted to run the school without any personal publicity. With the Chief Rabbi on board, that wouldn't be possible. A report on the headmaster's background could have been very embarrassing.

The school was also the Rothschilds' baby and they would have wanted to retain control of it. A subsidy of £20,000 a year gave them a very good case. Furthermore, good teachers for a Jewish school were very hard to find, and Angel proved himself to be, effectively, irreplaceable.

As far as the JFS President at the time was concerned, Sir Anthony Rothschild: 'loved the Jews' Free School as a parent watches the infant he fondly loves, because he saw in the progress of the School the progress of the community in which he took so great an interest'.[5]

When Adler spoke some years later at the opening of Jews' College, he mentioned JFS as a school for the poor. His own school, part of the new College, would be intended for the middle classes. He would be supportive of both and he would always be more concerned with the progress he was making in achieving his objectives, than in achieving outright victory. As he would say at the Westminster Jews' Free School anniversary dinner in 1868: 'When I first came to England about twenty years ago, the question of education was almost looked upon with ridicule ... .I thank God that now we have Jewish schools in every part of the metropolis.'[6]

The Chief Rabbi would also attend prize-givings when invited, though his day-to-day interest would always be Jews' College, for which he felt the same degree of affection that Rothschild felt for JFS. It would always, however, be difficult to get the community interested in the practice of supporting education, rather than the theory. Baroness Lionel Rothschild, reporting on a poor turnout at the Free School prize giving in 1866, said: '[Uncle Anthony] was surrounded by just four gentlemen connected with the institution. Dr. Adler – after having said a few words – rushed away, as if the plague had been in the building.'[7] It seems unlikely, however, that the Baroness would have known much of the Chief Rabbi's schedule that day, and he had made an appearance. The fact remained that the case for education had to be promoted with great vigour if it was not to be lost.

The charitable activities of the Jewish community continued to extend far and wide. In the spring of 1846 Adler was present when the foundation stone was laid for the Jewish Orphan Asylum Board, and by this time he could speak haltingly in English. In May he was at the anniversary festival of the Jews' Hospital at the London Tavern, though the hospital was really an orphanage and old people's home. From small beginnings, where just a few old people and children were looked after, the hospital could now point to its occupation by twelve old people, fifty-seven boys and seventeen girls. At the dinner £800 was donated and *The Times* was impressed, though it commented: 'We are at a loss what to say of the dinner, as it was given in the Jewish fashion. The wines, however, were excellent.'[8]

Fund-raising dinners were regularly held at the London Tavern, which was very popular. It was the location for the founding of the MCC in 1863, to the great benefit of cricket. It was a great pity that there was no fund-raising dinner for Jews' College until long after Adler had died. It can only be assumed that they were considered infra dig by the good and the great who served on the College Council.

When the original audit had been completed, Adler set about writing the Rules and Regulations that he wanted applied at all the synagogues which acknowledged his authority. This was not an exercise in egotism, some new system called Adlerism. It was just another clear exposition by the Chief Rabbi of what was the *din* and what, therefore, had to be obeyed without question. Adler was doing his job, as he had in Hanover.

Agreed, there might be some communities which resented taking instructions from his office – there was no audit response from Gloucester or Ramsgate – but most cooperated in providing the information he needed, and were glad to now have an experienced hand on the tiller.

Over the years he wrote first to 'All the synagogues in the United Kingdom', but this was extended as time went by to 'In all the synagogues of the British Empire in the charge of the Chief Rabbi', and finally to 'The synagogues of the United Congregations of the British Empire'. For decades after, the Standing Orders of many congregations in the Empire specified that services should be modelled on those of the Great Synagogue in London.

Those services were conducted according to the German and Polish rite, as had been agreed when the Ashkenazim first returned to England in Stuart times. Only in later years were they described as *Minhag Anglia*, as if the Germans and the Poles had hardly had an influence. When Adler arrived there was no *Minhag Anglia* (English usage).

There were forty-two points in the list of Adler's instructions distributed in 1847, and the document ran to twenty-three pages. It started with a clear explanation of what he was trying to do:

> The following regulations which are in strict conformity with the Law, are laid down for general guidance, and it is confidently hoped that all congregations, as well as all the individuals who attend the synagogues, will adhere to these laws, remove all differences, and conduct themselves so that every one shall feel impelled to exclaim:- 'How awful is the place; this is truly a house of God.'[9]

The next point, also made very clear, was who was in charge overall: 'The duty of superintending the synagogue, as far as religious observances are concerned devolves on the Chief Rabbi, when present.'[10] The authority then moved to a dayan, representing the Chief Rabbi, and then to the minister: 'provided these latter offices be authorised for that purpose by the Chief Rabbi and their respective Congregations'.[11] Otherwise the responsibility belonged to the honorary officers, but only when the ranks of all the possible religious officers had been exhausted.

Adler was well aware that synagogue politics had a constant potential for disruption. That had been the case in Hanover as well. The founders usually felt they deserved total authority because, without them, there would have been no synagogue in the first place. This, of course, was true, but it didn't command automatic obedience, even if they felt any serious opposition to their wishes should be condemned as ingratitude. By contrast, newcomers who were not founders often resented the fact that they paid their dues to keep the synagogue financially afloat, but continued to have no say in its functioning.

The Chief Rabbi didn't want to be involved in personalities but in the *din*. He could handle the personal problems if he needed to – there had been plenty of delicate negotiations to be undertaken in Hanover – but if he could stay out of the squabbling, so much the better. If he couldn't, the rules and regulations were specific on this point too: 'Should anyone think himself aggrieved, he shall apply for redress, if in religious matters, to the Chief Rabbi.'[12]

Religious matters were carefully specified to absolve the Chief Rabbi from accusations of interference in personal spats. A reasonably typical instance arose with the Southampton community. They had divided into two congregations and were not on the best of terms. They also had concerns about their *shochet*, who they suspected of authorizing non-kosher meat.

Adler investigated the position at their request, and suspended the *shochet* for six months. In future, by dint of his regulations, he would examine all the *shochetim* to see that they were suitably qualified, but the question of two congregations where one would do had to be solved on the South Coast.

If there was opposition to religious central control, Adler had a full arsenal of weapons with which he could apply pressure on the individual synagogue if he so chose. The Marriage Act of 1835 gave the Board of Deputies the sole right to authenticate a Jewish community as suitable to have a Marriage Secretary. Without such confirmation, all the marriages within the congregation had to be first held in a Registry Office.

It was a powerful incentive not to rock the boat with the Board but, in its turn, the Board's 1835 constitution laid down clearly that all the community's spiritual decisions would be made by the chief rabbi. So, effectively, Adler could block a synagogue's application for a Marriage Secretary.

The synagogue also couldn't make any ministerial appointments without Adler's approval of the candidate. This was in line with the law in Hanover, even though the office of chief rabbi in England was not a quasi-government position. No synagogue could even be officially created without the approval of the Board of Deputies and, therefore, the chief rabbi. There were always, however, always a number of small synagogues – *chevrot* – which decided to remain independent; some in the City, some elsewhere.

This was due to a development in Britain in the eighteenth century. *Chevrot* were immigrant community congregations, devoted to the practices they had brought from their home countries. They were not numerically significant and, in the East End, Adler's tenured *dayanim* would be a major influence. Nevertheless, the *chevrot* would cling to their old customs. It was part nostalgia, part a strong belief that the *din* supported their procedures, and part a way of proving – at least to themselves – that they were theologically superior to the community of which they had now become a part. They were *frummer*.

An example was the Beth Hamedrash in Sunderland, which would never acknowledge Adler's authority. After a disastrous fire at Krottingen in Lithuania, where they all lived, there was a mass exodus to Sunderland, where an earlier arrival from their congregation had settled and, reported back very favourably on his new life. So the congregation left Lithuania in a body and settled in Northumberland. They started their own synagogue and every element of their practices back home was replicated, even down to reading and studying a page of the Talmud chronologically every day. This is known as the *Daf Yomi*, and to complete the mammoth task took them about 25 years. During their existence, the Beth Hamedrash would manage the *Daf Yomi* cycle four times. Such a concentrated effort would have been totally impossible to achieve in any of Adler's synagogues. So, because they were unhappy about the standards of observance they found in the existing Sunderland Jewish community, the Beth Hamedrash remained strictly aloof. It was hopeless to expect them to change and, during his ministry, Adler would settle for a large majority of congregations acknowledging his authority, rather than trying too hard for 100 per cent.

Among other rules and regulations, measures to improve decorum during the services laid down that children under 4 were not to be admitted to the synagogue. It had been under 5 in Hanover. Adler also decreed that there should be no talking during services and nobody should leave before the end. As he put it in 'The Rules and Regulations for the Synagogues in the British Empire': 'It is necessary that quiet and decorum, dignity and solemnity should prevail there during divine worship, so that it may awaken the fear of the Lord, foster feelings of devotion and promote brotherly union.'

Legislation in this area was much easier to set down than to enforce, but Adler knew that better decorum was an attraction of the secessionist services. He wanted services to be more attractive and he welcomed the creation of choirs at the Great and the New, as he had in Hanover.

The division of men and women was confirmed, with synagogues requiring a ladies' gallery rather than a *mechitzah* (a partition) It was laid down that crinolines were not to be worn because they took up too much room. It was also ruled that the women were to sit in the ladies gallery at weddings, and not on the same level as the men. The reasoning behind this was hardly flattering to the men, suggesting that the visible presence of women could distract them from their devotions. On the other hand, there is an old tradition that during the wedding service the bride circles her husband seven times, either to remember the creation of the world or as a symbol of the walls round a happy home. Adler banned this practice, as being demeaning to the bride.

On occasions, improved decorum could come at the cost of much loved traditions. Adler's rules and regulations also stated that: 'Knocking during the reading of the Megillah (at the festival of Purim) is strictly forbidden'. It was true that the derisory knocking when the name of Haman, the arch-villain, is mentioned in the reading of the Book of Esther, does not improve the decorum. On the other hand, it makes the service enjoyable for the children who become personally involved in the service in the synagogue, and that is a worthwhile objective as well. The children knock today.

Antisocial behaviour was also addressed. For example, it was laid down that if any male congregant was caught chewing tobacco in synagogue, the fine was a hefty two shillings and sixpence (12½p – over £10 today).

Sometimes the decorum of the synagogue was affected by the length of the service. During a Sabbath service of two hours or more, it was difficult enough to expect total quiet. To reach that standard during a major festival like the New Year, was even harder to achieve. So Adler decreed that the Rosh Hashanah service should not last longer than five and a half hours.

He also decided to prohibit the auction of synagogal honours. The 'Penny to open the ark' cry was abolished for good. It was agreed that seat rentals should rise to make up the shortfall. He also dealt with the division of the *sedra*, the portion of the Torah read each week, which is divided into at least seven parts. A member called up for a section of the reading could ask for blessings for his family (a *Mi Sheberach*) and would make a donation to charity.

So the more people called up, the more money the synagogue could raise. Adler insisted that the maximum number of call-ups on a Sabbath should be ten. This system was generally maintained, though the independent Western Synagogue abolished *Mi Sheberachs* altogether in 1852.

If the congregation couldn't agree on who should be given a particular part of the service, the Chief Rabbi was prepared to arbitrate. For example it is considered a great honour to be called up on Yom Kippur, especially to open the Ark for *Neilah* (the final service), and arguments would break out on who had the right to be chosen; another cause of friction between the *baalei batim* and the seat holders. With some reluctance, Adler would make a ruling.

There were many other areas where Adler insisted on control. If, for example, a synagogue wanted a visiting preacher, they had to have his permission. This was a precaution to ensure that non-Orthodox or unqualified preachers should not be provided with an Orthodox pulpit. Finally, to make sure the rules were set in concrete, the Chief Rabbi stipulated that any alteration to the rules and regulations must have his written approval.

In 1850, for example, the Seel Street Synagogue in Liverpool decided, without consulting Adler, to include instrumental music in their Sabbath services. The change did, indeed, increase the attendance, but it was not part of the Ashkenazi ritual and Adler asked them to stop it. With regret, they agreed. When the Laws and Regulations had first been produced by the Chief Rabbi, Liverpool objected on the grounds that they had not been consulted before they were issued. Adler told them that there had been no need to consult with any congregation:

> First, because that code consisted for the most part of such laws as are beyond all question and indispensably necessary before any ulterior improvement can be effected; and secondly because it is obvious, that if it were competent for the smallest provincial congregation to throw its dissent into the opposite scale, no general measure for the benefit of all would be effectively promulgated.[13]

It wasn't unusual around the world for a suitably qualified rabbi to restate the regulations for a congregation, based on the authoritative codes of Jewish law. The rules of Orthodox Judaism date back hundreds of years. In the late twentieth century a dayan in London was asked whether it was necessary to observe the second day of festivals in Israel. He said it wasn't, as had been laid down by Rabbi Zevi Ashkenazi, the chief rabbi in Amsterdam, in the early part of the eighteenth century!

Equally, in Britain, accepted rules and regulations included, of course, the times of the Shabbat services, and these were designated according to a table produced by the Sephardi Haham, David Nieto, also in the eighteenth century. The Haham worked out what times the Sabbath should start and finish in Britain and that remains the standard to this day.

For the Orthodox, the prime consideration is still whether what is in their rules and regulations is acceptable to congregations around the world, because they are in line with the authoritative Shulchan Aruch (a sixteenth-century compilation). For the rabbis, to this day, the concept of 'modern times' has little relevance if the subject is concerned with ethics and morals, which are timeless.

Adler did not inaugurate new rules but simply restated what already existed, giving nobody any excuse for saying that they didn't know where they stood. The same applied when he presided over meetings of the Beth Din. He would state the law and if there was still argument he would plead: 'For my sake, let there be peace.' When they accepted his decision, the unsuccessful litigants could hold that they had only given in to make peace; they would get the credit for this. They would save face but Adler had settled the argument. One of his strongest principles was to always try to carry the community with him. The plea for peace was a disarming stratagem for getting his own way which could form a case study for a Business School today.

In 1847 he went back to Hanover for his mother, Rebecca's, 80th birthday. His successor there, Rabbi Dr Samuel Mayer, found a suitable house for him to stay in, but he preferred the more modest home of the family matriarch. The synagogue was plentifully decorated with flowers to mark the birthday and he was also able to join in celebrating the formation of a Commission by the Hanover government in 1846 to fulfil his great ambition to have a seminary to train Jewish teachers in the state. It consisted of Hanover councillors, the Landrabbiner and Cosman Behrens, the banker, who was still helping the ruler with his finances. In the end, the Hanover government not only gave the seminary an annual subsidy, but would increase it substantially in the years to come. The college started with seven students but quite soon had over thirty.

In England there would also be progress in the future, but the British government was not involved and the British Jewish community would not be as supportive.

As his English improved and his reputation solidified, Adler became more confident in trying to get the community out of bad habits. In March 1847 he went to Middlesex Street (Petticoat Lane) in the East End after the Shabbat service and announced firmly that he was against the pubs being opened and frequented by Jews on the Sabbath. It certainly didn't make him popular with the publicans but he had laid down the law. In theory his criticism would have been accepted by the congregation, but in practice it would probably have made but little difference. He couldn't win them all.

Adler also took up the question of the physically disadvantaged; another contentious issue. At the time those affected were often seen as an embarrassment to society and hidden away. They could even be committed to asylums even though there was nothing wrong with their sanity. Adler would never regard them in that light and in 1849, as just one example, he appealed for support for deaf mutes. It's only a footnote in his long life, but he was bringing succour to those who could not help themselves, and in this he was way ahead of his time.

In 1848 the last major area of discrimination against Jews in Britain was the parliamentary oath. Bill after bill had been introduced to make it possible to swear allegiance on the Old Testament, but all had been killed in the House of Lords. The Jewish lay leadership was still agitating for the change, but now the subject paled into insignificance because this was the year of violent uprisings all over Europe, with the overthrow of many governments. Britain was one of the few countries which did not suffer insurrection, but it was a close call. If there was no revolution in the United Kingdom, there was great concern that there could be. Lord Palmerston, the Foreign Secretary, even armed the staff in the Foreign Office against the possibility of serious rioting.

The primary organization which wanted change in Britain was the Chartists. The movement was strong and wanted many alterations to parliamentary practice. They advocated universal suffrage, paid MPs and the chance to become an MP even if the candidate didn't own any property. There had been fatalities in years gone by as a result of their demonstrations. It was, therefore, a matter of great concern to the government when they announced in 1848 that they were going to deliver a monster petition to Parliament, setting out their demands.

Revolution became a serious option, under discussion by the Chartist's leader, Feargus O'Connor, and his senior followers. As a result the government sent Victoria and Albert to the Isle of Wight for safety, got the Duke of Wellington out of retirement and recruited no less than 85,000 special constables to keep order. The Chartists wanted to present their monster petition to the Commons but, faced with overwhelming force, they eventually went home without there being bloodshed. Though the confrontation fizzled out, the government had been seriously alarmed, and for years any suggestions of alterations to parliamentary procedures were immediately tarred with the Chartist brush.

Indeed, Parliament set its face firmly against any radical moves for the foreseeable future, one of which would certainly have been the passing of an act to allow Jews to take their seats in Parliament without swearing as Christians. The Oath Act, which made change possible, wouldn't be passed until 1858.

Adler left it to the community's senior laymen to continue the battle. The precedents weren't good. The minor Jew Bill in 1753 would have made it easier for a few wealthy Jews to become naturalised, but after demonstrations in the country, it was necessary for it to be abandoned. In 1780 the anti-Catholic Gordon riots had led to mobs taking over London for days and threatening parliament. New proposed legislation affecting the rights of minorities had proved to be minefields. As Adler sought to improve religious standards, so did lay leaders like David Salomons work on the secular side, but the Jewish press were pessimistic. 'The voice of the people, which at the beginning of the session, spoke kindly in our favour, has now been hushed into silence by the thunder of the revolutionary Continent.'[14]

There was still work to be done.

Notes

1. *Jewish Chronicle*, 4 September 1846, p.211.
2. Gerry Black, *JFS: The History of the Jews' Free School, London, Since 1732* (London: Tymsder Publishing, 1998), p.93.
3. David A. Sher, 'Chief Rabbi Nathan Marcus Adler', *Jewish Affairs* (South Africa) (December 2015).
4. Portsmouth synagogue archives.
5. Gerry Black, *JFS: The History of the Jews' Free School, London, Since 1732* (London: Tymsder Publishing, 1998), p.57.
6. Ibid., p.76.
7. Ibid., p.62.
8. *The Times*, 24 May 1847, p.5.
9. *Jewish Chronicle*, 5 September 1845.
10. Bernard Susser (ed.), 'Provincial Jewry in Victorian Britain', Paper for a JHSE conference, 1975.
11. Laws and Regulations for all the Synagogues in the British Empire.
12. Ibid.
13. Cecil Roth, *History of the Great Synagogue, London 1690–1940* (London: Edward Goldston & Co., 1950), p.218.
14. *Jewish Chronicle*, July 1848.

7

A Pause for Manchester

Most of the communities which acknowledged the authority of the Chief Rabbi were very small. As such, they welcomed the opportunity to call on a highly qualified leader to help them with a multitude of problems; especially where to find synagogue officials and how to deal with conversions, marriages and divorces, as well as theological advice on the liturgy, and guidance on the resolution of personal problems. All this was now provided by Adler, free of charge.

Things were different in the provincial communities which were sizeable and growing; in the early days of Adler's ministry, that really meant Manchester, Birmingham and Liverpool. In these communities there was an almost universal desire of the founders to retain for themselves the highest possible status and control. If they were large enough, the attractions of independence from London were balanced with the advantage of being able to call on the help of the Chief Rabbi. In almost all these synagogues there had grown up the system by which the minority of founders maintained all the power, though the rest of the congregation still had to contribute financially.

There were critics of the handsome edifices the congregations built with the financial help of the founders. There were complaints, for example, that they were far larger than were needed. This was, however, to misunderstand synagogue finances. To look after those of the congregation who were in need, to pay the staff and teachers for the children, there were two main sources of income for those running the synagogue: seat rentals and burial plots. The larger the synagogue, the more seats could be sold, and even if the owners chose not to use their seats, the annual revenues would still keep coming in. It was all very well criticizing from outside; if the real grievance of the critics was that they lacked the influence they grumbled they deserved, the synagogue officers had the day-to-day task of dealing with the demands on the synagogue's resources, which were of real importance to those who asked for help.

Some of the Free Members were sensitive to criticism. In continuous defence of their own importance, they were inclined to resent occasions when they had to submit to the ultimate spiritual authority of the Chief

Rabbi. It upset their *amour propre.* Nevertheless, the large majority accepted that Adler made the final religious rulings and consequently they organized their religious lives on the basis of his guidance and advice.

It certainly wasn't always plain sailing for the founders though. In both Liverpool and Manchester the restrictive authority of the Free Members led to breakaway groups of seat holders starting their own synagogues. All were Orthodox, so there was no divergence in ritual, but if there were two synagogues there were two sets of honorary officers and two sets of opportunities for synagogal honours. They could become Free Members as well. There still remained opportunities for internecine squabbles and these were often aggressively conducted. Not surprisingly, Adler kept well away from the parties in dispute whenever he could.

He was happy to remain neutral as long as the synagogue squabbles were about status and not about theology. If he was asked to arbitrate the quarrels, he would make it crystal clear that he was passing judgement strictly according to the *din.* Then he could be seen as a judge carrying out the law, rather than as a prosecutor or defence lawyer.

The major provincial communities generally accepted this position over the years, with the notable exception of Manchester. There the situation was different and it was because of two men, Tobias Theodores and Rabbi Solomon Schiller-Szinessy. During the forty-five years of Adler's ministry they would present the single most serious challenge to his overriding authority.

Manchester's synagogue in Halliwell Street was built in 1824. There were about 250 Jews in the town at the time, where Liverpool had over 1,000 and Birmingham about 500. The Jews who paid for Halliwell Street formed a Select Committee and ran the *shul.* There was no minister, but they had a *shochet.* They made do. An optician became the honorary *mohel,* performing circumcisions until a competent surgeon was found a few years later.

The Select Committee were drawn from those founders who had lived in Manchester for many years. One factor which was driving the growth of the community, though, was the influx of new immigrants, who were attracted to Manchester as a major cotton town; twenty-four German cotton merchants arrived between 1836 and 1843.

It was the Select Committee who decided who might be added to their ranks, and how much the seat holders should pay for membership. They even split the cemetery they had bought into two sections; the left-hand side was for dead Free Members and the right-hand side for the rest. As might be imagined, this exacerbated the aggravation of those effectively designated second-class families.

The immigrants and the Free Members were two sections of the overall community, but there was also a substantial number of poverty-stricken Jews who couldn't afford to join the synagogue but rather needed financial support. The Jewish tradition was that charitable help for the poor was a fundamental responsibility for richer Jews to undertake. In Manchester the condition of the poor was often calamitous, and the wealthy accepted their duty. Like the East End of London they knew very well that there were a large number of cases where only charitable donations prevented the likelihood of near-starvation among the immigrants.

Among the original members of the community was Tobias Theodores, who had been much influenced by the German reformers and wanted to adopt many of their practices. He had little support for his views, however, because the community wished to remain Orthodox and had indeed voted for the appointment of Adler. Nonetheless, Theodores wrote and published tracts questioning the divine origin of the Talmud and arguing against rabbinism.

He was doing so in a town where opposition to established authority was widespread; Manchester was the headquarters of the anti-Corn Law League. The Corn Laws protected the profits of landowners by taxing imported corn. By contrast, the Manchester Cotton industry wanted Free Trade. The cheaper their exports could be, hopefully unencumbered by import taxes, the more they could sell. Overall, the agitation to replace the taxing of imports approved by aristocratic landowners put other proposed radical changes under the public microscope.

Manchester had a chequered history when it came to agitation. It was the setting for the Peterloo massacre in 1819 when the cavalry charged a demonstrating crowd, with many of the protesters killed as a result. The future Home Secretary, Robert Peel, had created the police as a consequence, to relieve the army from keeping order, but the memories remained bitter.

For the Jews seeking emancipation, their own decision to give the Chief Rabbi total autonomy in religious matters was an anomaly. How could they attack one central control while supporting another?

In 1844 twelve members of Halliwell Street broke away to set up another congregation at Ainsworth Court. It was still Orthodox, but the membership was comprised primarily of young and foreign Jews, who had come from humble origins but prospered. In September 1844 they opened their new synagogue and found the necessary financial support in David Hesse, a shirt manufacturer.

Against the wishes of Halliwell Street, Adler recognized the new congregation as eligible for a Marriage Secretary. As they were Orthodox there was no reason to withhold his approval. In 1846 Ainsworth Court also found a good secretary in Israel Levy, the son of the dayan in London. At the time Halliwell Street had no minister. It fell to Adler, when he visited

Ainsworth Court later in the year, to appeal on their behalf for funds to improve the synagogue and help more of the poor. He also called the two sides together to try to improve their relationship. They agreed to share the profits of *shechita* and to work together to alleviate poverty. Very impressed, Halliwell Street wrote to congratulate the Chief Rabbi on his efforts.

Thus far, Adler had no theological problem, but there were more rows in 1847 and Ainsworth Court withdrew from the agreements reached only a year before. Theodores and Hesse did not at the time have common ground on the question of orthodoxy. The two synagogues were equally committed to traditional Judaism. A visitor in 1848 could see no difference in the services, except that no sermon was preached in Halliwell Street and Ainsworth Court had a voluntary choir. Both services were poorly attended.

The two synagogues also had in common that they were embarrassed by the considerable increase in the number of paupers, which did not reflect well on the community as a whole. By this time the overall numbers were estimated to have grown to approximately 2,000.

After 1848 there was another influx of German Jews, this time fleeing from the uprisings in Europe. Many of these immigrants had moved from Orthodox to Reform at home. Their first task, however, was to settle down, and the Chief Rabbi continued to be called upon to make decisions in religious matters.

For example, just one question was whether a convert to Christianity could return to the Jewish fold because he wanted to say *Kaddish* (memorial prayers) for his mother. An authoritative decision was needed but there was no suggestion that there should be a separate religious authority in Manchester, as would have been the case in many parts of Germany. It was agreed that only Adler's judgements could be trusted to be correct.

In any event, if there was to be a separate religious authority in the future, there had to be a suitable candidate for the office. In a country where there hadn't been a single English rabbi available even for consideration as a candidate for chief rabbi in 1844, this was a major problem.

During Adler's ministry there would be only a very few able Talmudists in the country. Men like the Pole, Joseph Zedner, who would be recruited for the British Library as a Hebrew Librarian. Or Immanuel Deutsch who became an Assistant Librarian there. The Hungarian Adolph Neubauer would catalogue the Hebrew manuscripts in the Bodleian in Oxford and successive principals of the future Jews' College would be experts as well.

They did not, however, come to Britain to be synagogue ministers. The only synagogue which consistently employed a minister with *semichah* was the wealthy Hambro congregation in London. When Adler arrived they had Herman Hoelzel from Hungary, and from 1854–99 Samuel Marcus Gollancz.

In the future Gollancz's sons would become eminent in their own right and pressed for ministers with *semichah* to be addressed as 'Rabbi', but their father seemed satisfied to soldier on as 'Reverend'.

A group of members of Halliwell Street still liked the idea of disposing with authority coming from London. The potential solution for these advocates for local provincial authority came about in 1850, when a refugee from Austria arrived in the country. This was the Hungarian-born Rabbi Solomon Schiller-Szinessy, and he had all the qualifications possessed by Adler.

Schiller had a totally acceptable *semichah*, and a degree from the University of Jena, where he had been the first Jewish professor. He had written against the decisions of the Frankfurt Conference and was strictly Orthodox. He was also a spellbinding speaker, and he soon learned English. What was more, his ambition was to be the chief rabbi of the British provinces.

If the Talmudic qualifications of Adler and Schiller were very similar, their early lives were very different. Adler had lived quietly in Hanover and was surrounded by a strong family and influential friends. By contrast, Schiller was an activist who supported the Austrian rebels in the 1848 uprising. At 28 he blew up a bridge to stop the Austrian army's advance and was wounded and captured. He was sentenced to death and only escaped from prison on the night before his execution. To show his loyalty to the Hungarian cause, he adopted Szinessy as the second part of his name.

Now Schiller-Szinessy, he managed to get to Trieste and from there by boat to Ireland; the ship's doctor removed the bullets, which made his story even more heroic and dramatic. He then went on to England where he arrived in London in the summer of 1850. The immigrant rabbi had no connections in Britain, and had to build a life for himself from scratch. He was, thereafter, prepared to try short cuts where Adler had no need to take such risks.

It was Schiller's preaching that brought him to prominence. He accepted an invitation to speak in Birmingham on Rosh Hashanah in the autumn of 1850 and was enthusiastically praised in the Jewish press. As a result he was asked to preach in Manchester at Halliwell Street over Yom Kippur, and his addresses were so well received that he was invited to stay on for Sukkot.

At the time the community needed a school superintendent and Adler was consulted in December on whether Schiller would be an acceptable appointment for this post, as well as for that of minister. Adler welcomed the appointment, but reiterated that no changes could be made in the ritual without his approval. This was agreed.

There was a delicate technical point. A rabbi when called to the reading of the law in synagogue is entitled to be described as *Morenu HaRav* ('Our Teacher and Rabbi'). It remained, however, one of the planks of Adler's core objective that this description should be limited to himself, in order to emphasize the point that he was the only official authority for Judaism in the community. Schiller, however, undoubtedly had the necessary qualifications for the title and so the Chief Rabbi agreed that he could be designated *Morenu*, as long as Adler gave official permission each time. Schiller was installed in January 1851, at a generous salary of £250 a year, which included the superintending of the children. The Chief Rabbi opened a new school for them later in the year.

There was still the problem of having two practically identical communities in Manchester, and there would be obvious financial savings if they could be reunited. The discussions to achieve this, with the mediation of Schiller, dragged on, until the desired result was achieved in April 1851. There was a new constitution and, in future, Ainsworth Court members would be part of the governing body.

So far, so good, but Schiller still had ambitions to be the chief rabbi for the provinces. In the 1851 census he described himself as the Local Rabbi of the Hebrew Tongue. Such a title would appeal to those members of the community who wanted to be independent of London but this was now a direct challenge to Adler and to the national hegemony enjoyed by the lay leaders in the capital.

On occasions, other local leaders felt the same way about their independence. In 1851, for example, there was a dispute in the Liverpool congregation and the leaders in Manchester offered their services as mediators. This suggestion was immediately rejected in Liverpool, who said that they didn't need any help.

It was still the case that there were Manchester members who wanted changes in the ritual, whatever the Chief Rabbi decreed, and there were debates on the subject in 1853. It was realized by the potential secessionists that Schiller was the only minister outside London who could lead such a movement, but he was unlikely to be cooperative as he had always remained firmly wedded to Orthodox practice.

What was emerging were parties with two very different objectives; the first, to achieve more independence from London, and the second, to move towards Reform. Where there was considerable support for the former, there was little enthusiasm for achieving it by breaking away from Orthodoxy. Tobias Theodores continued to want Reform though and knew, of course, that Adler constituted the major stumbling block to achieving this.

Theodores told the Manchester community that the Chief Rabbi should only have responsibility for the Great Synagogue in London, protesting that there was no precedent in Judaism for the position of a chief rabbi. It wasn't a particularly sound argument as the Landrabbiner in Germany, from where many of the members came, had a very similar position, albeit subject to the approval of the government. It also weakened Theodores' argument, however, that it was well known that he wanted a fusion between Judaism and Christianity to reduce tensions between the two religions.

It was Theodores's core view that there would be a major advantage to the changes he proposed. That those who were, at the time, abandoning Judaism, because the Jews were not legally fully emancipated, would return to the fold if compromises could be reached. This was very much a bridge too far, however, for the majority of the now reunited community. If their numbers were also taken to include almost all of the poor immigrants in the town, they had come from much more Orthodox congregations on the Continent.

It was fully understood that if the reunited community moved towards Reform, the poor Jews would lose many of their traditions. This didn't concern Theodores whose two objectives were independence and Reform, but it certainly worried Schiller who wanted independence and Orthodoxy. Back in London, Adler and Montefiore faced up to the Manchester problem. They recognized that the move for independence could be best resisted if it were categorized as involving a move to Reform. This wasn't strictly true, but it did the image of independence no good at all.

In the coming years, the battle between Manchester and London would, primarily, be fought over comparatively minor matters. In 1851, for example, a marriage was sought by a member of the synagogue and a convert. Was the lady's conversion in Holland acceptable? It was the Chief Rabbi's approval that was normally needed to confirm this. Halliwell Street decided that Schiller's approval would be sufficient. The Chief Rabbi protested. As a compromise a dayan went from London to sit with Schiller to decide the matter. Adler wrote that such concessions would not be allowed in future.

Within weeks the Select Committee in Manchester recommended the election of Schiller for three years as Local Rabbi 'subject to the jurisdiction of the chief rabbi'. Schiller was elected unanimously to an office without precedent in Britain. Adler was not consulted and the functions of a Local Rabbi were not defined. No uniform strategy had been agreed on either side.

There were those on the committee who would have abolished the chief rabbinate, or at least his authority in Manchester, but they weren't at all sure they would get sufficient support from the community as a whole. As a compromise, Adler's supporters suggested to the Chief Rabbi that Schiller should be able to perform all the ordinary duties of a minister, but that extraordinary matters would still be left to Adler. What 'ordinary' and 'extraordinary' meant was also not defined. Adler chose the ground on which to fight the recommendation with care. All his experience in Hanover had drummed into him the value of well-judged diplomacy. He said he was sorry: 'that you should have finally decided on so important an ecclesiastical matter as the election of a Rabbi without previously requesting my sanction thereto'.[1]

Adler then gave a ruling that Schiller couldn't take up his office unless the Chief Rabbi endorsed his competence to take on the minister's role. As it had been agreed in 1850 that Schiller would not exercise any independent powers, Adler said that this agreement had now been breached. He made his views very clear. It was not his policy:

> to allow the performance of rabbinical functions in the Congregations under my charge to any gentleman, however he might be supplied with foreign Diplomas, without my previous examination ... [to find out] his capability of exercising such responsible duties ... In a country like this, when there exists no government control of qualifications whatever, such measures of precaution appears to me an absolute necessity.[2]

Of course, Adler's diplomas had also been obtained abroad and no British government was ever likely to want to be involved in the process of approving anyone's *semichah*. There couldn't, in fact, be any meaningful case that Schiller was under-qualified, but whether he had reformist leanings was another matter. He didn't but, if the resulting benefits were sufficient, Adler and Montefiore considered there was a danger he might change his mind. His financial position would always have to be a powerful consideration, which wasn't a problem for Adler.

Adler made the additional point that he had, personally, been elected on the basis he had described and with that authority. At his own election, he had been asked to take on the responsibility for all spiritual guidance of the entire community in Britain. The Select Committee was, in fact, openly questioning that authority. They made a half-hearted apology for not consulting the chief rabbi but considered a London visit to be interviewed by Adler, would be humiliating for their rabbi. In January 1852 they installed Schiller.

Both sides stood their ground, but in April Schiller made minor alterations to the services, again without consulting Adler. He sanctioned a choir and a Bat Mitzvah ceremony for girls. A committee was formed to make the necessary arrangements, at which point Adler and Montefiore decided that the situation was serious enough for them both to descend on Manchester.

The visit of the two national leaders was both flattering to the Manchester community and lent support to the traditionally minded members. In any forthcoming negotiation, they had the most eminent leaders on their side. At the subsequent meeting both sides compromised. Schiller agreed not to make decisions on marriages or divorces and not to introduce any innovations.

Adler approved the Bat Mitzvah ceremony and agreed that converts could have their credentials approved in Manchester in future. Furthermore, if a vacancy occurred for a dayan at the Beth Din in London, Schiller would be offered the position. As a result, the rabbi: 'salvaged his prestige, the congregation its pride, Dr. Adler his supremacy'.[3] There would still be niggles in the future.

There would, however, be another blow to Schiller's prestige. It occurred when he preached at the Great Synagogue in London and was not called up to the Torah as *Morenu*. It was held that this nomenclature was only appropriate for him in Manchester. That was either petty spite or a defence measure against the concept of local rabbis becoming a threat to the chief rabbi. Both sides were taking the view that big trees from little acorns grow. For his part, Schiller had stationery printed along the lines of that of the Chief Rabbi, with 'Office of the Local Rabbi' on the letterhead.

The supporters of changes in the ritual continued to press for action. At a large meeting in May 1853, almost 100 attendees voted for the desirability of changes in the form of worship in the synagogue. Theodores made a long and powerful speech in favour of change and the agitation continued over the coming years. Lip service was always paid to authority remaining: 'for the time being in conjunction with the Chief Rabbi', but Adler's overall rule remained under attack. The advocates for change were important, intelligent and articulate members of the community. They were, however, a small minority and the silent majority was not persuaded. Schiller sat firmly on the fence.

There was also a further weapon which the opposition could use against Adler. This was that the new Jews' College in London would not include training for *semichah* in its curriculum. It was the case, however, that there were no prospective students with a strong enough foundation in Jewish learning, to be even considered for a *semichah* course. Jews' College was in its infancy and had to be built from the ground up. It was simply a by-product that the lack of rabbis with *semichah* ensured that Adler was left as one of the very few ordained rabbis in Britain. This did admittedly reduce the likelihood of qualified challengers to his authority in the future. Additionally, there were good and sufficient reasons for Adler's decision not to concentrate on a *semichah* course, as the first need for most of the British Jewish communities at the time was for competent ministers, rather than Talmudic scholars.

Another attempt to introduce independence came in May 1853 when elections were held for the Board of Deputies. Four of those elected wanted to represent the secessionist community in London. The decision not to accept them was made on the casting vote of the chairman, Sir Moses Montefiore, and David Hesse, the Manchester delegate who was in favour of Margaret Street representation, moved further towards the secessionist position.

At a meeting of the congregation in December 1853, Hesse sought to get agreement that the *herem* against the London congregation should be repealed and Adler described the motion as 'an open rupture' with his authority. He also said that the community did not have the power to do any such thing. He had written to the congregation that: 'The ecclesiastical authorities have no power to alter the religious position in which they were at the time when the same was issued.'[4]

He called upon his friends in the congregation to oppose the motion. In doing so, the unity of the Manchester community was finally ruptured. Adler's supporters insisted that the Chief Rabbi and the Beth Din: 'alone are competent to pronounce a decision'. Further meetings were rancorous and on one occasion, 'the chairman not being able to obtain silence, adjourned the meeting'.[5]

Hesse produced a test case, asking whether a member of the Margaret Street secessionist synagogue in London could be accepted as a member in Manchester. If this had been approved, the result would have been that Adler's rulings were not binding on Manchester. The community prevaricated and decided to delay a decision.

Theodores insisted at public meetings that the chief rabbi's authority was 'fictitious', and Theodores was a powerful advocate for that position, particularly in view of the audience knowing no better. Theodores was a very fine academic; when the Shah of Persia visited the city, Theodores was the only Manchester representative who could speak his language.

Adler appealed for peace. At a general meeting in April 1854 it was unanimously agreed that the discussion should be postponed sine die. At the same time Schiller's contract came up for renewal and the community, with little thought for the likely consequences, decided that they would only contribute £50 in future towards his salary. The explanation was that the cost of helping the Manchester poor made savings in other areas a priority.

Everybody wanted Schiller to continue in office but the atmosphere had soured and they were no longer prepared to meet the cost. The pro-Adler party were now concerned that Schiller might become a pawn in the hands of the group of secessionists. It was noticeable, for example, that the terms of his reappointment omitted the condition that he would remain 'under the jurisdiction of the Chief Rabbi'.

Schiller had no option but to accept the new salary proposals. He reacted by saying that he would, henceforth, charge for carrying out marriages and other rabbinical responsibilities. He also said that nobody else had the right to conduct a marriage. With some reluctance the community accepted the position, but his support as the local rabbi was further eroded. So there was now a conflict between members and the rabbi, and another between those with Reform and Orthodox leanings.

There were discussions to try to mend the breach between the reformers and the orthodox parties. Adler was asked to give his approval. In April 1856 he declined to do so:

> I am sure that it is far from your thoughts that the avoidance of such an evil should be purchased by concessions which must undermine the very pillars on which the holy edifice of our religion rests. The propositions of the Reform Association, stated in the report, involve not only an organic change in the ritual of our Prayer Book, but a denial of the Oral Law, or the historic Judaism.
>
> So far as my authority is concerned, I am called upon to preserve our sacred faith against any encroachment; and, however anxious I am for the introduction of becoming decorum and solemnity in the house of G-d, I cannot conscientiously grant permission for any change in the ritual prescribed in our Prayer Book.[6]

There had been a crisis in January 1856 when Schiller said he wouldn't perform a specific marriage unless he was paid. The community decided to ask the Chief Rabbi to permit the *hazan* to conduct the ceremony. Adler asked the community to try again to get Schiller to change his mind and sanction the wedding. He pleaded for a peaceful outcome, but the wedding went ahead anyway with Schiller conducting the ceremony. The lay leaders stuck to their guns, making it clear that they considered Schiller subordinate to them.

At the same time, the rabbi was still looking to extend his authority to other communities. He went on to conduct a marriage for a breakaway congregation in Hull without the approval of his lay leaders, and without Adler approving them as entitled to have a Marriage Secretary. Adler had in fact refused to sanction the marriage. Adler wrote to Halliwell Street:

> I have the pleasure of knowing Dr Schiller and can scarcely believe it possible that one ever anxious for peace as he has always been, would rashly do any act which would widen rather than close the breach at present existing between the authorised Congregation [in Hull] and a few discontented persons.[7]

Adler's secretary wrote of his further comments:

> I sincerely hope that Dr Schiller will ponder well before he takes so fatal a step (as far as his reputation and character are concerned) as to come to Hull to act as the tool of despicable men who boast already of their success in inducing him to come to perform the marriage ceremony in Hull despite the Law of the Country or his courtesy and engagements to Dr Adler.[8]

The Hull community reported that Schiller had asked the breakaway community to call on him as: 'certain persons resident in this town had invited him to become their chief rabbi'.[9]

Schiller performed the ceremony and was, indeed, invited by the breakaway community to become their chief rabbi. He had, however, gone very much too far. Adler wrote to Halliwell Street and asked if there was any reason why he should not cease to recognize Schiller as the local rabbi. They agreed there wasn't and, on 20 February, suspended Schiller. On 25 March, without waiting for the results of an official enquiry, Schiller resigned. The school, nevertheless, appealed to him to continue to supervise the education of the children, to which he readily agreed.

Meanwhile those in favour of Reform had decided to form their own community. They agreed to adopt the Margaret Street prayer book and its practices. In April discussions with the Orthodox representatives to achieve a compromise were not successful. A request to Adler to meet the reformers halfway produced a response in June. He pointed out that:

> the prayer book of Margaret Street has not been adopted by any village, even not in America, where all kinds of experiment are exercised. [Congregations should] not be overanxious in introducing changes which, as experience teaches, leave the Synagogue [as] deserted as before when the charm of novelty has subsided.[10]

Adler also stood firm on the right of the *cohanim* (priests) to bless the congregation; he refused to allow the Sabbath service to be held in two parts; he insisted on the second day of festivals being observed, and took issue with the secessionists on a number of other points. The Halliwell Street Select Committee put up compromise proposals to the Reform group, but these were declined, in their turn, in August. They had become determined to reject the authority of the chief rabbi. Both sides dug in.

By July the breakaway group in Hull had rejoined the main congregation and reported that its relationship with Dr Schiller was, therefore, at an end. An announcement in the *Jewish Chronicle* on 10 October confirmed that Schiller had been appointed minister of a new Manchester Reform synagogue and, towards the end of the month he was also to be found preaching at Margaret Street. He had, however, insisted on the second day of festivals being kept. Otherwise he now found the Margaret Street order of service quite acceptable.

To further complicate matters, Halliwell Street was now requisitioned by the council in a road widening scheme, and both groups needed to build new synagogues. Schiller laid the foundation stone of the Reform synagogue in March 1857. In his address he gave his justification for the proposed changes envisaged by the new congregation: 'The spirit was made subordinate to the letter, that religious progress was negated by modern conservatism.'[11]

It was difficult to respond to such generalizations, but the majority of the community was looking for stronger arguments. Adler consecrated the Orthodox building on 11 March 1858 and David Woolf Marks the Reform synagogue two weeks later. One hurtful result of the split was that members of the Reform congregation were no longer allowed to be buried in the Halliwell Street cemetery where, so often, other members of their families were interred. Over the next few years, though, the relations between the two communities did improve, as congregants put their personal relationships with family and friends ahead of their differing religious views.

The main problem in the future would come when the Reform synagogue converted non-Jews. Children of a resulting marriage would not be considered Jewish unless it was the husband who had converted; a Jew is the child of a Jewish mother. Which meant that acceptable conversion had to be approved by an Orthodox body. Orthodox conversion is usually a very protracted process. It could be easier under the Reform aegis, but where the future non-Jewish bride was converted by the Reform congregation, the Jewish husband, effectively, was regarded as having left the Orthodox community, often to the great distress of his parents and family.

There was no doubt that, overall, the controversy had been a victory for Adler. The arguments about local autonomy had been subsumed into a debate on Orthodoxy vs. Reform. In refusing to join the Reform, the majority of members had, in effect, also voted for the reconfirmation of the sole authority of the Chief Rabbi in religious matters. In the spring of 1860 Theodores managed to get the Reform community to agree to abolish the second day of festivals. To some extent this was a pyrrhic victory as it was unacceptable to Schiller, and he resigned again.

In May his school pupils were examined on their Jewish knowledge. They put up a very creditable performance and David Hesse spoke very warmly of the efforts which Schiller had made in teaching them so well. The rabbi had certainly improved the level of tuition to a great extent, and had done so for nine years without receiving any extra fee. Many of the children were reported to have been in tears when eventually it came time for him to give his farewell address.

For the next few years, without a congregation, Schiller made a living teaching children privately, but his hope of becoming a chief rabbi for the provinces was in ruins. Schiller had been through worse times though.

At the home of a friend, he met a Unitarian lady called Georgiana Eleanor Herbert and they fell in love. The lady's conversion in England would have involved the Chief Rabbi, which was the last thing Schiller wanted. He had, however, communicated with the chief rabbi of Paris some years before on the arrangements for an Anglo-French marriage, when he was at Halliwell Street. He now used that friendship to arrange for his future wife to be converted, with the name of Sarah, and the couple were married by Rabbi Isidor at his home in Paris in 1863.

It does suggest that conversion was something of a movable feast, but the most important criterion was, as always, that the non-Jewish partner wanted to follow the religion rather than just get married to a Jew. The proof of their belief in the faith was a decision for the authorised rabbi who was asked to convert them, or for the appropriate Beth Din. Rabbi Isidor decided that Georgina Herbert was sincere in wanting to convert.

At the time of the marriage Cambridge University was looking for a scholar who could catalogue their Hebrew manuscripts and Schiller had all the necessary qualifications. So he switched careers from being a rabbi to becoming an academic, and the family lived happily ever after in Cambridge until his death a quarter of a century later.

Schiller would die two months after Adler in 1890 as the Reader in Talmudic and Rabbinic Literature at Cambridge. He had catalogued the manuscripts and was awarded an honorary MA in 1878. He was also the first Jew to go on the electoral roll of the town. In Cambridge his tortuous career had finally reached a satisfactory conclusion.

Notes

1. Bill Williams, *The Making of Manchester Jewry, 1740–1875* (Manchester: Manchester University Press, 1985), p.212.
2. Ibid., p.213.
3. Ibid., p.215.
4. Bill Williams, *The Making of Manchester Jewry, 1740–1875* (Manchester: Manchester University Press, 1985).
5. Ibid.
6. *Jewish Chronicle*, 16 May 1856, p.587.
7. Letter to the secretary at Manchester, 10 February 1856, from Williams, *The Making of Manchester Jewry.*
8. Ibid., 13 February1856.
9. Letter from Hull to Manchester, 17 February1856, from Williams, *The Making of Manchester Jewry.*
10. Letter from Chief Rabbi to Halliwell Street, 3 June 1856, from Williams, *The Making of Manchester Jewry.*
11. Williams, *The Making of Manchester Jewry.*

1. Rabbi Adler as a young man.

2. The main street in Hanover in the 1830s.

3. Oldenburg Landesrabbiner in 1829.

4. The Chief Rabbi in Hanover.

5. The Chief Rabbi arrives in London.

6. Henrietta Adler.
photo copyright The Jewish Museum.

7. The official portrait by Solomon Alexander Hart.

8. Jules Mombach, the Great Synagogu choirmaster.

9. Rabbi Dr. Solomon Schiller-Szinessy - the competition in Manchester.

10. The future Chief Rabbi, Hermann Adler.

11. Elkan Adler - a stalwart of the community.

12. The Chief Rabbi in his old age.

13. Ida Adler.

14. The grave at Willesden.

15. Sir Moses Montefiore – the other side of the partnership.

16. Rabbi Simeon Singer – the Adler Prayer Book secretariat.

17. The Great Synagogue in the City of London.

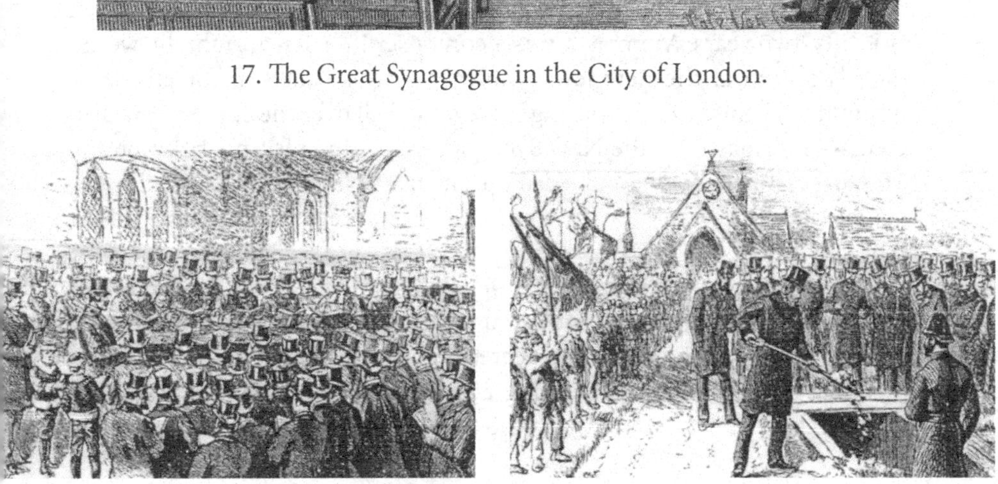

18. Two illustrations of the funeral in 1890.

8

Progress and Tragedy

In October 1849 there was the annual meeting of the Western Jewish Girls Free School to which Adler was particularly happy to offer his patronage. The meeting was conducted in the presence of the Duke of Cambridge and it was particularly noted how exceptional was the Hebrew knowledge of the girls who were, in some cases, no more than 5 years old.

The finances were a problem and £50 had to be drawn down from reserves to cover the deficit for the year. Subscriptions had only amounted to £80 and the school roll now numbered sixty-three. It was noted that it had been decided to abolish corporal punishment. This was a very liberal move for its time, even for girls.

The community might welcome small improvements of this nature, but it was still embarrassed by the judgements of academics from abroad. For example, Moritz Steinschneider, who was retained by the Bodleian Library in Oxford to prepare their Hebrew books for cataloguing, remarked on one of his visits to England that very few Jews could be found with even a modicum of rabbinic learning. The community couldn't ignore the shortcoming but it was a hard struggle for Adler to get them to do much about it.

At the Great Synagogue there was one area which could not be criticized and that was the singing of the choir. This was in the very safe hands of the choirmaster, Julius Lazarus Mombach (1813–80). He had come to London from Germany at the age of 15 and after joining the choir, he eventually led it for fifty-two years. Mombach was a composer in his own right, he would teach *hazzanut* at the new Jews' College, he was called in for all major community events, and he was highly regarded all over the country. He also acted as choirmaster of the New Synagogue, splitting his time between the two synagogues. When he arrived at the Great Synagogue at the time the Ark was opened, it became the custom for the congregation to stand out of respect.

The economic conditions in Europe had been worsening for a number of years. The crucial potato crop often failed and there were poor harvests, rising food prices and a serious increase in unemployment. Typhus also spread. In such circumstances, emigration became a possible solution and large numbers of Jews started to come to England from the Continent. The

European sea ports often had Jewish communities, and they facilitated the passage of the economic refugees.

The result was to put a great strain on the ability of the London Jewish community to cope with the substantial new influx. There were certainly more than enough Jewish poor in London who needed help, without adding to their numbers. Accordingly the wardens of the three London synagogues wrote to *The Voice of Jacob* pleading with the continental communities to stop giving encouragement to the migrants, and Adler signed the communication at the top of the list.

The letter pointed out that the emigrants were in danger of actual starvation, or falling into the hands of conversion societies, but this did little to stop the flow, particularly after the results of the 1848 revolutions which took place across the Continent. These were described at the time as the Spring of Nations, but most were eventually put down. One country benefited. It is now possible to see that many of the immigrants were very helpful in the development of the British economy; that is, however, to learn from 20:20 hindsight.

While there was no official discrimination against the Jews, apart from the unacceptable parliamentary oath, there was a degree of anti-Semitism which would have reminded Adler of what he had faced in Hanover. Nothing gross like accusations of poisoning wells or spreading the plague, but the perpetuation of simplistic unpleasant stereotypes. This applied even to notable newspaper like *The Times*.

In the spring of 1850, Lord Palmerston, the Foreign Secretary, would send a flotilla of warships to blockade Greece in order to get compensation for the head of the Athens Jewish community when a mob looted his house, led by a government minister's sons. The victim, David Pacifico, had asked to be recompensed for his substantial losses. The newspapers had a field day attacking the Foreign Secretary, condemning Pacifico as a confidence trickster. In the process of so doing, the Anglo-Jewish community was lumped in with its coreligionist: *The Times* commented: 'In other words, ask all you dare and get all you can. That may be a mode of dealing familiar to Greeks and Jews, but it is the reverse of those plain and fixed demands with which we are happily more familiar.'[1]

This was in line with the dictionary definition of 'To Jew' at the time, which was to cheat or to drive a hard bargain. However, it was made crystal clear in a debate in the House of Commons on the blockade, that Parliament took a very different view. As the future prime minister, William Gladstone, insisted:

> I say fearlessly, whatever may be the difference of opinion in this House as to the admission of Jews to political privilege, that no person

> could dare to stand up among us and allege his religion as a ground for mistrust or for the denial of justice, without drawing down upon himself, from all quarters of the House alike, universal scorn and indignation.[2]

The furore died down in a few months, Pacifico got his compensation, his reputation was restored and the fleet came home, but it was a nasty episode. It was also in 1850 that Adler lost one of his great supporters with the death of the Duke of Cambridge at the age of 76 from 'cramps in the stomach'.

The year before, the wish for the Orthodox to have a synagogue in the West End of London was finally approved by the decision to build the Central Synagogue near the new Regents Park which had opened in 1835. It had taken a long time; a subcommittee had been set up in 1848 to consider what should be done, but it didn't produce a report until 1851.

The Sephardim were invited to join in the new venture, but they eventually decided that their services were distinct from the Ashkenazim and it wasn't really feasible. Instead they created their own synagogue in the West End, which eventually became a new building in Maida Vale, now known as Lauderdale Road.

The Central was not to be an independent congregation, but a subsidiary of the Great Synagogue in the East End. For instance, no weddings could be solemnized there and it wasn't allowed to have its own officers or committee. It was run by the Great. It had some of the same problems as the older synagogues, though. It was almost easier to find the £6,000 to build the synagogue than to find a reader to take the service. When a *hazan* was needed in 1859, there would be no British applicants.

The Central would have many wealthy members and they liked their comfort. The question would arise of whether there could be a break in the Sabbath service. It normally started at 8.30 in the morning but many congregants found this too early. So they arrived at various times, as they still do today. The request was that there be an official break after the early morning prayers and the service should restart with the Reading of the Law, without the newcomers being so noticeable. Adler decided that this could be the practice in the Central which was a new synagogue, but nowhere else because a continuous service was the tradition. It is a well-known principle in Orthodox Judaism that what has stood the test of time eventually becomes the law. It is known as *minhag*, rather than *din*. Discussions on what the Central could and could not do were completed in twelve months. The Jewish community seldom moved in haste in Victorian times.

Adler's initial concern was that if he gave his approval, nobody would turn up for the earlier part of the service. At the same time, he recognized that the membership of the new synagogue was influential, so he approved the alteration for the Central. His concerns were well founded as there were occasions when the requisite ten men did not arrive for the earlier session.

Adler's eminence as an authority, from his time in Hanover, meant that he was well known in Jewish circles in many other parts of the world. Even after the American Declaration of Independence, the Sephardi synagogue in New York still looked to the Haham in London for responsa, and Ashkenazi Jews were equally able to ask for rulings from Adler as, of course, they could from other rabbinic authorities around the world.

Philip Levy, a trustee of the Elm Street Synagogue in New York, asked the Chief Rabbi's advice on the making of *matzot* for Passover. Adler's responsa was printed in *The Occident*, a Jewish periodical published in Philadelphia, on 7 Marcheshvan 5610 (23 October 1849):

> May the Lord grant you peace and life ...
>
> 1st Regarding your complaint, that they do not use water which has stood overnight, I have to remark, that although it is requisite to take care originally not to use such water, even if it be river water, still if they have drawn the previous evening a quantity which they deemed sufficient, they may be permitted to add ordinary water, so as to supply any deficiency which may occur.
>
> 2nd. Respecting the scruples you express that the doughs made are larger than ... a measure to the size of 43 eggs, equal 520 drachms of Egypt, about six pounds, I have to state that, although it is not true that in London they make the doughs larger than this, because I have given the workmen strict orders not to exceed it, and have given my personal attention to the matter: still, as the machine in question is so large and powerful, that it is almost impossible for any little piece to be left unbroken and unkneaded, it is not necessary to confine the size of the dough ... when such an instrument is used.
>
> 3rd. Respecting your scruples about the *Matzot Shimurim* (i.e. those especial cakes destined for the first two nights of the Passover) not to make them by a machine, it is to be remarked that, one who is truly anxious to fulfil the word of the Lord, should bake them through means of an Israelite only, nevertheless, it will be enough if an Israelite commences to mix the dough, and stands by whilst it is made. But, as respects your
>
> 4th observation, that the dough is cut into four pieces, and that a fourth-part is left without being handled within the influence of the heated steam of the machine full 18 minutes, I have to say that, if it be as you state, such baking is next to leaven, prohibited by Scripture,

> and it cannot be permitted to be used in many manner whatever; for not only that this time is ... [the time required to walk a mile] it is a well known decision of the *Possekim* that, if there be an additional amount of heat, the process of leavening commences in the dough in less than the specified time.[3]

There were many other occasions when eminent rabbinic authorities advised their communities that Adler's views should be highly regarded. During his time in Hanover, when he was only 32, he received the endorsement of the renowned Chatam Sofer (Rabbi Moses Schreiber), who gave his approval to a German translation of the Talmud by a number of scholars, because: 'according to my opinion this Rabbi was held as a *tzaddik* [righteous man] and a *talmid chacham* [wise scholar], I said the one part would testify on all'.[4] So if it was good enough for Adler, it was good enough for the Chatam Sofer, which was high praise indeed.

Another expert, Rabbi Shaul Nathanson, was considering a divorce case and told the people concerned that he had decided to consult Adler. Rabbi Isaac Bamberger, the author of the influential *Yad Halevi,* advised people to consult: 'The great Cohen Morenu HaRav Nosan Adler ... *Av Beth Din* of the *kehilla kedosha* [holy community] London'.[5]

Adler was happy to deal with problems on a very wide range of subjects. He was in frequent contact with colonial communities; for instance, he sent specific instructions to the congregation in Melbourne on how to build a mikvah and told them what religious functions their minister, Moses Rintel, was, and was not, allowed to perform. His involvement was very much appreciated. In 1852, for example, an 18-carat gold *Kiddush* cup arrived from Melbourne, crafted from some of the first gold discovered in the colony. In Britain there were now thirty-six towns with Jewish congregations.[6] They numbered as many as 1,500 in Liverpool, 1,000 in Manchester and 780 in Birmingham.

When he exchanged correspondence with *rabbonim* abroad, he would write in a number of different languages, though he had very little correspondence with non-Jews. He was particularly careful with the qualifications of overseas *shochetim* and, if necessary, would tell their community that they were inadequate and had to be dismissed. He withdrew the licences of butchers as well.

Another area where Adler was an acknowledged expert was the *kashrut* of different species of birds, and his office would get enquiries on the subject from across the world from rabbinic leaders. The Jewish community in Britain might well be unlikely to know of his eminence abroad, but his colleagues around the world held him in very high esteem. His views were certainly law for Moses Montefiore. Dr Louis Loewe was the editor of Montefiore's papers, and said he regarded: 'A word from him as decisive and obeyed its injunctions at whatever cost to himself.'

The congregations that did exist had all kinds of internal problems, from the rows over the poaching of members in the London synagogues to the split in the Liverpool community into two separate congregations, but then nobody ever suggested that Adler sought a quiet life.

In 1851 there was a national religious census to identify how many were attending places of worship on the Sabbath. The result showed there were only 3,000 Jews in synagogue in the whole country. By 1853 the Sephardi synagogue at Bevis Marks was only holding morning services during the week on Mondays and Thursdays. The decline was a grave problem.

The year of the Great Exhibition, 1851, drew over six million visitors to the magnificent pavilion in Hyde Park. A significant number of wealthy Jews bought season tickets which cost three guineas (£3.15p, and over £300 in today's money) for men and two guineas for women (£2.10). For those who were working during the week, the most convenient day to attend was Saturday because the Exhibition was closed on Sundays. The problem this created for the Orthodox was that season ticket holders had to sign their names when they showed their tickets. This they couldn't do on Shabbat and an initial request to the Commissioners to waive this necessity was turned down. It took an intervention by Moses Montefiore to arrange that if they went through Entrance 11 a signature wouldn't be necessary.

Adler accepted the compromise, though he knew very well that not signing wouldn't really solve the problem; the *din* also did not allow anything to be carried on the Sabbath, including tickets. The Chief Rabbi recognized, however, that he had to move slowly towards his goal of greater observance of the *mitzvoth*, for the secessionist minister, David Woolf Marks, was offering to make lower, rather than higher, standards officially acceptable. Moreover, the community's level of application of the *mitzvoth* was starting from a relatively low point in any case.

The danger was that, if Adler had repudiated the agreement, members of the community would have visited the Exhibition anyway, suggesting that his rules could be safely ignored. Trying to enforce not carrying on the Sabbath and missing the Exhibition was not a *mitzvah* he considered worth risking the undermining of his authority. Adler would choose his battlefields with care. He would start from the bottom and try to move up, rather than beginning with the full panoply of the *din* and risk having observance after observance ignored.

That Adler didn't make a fuss on this occasion was typical of his approach. He had to try to build the community as well as make it more observant. He lacked ministers, he had few Talmudic experts, not enough schools, not enough candidates for synagogue offices, few decent buildings for small communities and insufficient money to alleviate at least part of the crushing poverty which affected so many of his constituents. He couldn't solve the problem but he could show he didn't want it treated as out of sight and, therefore, out of mind. For instance, to show his personal support, he took care to attend the anniversary dinner of the Society for Distributing Bread, Meat and Coals to the Jewish Poor.

What Adler would have definitely approved was the number of Jewish children who were given tickets for the Exhibition by benevolent philanthropists. The Infant School and the Orphan Asylum were sent 150 each and at least another 100 tickets went to other Jewish schools.

By now Adler and Moses Montefiore had an agreed plan for achieving their objectives. The first, and most important of these, remained to prevent the spread of Reform Judaism in Britain. Throughout Adler's ministry he viewed with alarm the growth of Reform in Germany and America. It was promulgated by many spiritual leaders whose Talmudic credentials were sometimes as good as the average Orthodox rabbi living alongside them. As the office of chief rabbi didn't exist outside Britain, it was, therefore, the more difficult to insist that the Orthodox rabbis had a greater degree of authority.

Adler ensured that this was not the position in Britain. Throughout the Orthodox congregations he was determined that he would be the one Jewish spiritual leader. His authority would be based on the insistence of the Board of Deputies that other ministers had to be approved by him before they could be appointed by the synagogues.

The problem in Manchester highlighted the potential for disruption in the titles of his clergy. By refusing throughout his ministry to allow any other minister to be called Rabbi, he also put himself – and, therefore, his views – on a pedestal. There might be grumbles, which grew as the years went by, but his title would go some way to reinforce his supremacy in spiritual decisions.

The lay authority continued to be the Board of Deputies. Soon after Adler's election, there had been an effort to increase the Board's membership by bringing in more of the provincial congregations. At the time there had been little response, as the congregations said they couldn't afford the expense of attending meetings in London.

In 1853 things changed and the elections to the Board that year produced four successful candidates who declared that they would represent the views of the secessionist West London Synagogue of British Jews. There was then a tremendous row at a Deputies' meeting about whether this could be allowed. Montefiore, as the President, had to call the police to keep order.

When the constable arrived, he was stopped from entering the hall, an obvious case of obstructing a police officer in the discharge of his duty. To increase the confusion, Montefiore left the building in an undignified hurry with nothing resolved and the next meeting was equally cantankerous. Of the eight Bevis Marks delegates, only one voted to accept the four secessionist representatives, but Montefiore eventually had to use his casting vote to defeat a proposal to admit the West London nominees. He based his refusal on the first clause of the constitution of the Board which aimed to stop: 'infraction upon the religious rites, customs and privileges of the Jewish community'.

Montefiore held the view that the West London had done exactly that and he would block the proposal to allow their representation for the next twenty years. It was true that many secessionist leaders had important lay offices in Britain as a whole but, as far as he was concerned, they would still not be permitted to represent progressive communities on the Board.

It was all highly contentious, but, at the same time, the Chief Rabbi was kept well out of the fray. He was indeed asked his views but took all of two months to come up with a noncommittal answer. At the end of the year the Board confirmed their earlier decision, in spite of the fact that Montefiore was severely criticized.

Adler and Montefiore had, however, one major advantage. The secessionists had a bigger problem than trying to secure Orthodox acceptance; they were very much concerned not to be ostracized and criticized by the rest of the community. When Moses Mocatta, the warden at the secessionist synagogue, talked of changes, he opined that, 'For any least deviation, unqualified censure will be heaped upon us and the self-styled Orthodox of our co-religionists will gladly seize on the minutest point to vilify our Minister and cast obloquy on our congregation.'[7]

The Council of Founders hated the idea of this. They wanted to retain the respect of their friends, colleagues and family. They were only a tiny minority of the total Jewish community and they didn't want to emphasize the ways in which they differed from the Orthodox. They might want to protect David Woolf Marks, their minister, but they made sure that any new changes he recommended would require their approval before being introduced. Even thirty years after the formation of the community, they defended their general adherence to Orthodoxy. The *Jewish Chronicle* would report in 1874:

> We may state that the members of the new congregation deny altogether the impeachment of having renounced the Oral Law. Professor Marks and Mr Elkin, in the earlier days of the Reform,

> strenuously maintained the general fidelity of their congregation to the Jewish tradition ... There is probably less discrepancy between the Jews forming what are called Orthodox congregations and Jews who are members of the Reformed Congregation of London than is apparent within the bosom of a single denomination of Christians, we will say the Church of England. [The Reformed synagogue] cannot be characterized other than as a secession.[8]

Within the ranks of the secessionists there was, indeed, every kind of member, from very Orthodox to comparatively non-observant. It was soon recognized by the Council of Founders that, in order to avoid antagonizing the majority of the community even more, it was best to avoid lengthy discussion on the minutiae of the *din*.

To that extent Adler and Montefiore had an easier task in keeping the majority of the British Jewish community within the Orthodox camp. Their attitude could grant – or deny – the secessionists a degree of respectability, or at least toleration, and that was a powerful incentive for the Council of Founders.

Beneath the surface, however, both Adler and Montefiore exercised a steely determination to hold the fort. To them, the beliefs of the Reform movement were not a question of intellectual discussion and academic philosophizing. As far as both Orthodox leaders were concerned, this was a fight for the soul of the community, and neither had any intention of losing a single round.

The Chief Rabbi did, however, suffer a terrible loss in 1853. On 23 June 1853 his beloved wife, Henrietta, died. She had been suffering from ulcers in a world where medical science could do little to cure the condition. She was in great pain for many months and an ulcer must have burst without warning because it was her servant, Mary Doyle, who was there when she died, and reported her passing. Henrietta Adler was only 53 years old and the devoted couple were shortly to celebrate their silver wedding. It was a devastating blow.

She had been a fine wife to Adler since they were married in 1829. She had given him three daughters and two sons, the youngest of whom was only 13 when she died. In the obituary in the *Jewish Chronicle* we get a rare glimpse of the lady herself, and the impermanence of Victorian life: 'Not a nature to shine and dazzle. She shrank from display ... within a fortnight of her death, her position became alarming and every hope – humanly speaking – for recovery vanished.'[9] Her public image was appropriate for the time: 'With increasing simplicity and singleness of heart, she discharged her domestic duties of a wife and mother.' She was also very generous: After her death, the family found several parcels of money, labelled with the names of the pensioners, to whom she had dispersed weekly allowances.'[10]

Henrietta was the last person to be buried at the Alderney Road cemetery in the East End of London, which had been opened as long ago as 1696. The former chief rabbi, David Tevele Schiff, had also been interred there. The death certificate identified Henrietta as the wife of the High Priest of the Jews. It was a sweltering day and the Friday temperature reached 74 degrees[11] as the fifteen-coach funeral cortege, with the Chief Rabbi and Sir Moses Montefiore leading the procession, made its slow journey to the cemetery. The coaches of the honorary officers of the five main London synagogues followed behind. There was, after ten years in office, a very high regard for Adler but nothing could be done. When the tombstone was finally erected, it read in both the Jewish and Victorian way: 'Here lies Mrs Rachael Hitzuel, wife of the Gaon Morenu, the Rabbi Nathan Marcus Adler Hacohen. She was gathered on 17 Sivan 5613.'

Adler soldiered on. Within a month he lent his name and made a donation to the fund raising needed to send twenty young Jewish women to Australia, where Jewish wives were in short supply for those transported over the years. His daughters donated an additional amount to the cause in memory of their mother. There was also a celebration a couple of years later in 1855 when Jeanette, his second daughter, married Rabbi Anschel Stern, the Chief Rabbi of Hamburg.

Adler had recognized early on that if he was to be a role model, he needed to be a visible one. Where his predecessors had stayed in London, the Chief Rabbi, with the help of the railways, could visit the provincial communities on a number of occasions. He did so and was always treated with the utmost respect by the congregation and the non-Jewish townsfolk. He would often address large meetings where both Jews and Christians were welcome to attend, and he was, as always, a dynamic speaker. The welcome he received from the civic authorities enhanced his reputation still more.

In a country where religion played a far greater role than it does today, he was, to the uninitiated, the epitomisation of the Biblical prophet. Most of his non-Jewish audiences may never have seen a rabbi before. On these occasions Adler was always careful to deal with moral and ethical, rather than doctrinal subjects.

One event which brought him to the attention of a wide non-Jewish audience took place on the National Day of Humiliation and Prayer at the beginning of the Crimean War. It had been a custom in Britain on many occasions in the past for a day to be designated for the country to pray for success in war. The government decided to continue the tradition on 26 April 26 1854 and Adler gave a stirring address from the pulpit. *The Daily News* was only one of the papers which covered the story and pronounced the sermon: 'instinct with a fire and genius such as must have anointed the prophets of old'. Adler's themes were to point up the evils of the impending war, the blessings which might emerge from it and the duties incumbent on the community to contribute liberally to the support of the families of those who might be killed or wounded in the war. In fact, 21,000 British troops would die in the war, though 16,000 of them perished from disease.

There was another day designated for national prayer in October 1857 when the British in India had suffered grievously during the Indian Mutiny. The community observed the day with somewhat less enthusiasm; the use of pork grease in the bullets, forced on the Indian soldiery, might well have resulted in serious protest from Jewish soldiers as well.

Adler's serious potential opposition was from some of the lay leaders of the community, even though the Board of Deputies had acknowledged his spiritual pre-eminence. If members of the Board wanted to challenge him, though, there were serious obstacles standing in their way. The first was Montefiore's unswerving support and the chief rabbi's constitutional position. The second was the Board's relationship with the provincial communities.

Since the readmission in Stuart times, the centre of Jewish life in Britain had always been London. It was typical of its status that members of the new Jews' College Council would be expected to have a home in the metropolis. Decisions were made by the London delegates on occasions, without even informing the provincial members. This led to complaints and aggravation, but the London Board of Deputies delegates were far too powerful to be diverted from this discourteous approach.

The dislike of the provincial communities for the overbearing behaviour of London did not extend to Adler. He treated every one of his communities with great courtesy. Throughout his ministry the pattern of Jewish settlement widened as new manufacturing towns emerged, and Jewish merchants moved to take advantage of the commercial opportunities. In Adler's time Britain was the world's No. 1 exporter, and sold abroad more than countries two and three put together.

The provinces would also begin to grow more important as part of the Board of Deputies. Before the 1853 election London had twenty-eight deputies and was dominated by the fourteen representatives of Bevis Marks and the Great. The new Board had twenty-six provincial congregation representatives, though twenty-one of them lived in London. As the years went by, the London share of the delegates would reduce to well under half in the early twentieth century.

The community became much more diverse and Adler tried to be involved with every congregation. For example, the new communities needed new synagogue buildings and if these were to be highly regarded, what better way was there of establishing their importance than to have them opened by the Chief Rabbi. There was no other equivalent choice. Moreover, when they needed money, there was always the Chief Rabbi's name at the top of the donor's list.

It was not surprising that Adler took the starring role on these important synagogue occasions. From the consecration of the Canterbury Synagogue in 1848 until the opening of Princes Road Synagogue in Liverpool in 1874, the Chief Rabbi would be in the pulpit on the great day, to invoke the blessing of the Almighty on the new sanctuary. Such synagogues included Norwich in 1849, Exeter reopened in 1854, Birmingham in 1856, Southampton in 1865, Chatham and Coventry in 1870, Bristol in 1871, Sheffield in 1872 and Middlesborough in 1874. The typical reaction on these memorable days was reported in the *Jewish Chronicle* in 1862: 'The congregation was a crowded one and the impression which the Reverend Doctor Adler has made upon them will never be effaced.'[12] After Birmingham, where he inspected the schoolchildren and preached in the synagogue, he was reported to have: 'Riveted the attention of the congregation by his eloquent and skilful exposition.'

It wasn't just the great occasions that Adler graced. He wasn't looking for photo opportunities. He conducted pastoral tours and always included in his itinerary a visit to the school of the Jewish children. In 1862 he was in Sunderland, Newcastle, North Shields and Hull. In 1871 he was in Dublin, Swansea, Glasgow and Bristol. Each visit strengthened the community's commitment to the Orthodox camp.

Adler didn't just rely on visits. He remained the only umpire in town when the provincial congregations had disputes and called for judgements, which they did with some frequency. As the *Jewish Chronicle* would lament: 'the want of concord that prevails amongst some of these [provincial] congregations is a source of some uneasiness to those who wish well for the progress of the Anglo-Jewish community at large'. The paper referred to a large number of: 'angry and acrimonious letters bearing on points of dispute of the most unimportant and most uninteresting character', which it constantly received. It recognized, however, that the Chief Rabbi, 'on occasions too numerous to narrate has given the energies of his powerful mind and the influence of his amiable character to the promotion of harmony in his flock.'[13]

Sometimes the discussions on changes could go on for years. The Great Synagogue had its constitution carefully set down, but in Yiddish. In 1853 a committee started to see if there were changes which needed making and translating the new proposed regulations into Hebrew and English. The recommendations, as far as they were spiritual, were submitted to Adler for his approval, but the whole process took until 1861 when the final draft was agreed.

There was no chance of any other Jewish spiritual leader attaining Adler's eminence. There were very few non-Orthodox congregations, still practically no ministers who could be relied upon to state the *din* unequivocally, and nobody with Adler's status. There might be some arguments on occasions about Adler's decisions, but at the end of the day, nobody could gather a majority of votes in their congregations to oppose them.

Where Adler's opposition was less effective was on the rare occasions that he became involved in parliamentary legislation. One such instance involved the laws on divorce. In 1850 a Royal Commission had been set up to consider the current legislation which, effectively, made divorce impossible for all but the very rich. The church considered marriage indissoluble and only a private Act of Parliament enabled a divorce to be granted. Otherwise only ecclesiastical courts could grant a divorce and they didn't. By contrast, divorce according to Jewish law was permitted and cases were dealt with by the Beth Din.

From the conclusions of the Royal Commission eventually came the original Matrimonial Causes Act 1857 which moved divorce from ecclesiastic to civil courts. The government was, however, quite prepared to make an exception, to take Jewish law into account by accepting rabbinic divorce, and the Lord Chancellor presented a clause in the House of Lords to that effect.

Representations were, however, made by Lionel de Rothschild and Sir David Salomons that this clause be omitted. They were both deeply involved in trying to get an Oath Act passed, which would enable Jews elected to parliament to take the loyal oath on the Old Testament. They considered that asking for Jews to receive special treatment on the divorce bill would support the argument of the anti-Oath Act lobby that the Jews were not 100 per cent British and should not be treated as such. As a result of the lobbying of Rothschild and Salomon the clause was deleted.

Adler fought hard, with the help of the Board of Deputies, to get the decision reversed. He pointed to the inexpensive cost of a Jewish divorce which helped the poor. He stated that without divorce, any children of a future liaison would be illegitimate. He said that a mere civil divorce, which had not the sanction of the Beth Din, would put the clergy in a difficult position if they were asked to perform a second marriage.

It was something of a travesty that the new bill protected the position of wives to a far greater extent than before, often by adopting the Jewish divorce laws rather than the Christian. The Beth Din continued to administer religious divorce even after the passing of the Act.

When the 1857 bill was passed, Salomons tried to go further and made the case for the wardens of synagogues to be able to appoint registrars of marriages, rather than the Board of Deputies. It was ironic that Salomons had himself served as President of the Board for periods of months in 1838 and 1846 when Sir Moses Montefiore had gone on overseas missions.

The Board argued in rebuttal that the danger of such a change was that any group could set itself up as a Jewish community, even if, in an extreme case, they were intent on amalgamating with a branch of the church. The Board felt such a loophole was highly undesirable. The Committee's report came down on the side of the Board on this point, but not on all the instances where the *din* differed from English law.

The problem for Adler was that English law and Jewish law were not always identical. One area of difference, for example, was the question of whether a widower could marry his deceased wife's sister. This was permitted in Jewish law and indeed encouraged, in order to continue to provide the surviving children with a mother. Such a marriage was, however, forbidden in English law because of an incorrect reading of a passage which covered it in the Biblical Book of Leviticus. In spite of the urgings of Adler before the Royal Commission, the law was maintained that it was not legal. As a result, such Jewish marriages were often contracted abroad. Adler had officiated at them himself in Hanover and the Jewish community accepted the new couples into their ranks without demur.

Another problem arose when illegitimate children were left legacies. The question was whether they could be treated as equal to children born after the marriage had been solemnised later. In the case of Levy v. Solomon in later years it would be held by the court that if the legacies had been left equally between all the children, those born before the marriage could not inherit. According to Jewish law, the subsequent marriage legitimized the illegitimate children, but Adler had to agree that English law overrode the *din* in this respect.

In 1866 a case arose which concerned the legal acceptability of a Jewish *get* (bill of divorce). The Beth Din was informed that the courts could no longer recognize a *get* as constituting a divorce if there hadn't also been a civil divorce. From that time on, the Beth Din applied the law.

The secessionists, of course, did not accept the Chief Rabbi as the final word on spiritual matters. They also resented the fact that the Board of Deputies would not recommend them as a suitable body of Jews to have a Marriage Secretary. So in 1856 they had applied successfully in Parliament for a clause to be added to the new Marriage Act to allow them to appoint such an official. This was approved and it would, therefore, no longer be necessary for marriages in their synagogue to be preceded by a registry office wedding.

Adler was minded to address the long-term development of the community in Britain. From the outset he decided that his son, Hermann, would be his successor and carry on his programme. To this end, he sent Hermann to a continental Yeshivah to obtain his *semichah*. He saw to it that there would be no ordinations granted within Britain until long after he had passed away.

When the time came for Adler to take life more easily, it would be Hermann who would be the automatic choice to take over many of his responsibilities, and there would be practically no opposition to his appointment to that role.

In the absence of anything like sufficient ministers and teachers, both Adler and Montefiore set out to create a college to train suitable candidates. It would take time, but Jews' College did produce a number of ministers who were qualified for those positions. There would always be two schools of thought about their training. The lay leaders did not want to give up their supremacy in their congregations and allow their ministers to act with the authority of continental rabbis. They wanted them to be more functionaries, trained to be bureaucrats, capable of acting as secretaries of their communities, but only possessing the role of employees.

Within Jews' College this was not considered a satisfactory result of their education. Adler would ensure that the Principal of the College would concentrate on the teaching of rabbinic works. It was Michael Friedländer who would take responsibility for this for much of Adler's ministry after his appointment in 1865.

Notes

1. Leader, *The Times*, 27 February 1850.
2. Hansard.
3. *The Occident*, New York. 23 October 1849.
4. David A. Sher, 'Chief Rabbi Nathan Marcus Adler', *Jewish Affairs* (South Africa) (December 2015).
5. Ibid.
6. Todd M. Endelman, *The Jews of Britain 1656–2000* (Berkeley, CA: University of Californian Press, 2002).
7. Derek Taylor, *British Chief Rabbis, 1664–2006* (London and Portland, OR: Vallentine Mitchell, 2007), p.224.
8. *Jewish Chronicle*, 13 February 1874.
9. *Jewish Chronicle*, 1 July 1853, p.304.
10. Ibid., p.1.
11. Meteorological Office archive department.
12. *Jewish Chronicle*, 16 May 1862, p.5.
13. *Jewish Chronicle*, 28 November 1873, p.581.

9

A Pause for Jewish Education

The importance of learning is a core belief in Judaism. To emphasize its sweetness, the tradition is to give a child honey when it first picks up a book. The opportunity to study and teach the Torah every day is the ambition of the very orthodox. So there are formed Study Circles, or a Beth Hamedrash, where like-minded Orthodox Jews can study together. Through the generosity of past generations Adler had inherited one at 1, Smiths Court in the City. It had an extensive library and only lacked sufficient Jews keen on study, though there was always a hard core of devotees. The outstanding figure in Jewish bibliography, Moritz Steinschneider, on a visit to England, commented that very few Jews there could be found with 'even a tincture of rabbinic learning'.

So in 1841 it had been agreed to augment the objectives to include the need to train young people for communal roles. Not a great deal had happened after that either, though. Adler was keen to encourage the process and in 1849 raised £2,000 to revive the study of Hebrew literature and pay a librarian. The problem then was that few people used the library, though Adler set a good example by attending a study circle every Monday and Thursday evening to lecture on the Torah and the commentaries. On these evenings about thirty devotees made up the audience while he officiated.

Adler's problem was that, with a few exceptions, he was pretty well starting from scratch when it came to community organized education. There weren't the teachers, the books, the supervision, the curricula or the premises. To make matters worse, there was far too much lip-service given to religious study and far too little pressure exerted by parents on their children to settle down to learning about their religion. Adler devoted a lot of time and effort to improve matters, though it was many years before a network of Jewish schools would emerge and be supported by the community.

As early as 1846, Adler arranged a meeting to discuss a proposal for the formation of a college to improve the quality of Jewish education. This conference was to be chaired by a very senior and wealthy layman, Isaac Cohen, but unfortunately he died on the day it was supposed to convene and the project was delayed until its supporters could reorganize.

Adler knew very well that the future of Judaism depended on getting the maximum number of Jewish children to learn about their religion. He didn't believe this was going to come from their homes: 'To Adler, such an arrangement involved at best [Jewish] educational minimalism and at worst so scanty a Jewish education as to spell danger to the Jewish child in the Christian environment.'[1] He also recognized, however, that the advantage of a secular education was that it might enable the child to climb out of poverty. The problem was that the time spent on secular study meant that less time was available for religious tuition.

There were other problems too; first, that the community, as a whole, was indifferent to Jewish schools and Jewish education. The rich wanted their children to go to public schools in spite of the fact that there were strict limits to the number of places allocated to Jewish pupils, and there were the serious disadvantages that they would receive no Jewish education – indeed they would have to attend chapel – and they were likely to suffer anti-Semitism. Nevertheless, the status of a public school education was a key objective for a large number of families in their attempt to gain acceptance into society. As a consequence the majority of the children joining a Jewish school came from poor families, most of whom could not afford the fees. An early Jews' College Annual Report made the position very clear:

> It will usually happen that the majority of those aspiring to the honours of the clerical profession will be of the class little favoured by fortune; and it will therefore be vain to expect from the College students the payment of such fees as would be adequate for defraying the costs of their education.[2]

The Jews' Free School, the largest Jewish school by far, wanted to retain its independence. Efforts to introduce religious supervision by representatives of the chief rabbi would in the future be rejected. JFS had, of course, been founded well before Adler arrived in Britain. Its primary concern was to offer an alternative to Christian Conversionist Schools.

In 1806 the London Society for Promoting Christianity among the Jews was promoted as the largest in the world.[3] Jewish children whose parents could be prevailed upon to enrol them would be guaranteed a suit of clothes for their child and a midday meal. Both were substantial bribes but the generosity was not based on benevolence but on evangelism

JFS was already a large school in 1845 and the pupils were drawn predominantly from the multitude of poor Jewish families. There was, inevitably, an absenteeism problem due to the desperate need for the children to earn money to help feed their families. The children were often sent to run errands or beg for the pittance that such efforts might produce, instead of attending school.

The teaching of rabbinic subjects could not receive much of a priority under those circumstances. Adler's interest in the school was still much appreciated. When Sir Anthony de Rothschild, the president of the governors, gave the toast to the Chief Rabbi at the fund raising dinner in 1853, he said:

> Our worthy and revered Pastor takes a great interest in the institution of the Jews' Free School. We all know that his greatest study and care are for the proper education of the children of the poor. It is, therefore, a source of great pleasure that I have the Rev. Doctor's presence among and supporting me this evening.[4]

Adler dealt with the problem of poverty in his response:

> For poverty has nine lives; nay, has, like the polypus an endless succession of lives; but a sound and liberal education diffuses among the poor the means of intellectual riches – wealth that will direct their youth, support their manhood and cheer their old age; wealth that will break the very mainspring of poverty.
>
> (Cheers).

The school continued to owe its existence to the Rothschilds. They covered its losses and they provided the children with clothes, coats and shoes. They were kindness itself but they wanted the school to remain their personal charity. They didn't want the chief rabbi, no matter how experienced in educational matters, to be in charge; this had become the Rothschilds' traditional role.

The influence of David Woolf Marks was also considerable. In the early days of the school, he was one of the brightest pupils. On one occasion, in the absence through illness of the headmaster, Marks was even put in charge. In 1823 at the fund-raising annual dinner he wrote poems that were recited by the children and brought tears to the eyes of the audience.[5] If he was also good enough to become the Professor of Hebrew Literature he was, undoubtedly, a highly qualified educationalist. With his background it is unlikely that the man who wrote the secessionist's new prayer book would want the spiritual authority of the school to be placed in the hands of the orthodox chief rabbi.

The cost of staffing the Free School in an appropriate way would have been prohibitive. So Moses Angel, the head master, taught a limited number of the older children, who were called Senior Monitors, and they would teach younger children called Junior Monitors. Then twenty-odd Junior Monitors would impart the lesson to yet more children. It wouldn't be until 1858 that a Royal Commission on Education would recommend that teachers should be not less than 32 years old.

When Adler visited the school he found the house old and dilapidated. He convinced additional rich families to improve the building and they did so. Another problem remained though: the social status of masters teaching in a free school was so low that the recruitment of qualified individuals was very difficult. Nevertheless, under Angel, the school roll reached 2,000 by 1855.

At the anniversary dinner, the Whig Leader Lord John Russell presided and spoke of Adler as a gentleman well known for his learning and his virtues. In response Adler told his audience that it was the duty of society to provide the poor with food, clothing, shelter and education. The educational curriculum had to be both secular and religious and girls had to be offered schooling as well.

Opposition also came from those community leaders who were more concerned with emancipation than the future of Judaism; many felt that faith schools were against the spirit of the age. They were, therefore, against even the foundation of such schools. When Adler took office, he must have been surprised at the situation he met. He had been recruited partly because he had the reputation of a fine educationalist from his time in Hanover. Consequently, as it was generally acknowledged that the standard of Jewish education in Britain was totally inadequate, he would have expected to be given the authority and support he needed to improve the situation.

He did struggle throughout his ministry to provide more and better Jewish education. He may have resented some schools' reluctance to give him spiritual control, but his main objective was to increase the number of Jewish children receiving some religious education. He also would have put the interests of the children ahead of his own self-esteem, and keeping the Rothschilds onside was a key consideration.

There were discussions in 1851 between the government's Committee of Council for Education and the Board of Deputies about the possibility of the Board taking full responsibility for Jewish schools. Adler was naturally very keen on this, but the Board faced substantial opposition from a range of schools, from JFS to the West London Synagogue School and decided to stand aside, to Adler's disappointment.

Furthermore, the production of future Jewish teachers by the charismatic headmaster, Morris Angel, over many years, was a main source of staff recruitment for Jewish schools all over the country. That needed to remain undisturbed. Furthermore, Angel was much admired outside Jewish circles as well. In 1858 teachers would need a certificate before they could practise, but Angel was excused from the need to apply. It was taken for granted, anyway, that Adler was deeply involved in the school. In 1854 it was reported that: 'At the service on Tuesday last, HRH Prince Albert made a special enquiry of Dr. Adler about the Jews' Free School.'[6]

After the initial aborted meeting, sounding out potential donors for Adler's new Jews' College and deciding on the curriculum for the project took another six years. In 1852, though, a meeting was held under the Chairmanship of Sir Moses Montefiore. The chief rabbi had set the scene with a circular from his office on 8 December 1851.[7]

> The necessity of establishing a College for the training of Jewish Ministers and Teachers is so obvious and so generally recognized that it will suffice merely to call attention to the fact that among the numerous clerical offices of the united congregations in this Empire, some are vacant, and only a few are held by Englishmen. That although our community on the whole is advancing in culture and intelligence, the dearest interests of ourselves and our children, our pulpits and our schools, the most precious things on earth, our character, intellect and souls, are still not seldom entrusted to men of ill-furnished minds, untutored, or at least unprepared for the performance of their sacred functions. It is no less generally acknowledged that a public Day School for the sons of our middle ranks is urgently required, especially in London, where there are good educational institutions for our poorer brethren, but none for the classes above them. Attendance in the public schools of the general community subjects our sons to this disadvantage, that they are not only deprived of one school-day in the week, but are necessarily left unprovided with sound religious instruction. That whilst their minds are necessarily engrossed by the acquisition of secular knowledge, they, for the most part, receive at home but slender and inadequate tuition in the elements of Hebrew and of our sacred doctrines.

Adler was not afraid to call a spade a spade, and he then went on to outline his plan for a school which would: 'be established in London for the purpose of affording a liberal and useful Hebrew and English education to the sons of respectable parents, and training of Ministers, Readers and Teachers.'[8]

It would be for boys between the ages of 9 and 15, who could write and read English and read Hebrew and they would be day-boys. In the Hebrew department they would be taught the translation of the prayer book, together with Bible, grammar, Jewish history and religion. They would also dip into the Pentateuch and the Shulchan Aruch. (Code of Jewish Law). In the secular department they would be taught English grammar, composition and literature, ancient and modern history, physical and political geography, arithmetic and bookkeeping. They would also learn the elements of mathematics, natural philosophy, Latin, French and German. All this for five hours every day except for Shabbat and festivals. It was a major secular curriculum and certainly not available for most children at the time.

The school would be governed by a council who would choose six pupils as Clerical Students. They would be taught more advanced theology and classical literature, logic and elocution at University College, London. They would have to have good characters, be in good health, and either have been born in the country or have parents who had lived in England for ten years.

The non-Clerical Student pupils would also be able to go from the school to University College, London to get a degree. That College had only been founded comparatively recently. It was an initiative to rectify the fact that Oxford and Cambridge were strongly Church of England and members of other faiths could not receive degrees from them. So a number of influential non-Church of England dignitaries decided to start a purely secular college.

It had opened in 1826 but against great opposition from the established church. Dr Arnold of Rugby described Jews as infidels and heretics and labelled University College as 'the Godless Institute in Gower Street'. Klemens von Metternich, the Austrian Chancellor, instructed his ambassador to tell the King that its establishment would bring about the ruin of England. It was later renamed University College London and it was the obvious partner for Jews' College, if the Jewish college could be formed. It remained so for many years. Among the most important initial financial backers of the college was Isaac Lyon Goldsmid, a prominent Jewish financier and philanthropist, but it had not been until 1836 that a Royal Charter was obtained for UCL, allowing degrees to be awarded. UCL was happy to accept Jewish students and was so determinedly secular that no minister of religion was allowed to sit on its Council.

The staff needed to run Jews' College would consist of a headmaster, a second master, assistant masters and a Librarian. When it came to financing, Adler expected that there would need to be an annual budget of £1,000 which he planned would come from charitable support, the revenues of the Beth Hamedrash and school fees of £10 a year. If, however, anybody gave the College £250 they could have one pupil place free. For a one-off donation of £1,000 they would have a free scholarship and a free Clerical Student, including the fees at University College, London. If they gave £30 a year, there would be the same advantages. As far as the governance of the college was concerned, the council would consist of Adler as ex officio president, Sir Moses as vice president, five Council members and appropriate trustees.

Montefiore's meeting in January 1852 was well attended and promises of support were received from those present and many luminaries who could not attend. A Council was nominated, 'to obtain donations and subscriptions as may seem necessary for the constitution and consolidation of the Institution.'

In the main address Adler pointed out that there were less than ten ministers outside London who were British:

> Is it right that our country should have none who are able to give their brethren light, admonition, consolation in suffering and in sickness, to enter the dwellings of the poor, to be their friend, their guide, and to bring them to the side of their duties.[9]

He made his views on the present situation crystal clear: 'Our pulpits and our schools ... are not seldom entrusted to men of ill-furnished minds, untutored, or at least unprepared for the performance of their sacred function.'

There was no problem recruiting the community's present and future leaders to sit on a committee chaired by Sir Moses Montefiore. On the list were Joshua Alexander, who would become the secretary and solicitor for the Jewish Board of Deputies; Lawrence Levy, a vice-president of the Jews' Free School; Jacob Franklin, the father of Anglo-Jewish journalism; Sampson Lucas, a future elder of the United Synagogue; and George Jessel who, as solicitor-general, would be the first Jewish government minister. Aaron Levy Green, already a minister, was appointed honorary secretary.

Critics of the college in the future would attack members of the council as has-beens, but this was unfair to the vast majority of those who gave their time and expertise to support the institution. The Sephardim also asked to be involved and Joshua Benoliel, Nathaneel Lindo and Joseph d'Aguilar Samuda came to the meeting in April. They too were significant figures and practical men; Samuda ran the largest ship building yard in the country on the Isle of Dogs.

The Sephardi elders had voted to give £500 to the college and were warmly welcomed. What they wanted in return for the largesse was, primarily, three representatives on the council, at least one Hebrew master who could teach the Sephardi pronunciation, and at least one Clerical Student. In the end the council consisted of ten Ashkenazim and two Sephardim.

It would still take nearly three more years for sufficient funds to be collected for a suitable building to be equipped in Finsbury Square, near the Chief Rabbi's home.

The problem of successfully financing the College was a sine qua non, but much of the thinking among the community proved highly optimistic, if not positively illusory. *The Voice of Jacob* discussed the prospects in 1849 and airily proclaimed:

> Our answer is simply, that every congregation will gladly contribute to the establishment of an office which will and must ultimately lead, not only to the moral improvement of the congregation, but likewise to the increase in the Synagogue funds, there being no doubt that the Synagogue would be better attended, and its frequenters be more liberal in their offerings, if a soul-stirring lecture appealed to their hearts and their purses.[10]

No, they wouldn't. The synagogues would like qualified preachers, but the great majority of the congregations were definitely not ready to contribute to the cost of educating one. It would be a major and justified criticism of the British Jewish communities over the years ahead that they felt the cost of educating ministers should fall on other shoulders than theirs.

Generous individuals would have to come to the rescue of the college finances time and again, but in the years to come the support of new organisations like the United Synagogue and the Federation of Synagogues would usually be miserably inadequate. Their justification would be the financial pressures they themselves had to contend with, but with a number of congregations, this was often only an excuse; much more could have been done.

Where *The Voice of Jacob* was right was when it said:

> We candidly confess that it is, to our view, rather degrading than elevating the sacred office, that the people are, under the present circumstances, compelled to seek abroad for those who can serve them. We are anxious to obtain full emancipation; and would it not be a disgrace if we were told by our Christian opponents that the Jews of England are so ignorant that they cannot find a lecturer in their community?[11]

For years, many communities couldn't.

The training of the Clerical Students would include taking services in the Beth Hamedrash synagogue and teaching on occasions in the day school. It was hoped, if necessary, to provide them with board, lodging and clothing. At the end of their time at the college there would be an examination for their diplomas, but not to provide them with *semichah*. At the outset Adler was aiming for a theological college rather than a yeshivah; the former produced ministers and the latter concentrated on imparting Talmudic knowledge.

There was one absolutely crucial error in the structure of the Council which would not be corrected for seventy-five years: 'it had previously been tacitly agreed among the Governors that residence in London was an essential qualification for membership of the Council'.[12] This was pure snobbery and not written into any constitution. It ensured that the council would only include those considered the 'right kind of people'. It was disastrous because it meant that the College was seen in the provinces as run by the London Jewish establishment which, of course, it was.

The council was full of eminent and dedicated men, but if the objective from the start was to get national support from the community, it should have automatically followed that provincial councillors would be recruited in order to at least feel they had a say in the way the college was run. Yet the provincial communities were effectively excluded from the seat of power.

Those communities continued to be very conscious of their status. There was the considerable support for local chief rabbis, rather than just one based in London, and the irritation grew. The leaders in the provinces were every bit as proud of their positions in their communities as their London opposite numbers, but the council took it for granted that they would support the college financially without any say in its operation.

From a fund-raising point of view, this was exactly the wrong approach, and the support the college would receive from provincial communities in the years to come would be very limited. After all they were far more remote from London than in modern times, when telephones, facebook and emails make communications easy. They had their own financial priorities and plenty of demand for their available financial resources. If London was to train ministers without involving local communities, then that could be the price for excluding the provincial communities from serious involvement.

The problem with getting the support of the overseas communities was not their exclusion from the council; they wouldn't have expected to come to London to attend meetings. There was, however, no real effort to get their support for the college, even though many were very happy to accept graduates in future years.

Raising sufficient funds involved a lot of hard work and, for Adler, 1853 would prove a particularly difficult year in both his personal life and as the chief rabbi, losing his wife and having to deal with the problems in Manchester.

One additional root problem was still that of convincing those who wanted emancipation to support the school and college project. This was well illustrated by a letter Sir David Salomons sent to Adler in 1852. He wrote:

> Although I feel confirmed in the opinion first expressed to you that your proposed educational scheme as a whole was open to grave objections, I fulfil my promise of sending you a contribution. I must, however, make special conditions in respect of it. I wish to promote the education in this country of such of our Jewish fellow subjects as are destined for the Ministry of Her Majesty's Dominions and I offer my donation with that sole object in view. I wholly disapprove of the proposed day school as unadvisable and unnecessary. I also desire that my contribution be left distinct from the funds of the Beth Hamedresh.

There was in fact no existing method of preparing school children to be sufficiently knowledgeable to enter a college to prepare them for the ministry. So where they were supposed to come from, if there was not a school, was left in the air. The solution, as far as Salomons was concerned, was for more Christian schools to accept Jewish children, offering a greater degree of toleration and still providing an excellent education; City of London School and University College School came into that category. UCS had been founded by the University College London in 1830 and followed in its secular footsteps. City of London had been created by an act of Parliament in 1834 for poor children and was also happy to allow Jewish children not to be influenced by Christian teaching. Adler sent his son, Hermann, to UCS.

The need for a college was still widely recognized. The somewhat lofty ambition, according to the *Jewish Chronicle*, was that:

> the future ministers of the Anglo-Jewish congregations will be men of thorough English feelings and views, as conversant with the classics of their own language as with those of the sacred tongue, as acquainted with modern science as versed in ancient lore; men in whom the flow of the burning thought will not be impeded by heaviness of tongue, and whose ardour of enthusiasm will break forth and rouse and kindle with Shakespearian vigour and Miltonian sweetness.[13]

Agreement on what kind of graduates should emerge from Jews' College would never be unanimous. The lay leadership wanted a trained Anglo-Jewish ministry. That was non-contentious. The question would always be, trained for what? Before the Enlightenment the Ashkenazi rabbi in Europe would be scholar and teacher, judge and legal authority. In Britain the Church of England vicar was now the model for a lot of people.

Pastoral duties were not generally intellectual or academic. It is no wonder that Jews' College for many decades would not set out to produce rabbis; the lay leadership would often take the view that the graduates had no need for the extensive rigours of Talmudic scholarship though successive principals would all be insistent that they did. The lay leaders wanted their focus to be on the pastoral and their training weighted towards the secular.

The inaugural ceremony for the opening of Jews' College eventually took place in the fashionable heart of the City, on Sunday, 11 November 1855. After the afternoon service, conducted by Rev. Aaron Levy Green, Adler addressed the assembly. It had been a long struggle to reach this point and his speech expressed his displeasure with many who had let him down over the years. He obviously resented the lip-service. He also forecast the future with considerable foresight:

> Gentlemen, – It is my pleasing duty, a duty which fills my heart, and I am sure your hearts, with gladness, to open, this day, the Jews' College; an institution which is so important that it forms a new period in the history of our community. Allow me to address a few words to you on this occasion. After a long, very long interval between the stating of the idea and its accomplishment, we have, at last, by the assistance of the public, by the perseverance of the Council, and especially, by the aid of Almighty G-d, succeeded in opening this college to the use of the Jewish public.
>
> This is not the place to speak of the numerous difficulties which surrounded the realisation of the scheme; how some regarded it as unnecessary, nay, injurious to the progress of the community; how others were in favour of one leading principle, but against another; how those whose support was expected left the project to its fate; how often, not without sighs and tears, I myself despaired of its attainment.
>
> It suffices to say that the doubts were dispelled, the impediments removed, and the difficulties surmounted; we are able to open it. And if it be true that the beginning is half the accomplishment, we may justly rejoice in the fact. There may be some who have anticipated something more important, something grander and more striking, but we have, thank G-d, a house to work in, teaching power to work with, and minds to work upon.
>
> We have, in the school, the very number of pupils on which we originally founded our plan, and, in the college, we require only a very small number of students; so that the supply may not be greater than

> the demand. Besides, it is a known fact that every good and sound idea begins in a small degree, and grows and prospers with years ...
>
> Without exaggeration or metaphor, we may truly hope that young men will obtain, in this College, a sound scientific and theological instruction, so that in the course of time our schools and our pulpits will be filled with well-trained, well-furnished teachers.
>
> We may sincerely hope that this school will afford to the youth of our middle classes a sound religious and secular education, which will go hand in hand without – as is frequently the case – injuring, curtailing and thwarting each other; we may reasonably hope and expect that the school will enlighten the intellect, warm the heart, and render them good men, faithful citizens and pious Israelites ...
>
> The permanent success of this institution will depend on some conditions and suppositions. It will depend on the support of the public at large, both in the Kingdom and the Colonies .... again the institution requires patience and perseverance. If the public expects a distinguished ministry in a very short time, or if parents hope to see immediately both blossoms and fruits sprouting, as from the rod of Aaron, or if parents will not assist the masters in their difficult task, they will be dreadfully disappointed; they will reap no fruit but that of delusion.[14]

Adler was still laying it on the line. He went on to encourage the pupils in his audience to try their hardest and encouraged the staff in similar terms. The work could now begin.

English was not Nathan Marcus Adler's first language and his correspondence is, as would be expected, very formal. The family wrote to each other in a local German dialect and Germanic script, which is very difficult to decipher today, and his sermons were, again, carefully crafted to reflect his office rather than his inner thoughts.

At this distance in time it is helpful to have a record in English of him talking more informally. One occasion which survives from the Jews' College annual reports was when he took the chair at the first General Meeting of the Governors of the college on 8 February 1857. He was talking to a smaller gathering than would have listened to him in the pulpit. What he had to say is, therefore, more intimate than can usually be found:

> ... you will allow me to make a few remarks in fuller explanation of some of the statement and details [given by the Secretary before]. And I more strongly desire your permission to do so, because I took the liberty of addressing you at the preliminary meeting at some length

> [a year before], and I am perhaps now able to demonstrate and make manifest in practice what at that time I could only prove in theory.
>
> ... Let me confess that there were times when I almost despaired of its [the College's] realisation, and I am not afraid to say that I should have given up the project had I not kept steadily in view the greatness of the object at stake, had I not been encouraged by the conscious purity of those motives which I had so warmly cherished from the first moment of my arrival in this country – the hope to provide my community with efficient ministers and teachers for the improvement and benefit of generations yet unborn ... that while the expenditure of the year amounts to £900, the income is £700, and that this deficiency will be easily met by the usual benevolence and public spirit of our body ... and will reflect on the already proved groundlessness of those objections which are still urged against it.

In actual fact, this confident expectation of benevolence and public spirit was not to be forthcoming. For most of the future 150 years the financial situation of the college would be parlous and reliant on the generosity of a very small fraction of the community.

On a number of occasions the death of supporters of the college and their subsequent bequests would alleviate the annual deficiencies. Over £3,400 was raised to get the college and school started but, as time went by, the capital sum was slowly drawn down. Adler had other problems as well.

> Allow me to state openly some of the gravest objections referred to, which are brought forward against the College or School, and to meet those objections by facts.
>
> Against the training of ministers it is contended that instead of bringing boys up to an advantageous career in life, we shall render them unhappy, because they will either find no situations at all, or only poor and dependent ones ... even if we look no further than this kingdom, the demand already far exceeds the supply ... We think that were our teachers well educated and well furnished with religious and secular knowledge, they would have means and ways through public and private tuition to find an excellent living.[15]

Again, it was a pious hope, and the salaries of ministers would remain the subject of concern for chief rabbis to the present day. Happily:

> Besides, can it be denied that we have some young men, whose feelings and tastes lead them to the ministerial profession, in whom nature's

> hand has implanted an unconquerable love for it, and imprinted a higher bias than that for common toil? That there are some who feel a burning desire to fulfil the mission of Israel, to teach the Word of God, and to make souls happy – who would prefer this avocation to any other of worldly lucre and ambition, did not the cold voice of relatives chill such feelings and tastes.[16]

It would indeed be fortunate for the community that there would always be young men with a vocation for the ministry. That, in fact, would be Jews' College's ongoing gift to the Jewish communities both in Britain and abroad: the training of men who had the vocation but needed the right education. And also, in time, to train women to be teachers.

If they were not all Talmudic giants, they still brought a great deal of carefully acquired knowledge to their future pulpits, parishes and classrooms. According to the *din*, the study of the Talmud was an obligation on every Jew and no financial reward was appropriate for it.

On many occasions the men would arrive at the start of a congregation's life and by sheer hard work build it up into a viable body. As Jewish communities declined and vanished, often because the commercial rationale for living in the town had disappeared, new congregations had to be formed, and Jews' College graduates would be crucial to that development.

They would perform their duties diligently, visiting the sick, comforting the mourners and supervising the teaching of the children. They lived by the motto of the College – 'The fear of the Lord is the beginning of knowledge'. Adler would expand on the mission statement and spend a lot of his time ensuring that it was their guiding light. His view was that:

> Whether right or wrong, it is a fact, that the community prefers natives to foreigners; now I ask you, is it not paradoxical to want and desire them anxiously, and yet to do nothing for their qualification? Is it reasonable to wait until they might fall from the sky like manna?[17]

They certainly wouldn't fall like manna. Their recruitment would always be a problem and there would be numerous struggles to encourage and sustain them through to their eventual qualification. Adler was continuously involved, visiting the school on innumerable occasions and taking a close personal interest in every aspect of the operation. Big trees from little acorns grow and Adler deserves the credit for the eventual results.

Rev. Aaron Green had been appointed as one of its secretaries and would serve until 1883. He reported at the first meeting: 'Whether a time will come when the school may be dispensed with, and the connection between the two branches may be safely severed, the future alone can answer.' Was the Jews' Free School, set up for poor children, a possible alternative? Adler was dismissive:

> I answer, No ... In the short time that our College has existed, it has already proved that it has its own field of culture, without interfering in the least with the work of others ... What would become of our holy religion amidst the present and future attacks from within and without, were its teachers restricted to a petty allowance of one or two hours a day?

Which was the case at the JFS. Adler recognized that the Jews' Free School educated its pupils to survive in the adult world, not to become ministers. There were far more poor children than prospective clergy. Many of the orthodox dismissed JFS as a school for Jews rather than a Jewish school. Adler went on:

> Why clog it with a school? ... Gentlemen, I said at the first general meeting and I repeat it this day, supported by experience, that the School is indispensable for the support of the College both intellectually and financially ... the school teaches the man, the College the individual. The School is general, the college is special.

The problem for the college at the outset had been that there were practically no candidates sufficiently knowledgeable to attend it. In the future they would only be recruited in very small numbers, but the problem remained that the institution would still need the same number and quality of teachers as if there was a far greater roll of students.

They would need a building, furniture, books, and all the other elements of an academic institution. Without the school fees, the college could never hope to be financially viable in the early years. Furthermore, the school was expected to be the feeder body for the college, like the public schools who had connections with primary schools for the same reason. As it was spelt out in the annual report:

> The present attendance of 40 pupils raised an income of £400 in school fees. This income might be regarded in many respects as an important aid and support to the College ... there is no other Jewish day school for the higher and middle classes ... We know [however] that there are gentlemen who tremble at the idea of an exclusive Jewish school, and think it injurious to our present or future social position.

The snobbery and class system of Victorian Britain was a core fact in everyday life. In the Jewish world, too, status mattered a great deal. There is, however, no point in trying to judge the Victorian culture by twenty-first-century standards; to visit the past is often a visit to a foreign land. To add to the varying opinions, the Jews keenest on emancipation were looking for a different kind of minister from those on the Continent. There:

> The modernists weighed their rabbis in a notional balance and found them wanting. The rabbis did not conduct themselves with enough urbanity, compete with the leaders of opinion and culture in the newly open European society, or couch their message in the local idiom or vernacular.[18]

Continental rabbis were still theologically learned, though. Adler pointed out the dangers of children growing up in non-Jewish schools, and lacking real knowledge of Judaism. Those who don't know what they are giving up, are more likely to leave the faith when they reach adulthood. Convincing upwardly mobile Jewish families of this though was never going to be easy.

> If they would consider all this, they would be not merely reconciled but even delighted with the existence of the School ... provide the necessary aids for the support of the College by annual subscriptions; the more so, as hitherto besides the munificent annual gift of £100 from the house of Rothschild, the amount from such resources is limited to £48.[19]

In reality, the shortfall in the accounts in the next fifteen years would seldom exceed £100, but the simple solution chosen by most charities was not adopted by the college; there would be no annual fund-raising dinner until the Jubilee year in 1906. Concern about a possible lack of dignity involved in holding such events would seem to be the hidden agenda.

Life Governorships, donations and bequests were more respectable and did not involve dedicated fund raisers. As a consequence, the deposit account steadily dwindled. In fairness, the alternative use of charitable offerings to help the impoverished and the disadvantaged made a powerful argument for that use of the money.

Solid support did continue to come from the Rothschilds, and the old Beth Hamedrash had funds which provided another £50. It was also possible to become a Life Governor with a donation of £10 and, in 1857, there were over seventy of them. When the Liverpool banker, Israel Barned died, his demise was sincerely regretted, but he did leave the College £1,000. Such a large benefaction was, unfortunately, a rare occurrence.

There were only twenty-four hours in the day and time spent on secular subjects reduced the hours available for rabbinic study. Many influential laymen totally underestimated the time it took to achieve even a rudimentary understanding of the Shulchan Aruch.

In the future the College would not only train good men who became rabbis and dayanim. The graduates would occupy overseas pulpits where, without them, an English-speaking minister would have been almost impossible to find. As a random sample. they served congregations in Melbourne, Tasmania, Perth and Sydney in Australia, in Nairobi and Shanghai, Bulawayo in Zimbabwe, the Philippines and Denmark. In all these locations they were vital to the communities they served and often won great affection and regard.

Finsbury Square soon had a family atmosphere, as James Loewe, the future headmaster's son, later recalled. He remembered, as a 6-year-old, Lady Montefiore arriving with sweets for him, and his being allowed to play in nearby Artillery Park, while a pupil was being taught Talmud in the Great Hall by his father, and Sir Moses Montefiore was in deep discussion with the Chief Rabbi.

Adler would be deeply interested in the progress of the College all his life. As a former student, the future Sir Hermann Gollancz recalled in the *Jewish Chronicle*:

> And there was another member of the Council who made the deepest and best impression upon us all – the Chief Rabbi and President of Jews' College, Dr N.M. Adler, whose dignified and venerable figure we saw constantly, and whose devotion to the interests of the College seemed the master passion of his life. Hardly a day passed that he did not visit the institution. The Council minutes show that he was rarely absent from a meeting. He lived opposite the College, or he could not have spared us so much of his precious time. As College students, he frequently examined us to see what progress we were making in his favourite subject, the Talmud. His interest in us personally manifested itself in so many gracious attentions, as when a student who had matriculated would be invited to spend a weekend with him at the seaside – an honour, the pleasure of which was only marred by the consideration that Dr Adler's student-guest was expected to conduct the whole of the Sabbath service, which he held in his house.

Louis Loewe was the first principal of the college until he took over the Judith Lady Montefiore College in Ramsgate. He was succeeded by Barnett Abrahams, a charismatic young leader who unfortunately, in 1863, died at the early age of 31, to the great dismay of the community. The effect of Adler's participation on these sad occasions goes far to illustrate the regard he achieved throughout his congregations. As was reported at the time: 'The sobbing accents in which the Chief Rabbi pronounced his funeral oration in the courtyard of Bevis Marks left an indelible impression.'[20] Adler stepped into the breach after Abrahams' death and gave daily lessons at the college in Hebrew theology until a replacement could be found.

One of the legacies of Abrahams was the Jewish Association for the Diffusion of Religious Knowledge which he started in 1860. This was a group of volunteers dedicated to spreading a greater understanding of Judaism to sections of the community who were unlikely to get the benefit otherwise. They would visit prisons, asylums, hospitals and communities who couldn't afford a minister. Again, always in financial difficulties, the volunteers soldiered on for many years and eventually became the Jewish Religious Education Board. Elkan Adler, the Chief Rabbi's son, held the post of JREB Superintendent for many years. As the President of Jews' College, Adler obviously had a major influence in the choice of a principal. Abrahams was under 30 when he was appointed and would have looked to Adler for advice. So the idea of the Jewish Association for the Diffusion of Religious Knowledge was very likely a concept of Adler's. It would be another example of the Chief Rabbi achieving a personal objective, for which someone else would get the credit.

In 1864 Adler was happy to be involved in a new educational venture in the East End. This was the Stepney Jewish School, situated alongside the Stepney Green Synagogue and an old people's home. Marcus, his son, would become the President of the Governors even though he would also be busy designing London tram and train fares. The first term of the new school was scheduled for the autumn and a girls school would follow.

The Stepney Jewish School would be far smaller than JFS and, as can now be expected, would struggle throughout its existence to keep financially afloat. Nevertheless, though it started with only a handful of children, ten years later it would be have a school roll of 250. It was a very necessary addition to the Jews' Free School because there could never be enough schooling available for the families of the increasing number of poor Jews in the City and East End. The founders bought a freehold and put up a decent building. As was so often the case with Jewish charities, it was the Rothschild family who picked up most of the construction bills. The annual shortfall would be around £150 a year, but, as the governors wouldn't hold a fund raising dinner, it was left to Marcus to appeal for funds through the press.

Whatever educational initiatives Adler wanted to promote, he could always count on the support of his sons; Hermann in the ministry and at Jews' College, Marcus with the Stepney Schools and Elkan with the Board of Jewish Religious Education, as well as chairing the library committee at Jews' College. All three sons were committed to the task of educating Jewish youngsters and the community at large, but it was also a way of showing their affection for their father. For his own part, Adler compiled the Chief Rabbi's Code, with syllabuses for various age groups, as well as recommending text books, and lobbying for competent teachers wherever they were to be found.

The emphasis in any school where Adler was involved would, naturally, be on religious education. In 1870 when he went with the new Haham, Benjamin Artom, to inspect the Stepney School, there was, 'a searching examination in Hebrew, religion and Biblical history'.[21] He left it to Artom to repeat their joint belief: 'He warned his brethren that instruction, to be of avail, must be religious. For the safety of Judaism, religion and education must be combined.'[22]

Adler's feelings on the subject of the education of Jewish children can be gathered from his speech at the anniversary dinner of the Westminster Jews' Free School in 1868:

> When I first came to England about 20 years ago, the question of education was almost looked upon with ridicule ... 4,000 years ago the Almighty impressed upon the Jews the duty of teaching their children; and the Rabbis, 2,000 years ago, taught that the city which did not possess a school deserved to be destroyed. I thank God that now we have Jewish schools in every part of the Metropolis.[23]

In fact, within ten years of his arrival to look after a community approximately 40,000 strong, there were about twenty Jewish schools. Out of approximately 6,000 Jewish children, over 3,000 went to Jewish schools. That had been Adler's objective. That was why he had included questions about educational facilities when he wrote to the congregations so soon after his installation. That was why he encouraged their support whenever he visited a provincial community.

By the time of the Forster Education Act in 1870, JFS would talk of not being able to take any more pupils because of the enormous size of its school roll. In addition in London there would the school at Jews' College, Stepney Schools, Borough Schools, and the Westminster Free School. On his pastoral tour to the North-East in 1869 Adler again pleaded for more schools to be founded. The Brighton, Cardiff and West Hartlepool communities created schools as a result. Chatham was to come, plus a new school in Manchester and others in Liverpool, Cheltenham, Birmingham and Sunderland.

The Forster Act saw the government invest enormous sums in new schools. The London School Board opened a brand new school a few hundred yards from JFS. It was state-of-the-art and planned for 1,200 children. Nevertheless, in the first few months it attracted less than 100 pupils; the Jewish parents in the East End only wanted to entrust their children's education to a Jewish school they could trust to advance the education of the faith. They, therefore, were disadvantaged because, in its final form, the Act allowed no public funds to denominational education.

Adler still had to convince the wealthy families to send their children to Jewish schools. The best teachers were not available in sufficient numbers and the alternative Christian teachers could not be expected to inspire the children in their Judaism, but a lot of progress was being made.

There would continue to be an ongoing battle between the lay leaders who wanted ministers who were trained bureaucrats and the college principals and presidents who were determined to concentrate on producing rabbinic scholars, even if the graduates were not sufficiently knowledgeable to be given *semichah*, which entailed a great deal of additional highly concentrated study.

A few years after Adler died, Sir Moses Montefiore's great nephew, Claude Goldsmid Montefiore, was invited to present the prizes at the college and spelt out the conflict of opinions with which Adler had battled, as did his successors:

> I should not mind the stigma attached to Jews' College that no single student has ever received the Rabbinical Diploma at its hands. I should not mind the stigma if it be frankly said the Rabbinical Diploma cannot be given without the acquisition of a mass of knowledge which has now become obsolete, the possession of which would be of no use to a minister whose task it is to inform the lives of modern English Jews and Jewesses, who live under conditions wholly different from those under which their forefathers lived in mediaeval ghettos.[24]

In spite of all the problems, however, Adler had successfully founded the College and it would continue to produce trained ministers for more than a century into the future.

Notes

1. Sonia Lipman and V.D. Lipman, *The Century of Moses Montefiore* (Oxford and New York: Oxford University Press for the Littman Library of Jewish Civilization in association with the Jewish Historical Society of England, 1985).
2. Jews' College annual report, 1858.
3. Todd M. Endelman, *The Jews of Britain 1656–2000* (Berkeley, CA: University of Californian Press, 2002).
4. *Jewish Chronicle*, 25 February 1853, p.162.
5. Gerry Black, *JFS: The History of the Jews' Free School, London, Since 1732* (London: Tymsder Publishing, 1998), p.65.
6. *Jewish Chronicle*, 7 July 1854, p.343.
7. Isidore Harris, *History of Jews' College* (London: Luzac & Co., 1906), p.vii.
8. Ibid.
9. *Jewish Chronicle*, 4 January 1852, p.106.
10. *The Voice of Jacob*, 12 January 1849.
11. Ibid.
12. Albert Hyamson, *Jews' College London 1855–1955* (London: Jews' College, 1955), p.103.
13. *Jewish Chronicle*, 24 November 1855, p.65.
14. Jews' College Annual Report, 1856.
15. Jews' College Annual Report.
16. Ibid.
17. Ibid.
18. Rabbi Raymond Apple, a paper on Jews' College and the Jewish Ministry, Tel Aviv.
19. *Jewish Chronicle*, 24 November 1855, p.387.
20. *Jewish Chronicle*, 6 December 1863, p.6.
21. *Jewish Chronicle*, 18 February 1870, p.10.
22. Ibid.
23. Harris, *History of Jews' College*, p.vii.
24. Jews' College annual report, 1895.

10

Building the Community

In America, Judah Touro, a New Orleans Jewish merchant, died in January 1854 and left $50,000 for relief in the Holy Land. His friend, Moses Montefiore, was appointed an executor and was made responsible for its distribution. Montefiore created a charity with the Chief Rabbi as his co-trustee. This was the Appeal Fund on Behalf of the Suffering Jews in the Holy Land which would continue to try to raise additional monies for many years thereafter. At the outset Marcus Adler was employed by Montefiore as his confidential secretary and worked hard on the fund-raising, which initially produced another £20,000 (£500,000 in today's money).

Conditions for the Jews in the Holy Land had become disastrous, with cholera epidemics, long droughts and price inflation. Adler went to the station to say good-bye to Montefiore who, with his wife, would travel thousands of miles to Constantinople to call on the Sultan for help. The Holy Land was part of the Turkish Empire, and Montefiore managed to at least get the Sultan's nominal support. He went on to the Holy Land once again to see what more could be done to help but the challenges were immense.

In Adler's words, the objectives were to: 'bring about a unity of action among the different congregations there, to purchase land, to establish farms and factories and to devote part of the money annually collected to wages to those who will work.'[1] It would all take a very long time. Existing living conditions were so appalling that Adler was horrified to learn from Montefiore that parents were selling their children to strangers so that they didn't starve.

The Touro legacy went to found a Jews Hospital in Jerusalem, a girls' school and on a number of agricultural projects. The appeal had raised an extra £20,000 but it didn't go far when spread over an entire country. In 1866 another £5,000 was raised and contributions came from both America and the Empire. Even so, by 1867, only £89 was left. Just one example of the kind of core problem which had to be addressed was that, for years, with the drought, there was practically no water to speak of in Jerusalem.

There had been a great revival of interest in the Holy Land, with archaeologists and explorers from many countries trying to find evidence to back up the Bible accounts. Plans were laid to cleanse the natural water supply, which had become hopelessly contaminated over the centuries. A Jerusalem Water Relief Society was set up, under the patronage of both the Montefiores and the Rothschilds in 1864. It would take many years to solve the problem, but Adler continually preached of the necessity for the community to provide funds to do so. In 1867 the waterworks were at last rebuilt, and water brought from the nearby Pools of Siloam. The systems have now been modernised but there is one memento of Montefiore's earlier efforts and that's the 1857 Windmill in Jerusalem, which he built to make the grinding of corn more economic.

Montefiore's journeying on behalf of Jewish communities under pressure overseas was quite extraordinary in its variety, and heroic in view of his increasingly extreme old age. He started in 1827 when he was only 43 with a visit to Egypt on his way to Jerusalem and Constantinople. He was in St Petersburg at the age of 60, Jerusalem again at 71, Rome at 75, Constantinople again at 79, Morocco at 80, Syria at 82, Bucharest at 83, St Petersburg again at 88 and Jerusalem again at 91. It was often dangerous, but at least when he went to Morocco, the government provided a warship to carry him from Gibraltar to Mogador, and the Sultan came up with an escort to take him across the Atlas desert. His pleas to the rulers of those overseas countries often did produce some results, but not all that he hoped to achieve.

For his part, Adler was never distracted from his concern for the community in the Holy Land. He gave them a high priority and treated their cause with great sensitivity. Part of the funds raised went to build almshouses in Jerusalem, but the word emphasized the poverty of the inhabitants and so Adler declared that the area should be known as Mishkenot Shaananim – 'The dwellings of those at ease'. The houses were built by Conrad Schick, a Christian teacher fascinated by the history of Jerusalem. Another district he created became the home of the very orthodox and is now known as Mea Shearim. They were the first homes for Jews outside the city walls.

The Holy Land was not the only part of the Middle East where the Jewish community was in danger. In 1860 the Moslems attacked the Christians in Syria and murdered some 10,000 of them. The Turkish authorities eventually acted and hanged hundreds of the assailants, but they also sentenced 200 Jews to death for allegedly participating in the massacres. Montefiore intervened again, as did Lord John Russell for the British government. The Jews were eventually released, but it had been a close shave.

Disease was widespread in London as well, with cholera and smallpox carrying off thousands of sufferers. *The Builder* magazine noted an anomaly in the East End where the Jewish community seemed less affected by the epidemics. They put it down to the high standards of cleanliness maintained in even the poorest Jewish homes.[2]

In 1856 Adler became a naturalized British citizen and in May 1857 he announced his betrothal to Celestine Lehfeld (1821–90), the sister-in-law of the Chief Rabbi of Berlin. The daughter of a Berlin doctor, she was 36, eighteen years younger than Adler, who was 54 by this time. The family were Rittergutsbesitzer, landowners with estates in Silesia, and they included the foremost Shakespearian actor in Germany.

Brought up in highly intellectual surroundings, Celestine was passionate about German poetry and both elegant and courageous. During the 1848 uprising, she had helped to tend the wounded who had been fired on by the German soldiery and went on to reject a suitor who had kept out of the way, presumably feeling that discretion was the better part of valour.

Nathan and Celestine were married in August and they were able to welcome his brothers Gabriel and Baer to the wedding. Gabriel was now the chief rabbi of the Schwarzwald and Baer was still providing spiritual leadership in Frankfurt. Baer's daughter, Hitzel, had married Moritz Budge, whose sons would found the firm of Budge, Schiff and Co. in New York, which became one of the major American merchant banks

The wedding was in Halberstadt, still part of the State of Hanover. Nathan Adler had been a widower for several years and, as he said at the reception, he gave: 'fervent thanks, out of the depths of his heart, to G-d the Almighty Father, for having blessed him with a wife who would be a comfort and solace to him in his difficult office'.[3] For the next thirty years that would indeed be the case.

Adler, as always, made a great impression on those who met him for the first time:

> To our joy the Reverend Doctor stayed here till Sunday, August 30th and his great piety and profound knowledge, combined with the most friendly demeanour, have gained him the veneration and love of all who were so fortunate as to enjoy his presence.[4]

Rebecca Adler, his mother, died in Hanover in April 1858 when she was 94, but she had the pleasure of knowing that he was no longer a widower. The wedding would have also been one of the last occasions when Adler would see his brother, Gabriel, who passed away in 1859 at the age of 71. The new marriage was blessed with three children and this was a considerable achievement when it is remembered that Celestine first gave birth to Ida Rebecca (1859–1933) when she was 39, to Elkan (1861–1946), when she was 41, and to Rebecca (1865–90) when she was 44 and in early middle age.

The children of Nathan and Celestine would have adult brothers and sisters, and Sarah had already married Henry Solomon in 1850, after they had been introduced at Sussex Hall. Minna married Jacob Israel, a Berlin merchant, in the same year as the Chief Rabbi and Celestine. She didn't enjoy very good health in her life and only one of her children survived. This was Barthold, who would marry Sarah's daughter, Amy.

Marcus soon started working for the Alliance Assurance Company, of which Montefiore was a founder, and would become its actuary, staying in post for thirty-five years. During this time he was made a Fellow of University College, London where he had studied as a student, reading mathematics.

The Chief Rabbi, living in the City, had thought deeply about the depths of poverty which plagued so much of his Jewish community about him. Each synagogue, of course, gave charity to the poor, but simply providing a little financial assistance hardly touched the continuing problem. Intent on tackling the ongoing crisis, the three main London synagogues formed a conjoint committee in 1858 to coordinate their efforts, but their total budget was only £500 (£45,000 today). Adler set out to plead for a far more intensive effort. In a sermon in 1859 it is possible to recapture the likely effect of his words, as he quoted the sages:

> Ten things in the world are of a hard nature; the rock is hard, iron breaks it; iron is hard, fire melts it; fire is strong, water extinguishes it; water is powerful, clouds carry it; clouds are huge, wind disperses them; wind is strong, man resists it; man is strong, death vanquishes him. Death is surely strong, but charity is stronger still, for charity mitigates the sting of death and alleviates its pangs.[5]

Adler's practical solution was to create a Board of Guardians for the Relief of the Jewish Poor. A Board that wouldn't just give away money, but an organization which would befriend the poor and help them out of poverty. The three London synagogues worked together to create it, and Lionel Louis Cohen became its secretary and practically wrote its constitution. Today the Board is part of the communal charity organization, Jewish Care.

It was decided that every applicant for help should be visited by the Clerk of the Board and there were additional committees created to encourage apprenticeships, and to take care of such things as medical problems and the distribution of matzah at Passover. From one apprentice in 1863, there would be over 100 by the time Adler died. One form of assistance was to provide indigent families with a sewing machine, and the Singer company agreed to undertake the distribution.

Considering the sheer size of the problem which the community faced, the Board of Guardians was a good start, but still nowhere near well enough endowed to make a major difference. For those it helped, however, it was a godsend and particularly helpful to foreign Jews who had no connections to any of the synagogues. After some initial argument it was finally agreed that applicants had to be in the country for six months before they qualified for help, but then, like any other Jew in distress, they would be eligible for support. It was also an innovation which would be copied in many provincial centres, though it would take a long time; boards to consolidate relief work would be formed in Manchester in 1867, in Birmingham in 1870, Liverpool in 1876 and Leeds in 1878.

It was in July 1858 that the Oath Act was finally passed which enabled Jews to take their seats in Parliament, after swearing fealty on the Old Testament rather than the New. Comparatively few MPs voted on the bill at any of its readings. This was because it was a very hot summer and the stench from the Thames was so bad it even made a move of the whole Parliament to Oxford a distinct possibility. The odour permeated the whole building. The cause was the invention of the water closet, which enabled effluent to be carried through drainage to the Thames, instead of having to be collected at source. It wasn't surprising that few MPs wanted to work in the House under the oppressive conditions, but it did help to pass the Act. Lionel de Rothschild, who had first been elected to the Commons for the City of London in 1847, was duly sworn eleven years later as the first Jewish MP. Rothschild had persisted in advocating the Oath Act, but when he was finally able to take his seat, he never once spoke from the floor of the House.

There was still a degree of opposition to the bill, though, with the Earl of Shaftesbury, president of the London Society for Promoting Christianity among the Jews, refusing to accept a post as Chancellor of the Duchy of Lancaster because of the Liberal party's support for Jewish emancipation. The London Society did not lack for funds. Its budget from 1820–30 was £12,500 a year (about £900,000 today) and this increased to £30,000 from 1840–50. Its results, however, were not very impressive, with only 180 baptisms between 1843 and 1849.[6]

Palmerston, Shaftesbury's father-in-law and leader of the opposition at the time, saw the problems of the Jews differently. Apart from being a tolerant man, when he was Foreign Secretary he saw that defending Jewish communities could provide a good excuse for Britain to participate in Middle East politics. At the time, the French looked after the Catholics, the Sultan the Moslems and the Czar the Russian Orthodox. That left the Protestants and the Jews, and Palmerston instructed the British diplomats in the region to take them under their wing.

The first Protestant bishop of Jerusalem had only been installed in 1841. This was a former German Jewish minister called Michael Wolff (1799–

1845), who took the name Michael Solomon Alexander when he converted to Christianity in 1825. He had emigrated to Britain in 1820 and became the *shochet* in Plymouth after service as the minister for the Norwich community, before he converted. He was a good enough scholar to be appointed Professor of Hebrew at Kings College, London from 1832–41 when he went to Jerusalem, but unhappily he died of a heart attack in 1845 at the early age of 46.

Some suggested that Adler, himself, was against the idea of Jewish MPs because their parliamentary duties could infringe on their religious obligations; this was the view Montefiore had held. Adler, however, went on record that he was in favour of emancipation, even though he recognized the conflict of interest it might produce. Equally, there were misunderstandings on the part of the parliamentarians. One bishop, when he met the Chief Rabbi to discuss the treatment of Jewish communities abroad, apologized for the fact that he didn't speak Hebrew. Reassured that this wouldn't be necessary, there was a useful discussion.

In April 1859 Montefiore was abroad again; this time to Rome to seek an audience with the Pope to appeal for the return of a Jewish child to his family, after the child was forcibly removed by the Papal police. This was the famous Edgardo Mortara case, where a Catholic servant had performed a baptism on the Mortara baby when he was seriously ill. When this was discovered years later, the child was, effectively, kidnapped to be brought up as a Catholic. There was international indignation but the Pope refused to meet Montefiore and the child eventually became a priest. His mother died of grief. Montefiore had done his best, but this time without success.

Back home, Adler was involved in the case of Gordon vs. Goodman. In court he was asked whether or not the children of Jews who lived together were legitimate, for inheritance purposes? And was a Jewish/Christian marriage prohibited? Furthermore, should the minister marrying them find out first if the bride was Jewish? Adler replied 'yes' each time. It wasn't, however, the right answer in English law and that was the one which counted, as the Court of Appeal later confirmed.

A new synagogue was to be consecrated by the Chief Rabbi in Swansea in the autumn of 1859. Unfortunately he fell ill and his doctors forbade him to make the journey. So he sent Hermann, who had just taken his degree at London University. The lad was only 20 years old, but the chief rabbi already had plans for his son to succeed him. It was Hermann Adler's first time in a pulpit, but he spoke fluently for an hour to the general approval of the congregation.

As the Board of Guardians came into being, the General Literary and Scientific Institution, known as Sussex Hall, finally closed its doors. Set up to further adult education in 1844, its financial support was insufficient and it became another of the Jewish charities which withered on the vine. Without sufficient money, the road to hell – or at least oblivion – continued to be paved with good intentions.

Adler continued to have to deal with knotty problems. The new Central Synagogue wanted to make alterations in its times of service and Adler had given his permission. Now the Western Synagogue nearby wished to adopt the same timetable and asked for the Chief Rabbi's approval, as their community was split on the desirability of the change. Adler adroitly avoided taking sides by refusing to become involved unless the Western became a branch synagogue, recognizing his overall authority. As the Western wanted to retain its independence – initially it hadn't even voted for his election – that ended that potential problem.

There were difficulties as well involving individual ministers at home and abroad. In 1860 the minister in Cape Town felt himself under severe pressure and thought of resigning. He wrote to Adler for advice and the chief rabbi replied:

> If you wish me to speak of these to the community, I will readily do so. I will support you wholeheartedly and encourage them to pay attention to you and to strengthen what you have established. My advice is that you should not leave your position but carry on with your work.[7]

The influx of refugees from Continental Europe created new and larger Jewish communities in the North of England and, through the generosity of those who were successful in business, bigger and finer synagogues were built. It helped that the tax on bricks and the duties on glass had been abolished. When the time came for the buildings to be consecrated, the Chief Rabbi was invariably on hand if asked to conduct the service.

A typical example came in May 1862 when the new Sunderland Synagogue was completed. Accompanied by Hermann, the Chief Rabbi was greeted at the railway station by the honorary officers and accommodated in 'a superb suite of rooms' at the Queens Hotel. The consecration took two hours the next day, after which there was a gala dinner with a considerable number of speeches.

Adler did not just visit the congregation for the sake of the ceremony. He held meetings with the honorary officers to discuss their problems and went on to North Shields to visit the community there, in a 'carriage with four horses and postilions'. Where coachmen sat at the front of the carriage, postilions made the entourage much more impressive by riding on the horses. The Chief Rabbi also travelled to Newcastle to visit the Jewish school.

By contrast with the local grandeur, Adler's speech at the Sunderland dinner was, as was always the case, carefully self-effacing. He told his audience, as reported by the *Sunderland Times*: 'It has ever been my most fervent wish to be the humble instrument in the hands of the Almighty, to preserve our holy religion in its integrity, to promote the spiritual welfare of all those professing it, and above all to uphold peace and concord between all its members.'[8] When the community, like so many others, looked for spiritual guidance in the future, there was only one man they would rely on. It was very easy to warm to Adler when his persona was so benevolent and non-dictatorial.

Similar occasions took him to Southampton in 1865, Canterbury in 1868 and the Liverpool Old Synagogue on its refurbishment in 1869.

The training of Hermann to take over from his father had been meticulous. From the age of 4 he began to learn the Ten Commandments and was tutored by his father every day. Both Elkan and Marcus were also given ample opportunity to become Jewish scholars. The education at home was, of course, far superior to that available anywhere else. It was important to build up Hermann's credentials for the post and the first necessity was for him to have a superior education to those who were likely to compete with him for the office in the future.

Apart from his father's tuition at home, Hermann was sent to University College School and matriculated at 18. His career continued to follow a careful plan. In 1860 at the age of 21 he went to Prague, to Solomon Rapaport's yeshivah, to study for *semichah*, which he was awarded in 1863. From there he moved to Leipzig University to gain a PhD. From Leipzig he returned to London to act as temporary Principal of Jews' College and his father's secretary. When the new synagogue opened in Bayswater in 1863, he competed for the post of Lecturer and was successful.

Bayswater had been built to provide another place of worship for those living in the West End, in spite of the opposition of the City synagogues, who were still concerned at the likelihood of losing members if there were more conveniently located synagogues. Eventually the Great and the New approved the Bayswater plan but the Hambro opposed it. Adler eventually intervened to encourage its construction and consecrated the new synagogue in July 1863.

When it was opened, it was decided to have three ministerial officials. Isaac Samuel was chosen as the First Reader and Raphael Harris the Second. There was then the position of Lecturer to be filled and Hermann was the successful candidate. Although his title was not that of 'minister', he soon established a reputation as a fine preacher and by 1867 was referred to as minister of the congregation.

Bayswater soon had a wealthy membership. It was independent, unlike the Central, had its own Marriage Secretary, and had been sponsored in the end by the Great and the New. The Great also helped to find the money for the North London Synagogue, on condition that it adopted the same ritual as its benefactor, but would not help when there were appeals from the incipient community in Dover and from the Borough Synagogue in South London. Adler stayed at Bayswater for nearly thirty years and was so popular that he was always known within the community as Dr Hermann. Unlike the Great and the Central, the building would survive the Blitz, but was compulsorily purchased by the Greater London Council in 1965 to enable the Westway road to be built.

Hermann was doubly fortunate. He received not only a religious education from his father, but also learned the arts of diplomacy from him, and many of his favourable attributes were mirrors of the Chief Rabbi's approach to community leadership. When it came to preaching, however, if the Chief Rabbi was 'the father of the Anglo-Jewish pulpit', as the famous historian, Cecil Roth, put it, Hermann had a hard act to follow. James Douglas wrote for the *Morning Leader* about preachers and he listened to the best, all over the country. When he got round to Hermann, he was not impressed. He wrote: 'Dr Hermann Adler is no orator. He reads his prelection in a husky voice with a strong Teutonic brogue. His personality is invisible ... the voice is passionless, remote, aloof. He has no gesture, no trait, no eccentricity.'[9] There was, however, no common preaching tradition for ministers of the two religions for Douglas to judge by, and Adler was always considered a fine speaker within the Jewish community.

The challenges at Bayswater were many and one of the most important was the teaching of the children of the congregation. At first it wasn't even possible to gather a class together, but Hermann Adler persevered, and was so successful that the congregation presented him with a testimonial in 1869 to recognize his success in his educational endeavours. He had also gained permission from his father for girls to have their own Bat Mitzvah ceremony when they were 12 years old. This followed the same innovation in Hanover during the Chief Rabbi's incumbency.

After the death of Barnett Abrahams, Hermann took over the teaching of the Talmudic element of the Jews' College curriculum. This was before the appointment of Michael Friedländer as the new Principal. Hermann was only 24 years old, but he had the qualifications, and there was really no competition among the college staff.

For all the Chief Rabbi's careful planning, there was one aspect of his son's image he could do little about; Hermann couldn't be brought up to belong to the large and poorer section of the community. His father had arrived in the country with little known of his upbringing except that he was rigidly Orthodox. As time went by, however, it was recognized that while he was welcomed by the wealthiest and most powerful members of the community, he was also entirely at home teaching Talmud every week at the Beth Hamedrash. He belonged in both camps.

Hermann, by contrast, from an early age was welcome in the homes of the lay leaders of the community. His father was the Chief Rabbi and his eventual synagogue was one of the most prestigious in the country. He would act as his father's secretary and he would stand in for him. Although he had a guttural accent, he had *semichah* and was every bit as Orthodox.

His behaviour towards the poorer members of the community was rather more problematic. At the end of the day, he was not accepted as part of the East End family. It didn't affect his career but it would, on occasions, lead to clashes and adverse comment. He was also a good, but not exceptional, scholar. This didn't help. There would be criticism from highly qualified East End *rabbonim* about *schechitah*, and more from the principal of Jews' College, the brilliant Adolph Büchler, because of what he considered interference by a less Talmudically knowledgeable honorary officer; this would lead to Adler standing down as chair of the Council.

The death of Barnett Abrahams had been preceded by the demise of Judith Montefiore in 1862. It was a bitter blow to her devoted husband, Sir Moses, who originally decided to perpetuate her memory by building a college in Jerusalem. He changed his mind, however, and created the Judith, Lady Montefiore College in Ramsgate where they lived. It would compete to some extent with Jews' College, but the relationship of Adler and Montefiore ensured that the two worked in harmony during their lifetimes and the cooperation between the two communities continued thereafter.

In 1866 Moses Montefiore was 82 and Adler was 63. Montefiore was off to Jerusalem again where the plague had broken out. It was, not surprisingly, considered that a point might soon be reached at which he might consider retirement. The Sephardi elders, looking to the future, felt it would be a sensible precaution to safeguard their own spiritual leadership by at last replacing their Haham, Raphael Meldola, who had died as long ago as 1828.

The problem remained that there was no suitable British minister capable of doing the job. The Sephardim, therefore, cast their net wider and there emerged a candidate from Italy, a 31-year-old rabbi called Benjamin Artom. He would never be, in any way, a competitor to Adler, as far as national spiritual authority was concerned, but as a rabbinical colleague, he was well trained, had a good mind, and was on a par with the Chief Rabbi as a preacher. He was certainly a better musician.

He had been appointed a Professor of Literature in Italy and by the time he was 20 he was teaching Hebrew, Italian, French, English and German. Initially, though, his Italian background gave some cause for concern: 'It will take some time before a congregation of Englishmen, citizens of a nation singularly unimpressed, will get accustomed to his lively gesticulations.'[10]

Admittedly, this was no dry-as-dust instructor on DIY ark building in the wilderness. This was a vibrant, involved, determined, impassioned speaker. He also knew exactly how to get the attention of his congregation. The rule is, if in doubt, tell a story; 'once upon a time' is the ultimate crowd puller. So Artom's installation sermon began:

> Do you see that noble, hoary-headed figure rising before our mind's eye from the mists of antiquity? ... it is the historical figure of an aged man who, oppressed by cares and sorrow, and overwhelmed by fatigue, is yet hurrying his steps onwards and onwards to an unseen goal.

A classic example. Who was it? Why was he hurrying? What was the goal? Artom was going to tell his audience about Elijah.

The new Haham was much younger than Adler but the two were of like minds. Artom was determined to spread the word. As he said in his book of sermons: 'Our real doctrines are still imperfectly known to the followers of other creeds.'[11]

Adler's brother, Baer, died at the age of 80 in February 1866. He had attended the Frankfurt *yeshivah*, got his *semichah* and married Henrietta Adler's sister. Although he served on the Beth Din in Frankfurt, he decided to make his way in the commercial world, as did almost all the rabbis in his time, and he had been successful in that field too. That he was highly regarded at an early age is illustrated by his choice as a Frankfurt delegate at Napoleon's Sanhedrin in 1807.

It was now high time Hermann Adler got married. He had his own pulpit and it was traditional for a minister to have a wife and family. In 1867 he married Rachael Joseph, (1838–1914), and they had three children: Henrietta (Nettie), CBE (1870–1950), Ruth (1872–1952) and the Rev. Solomon Alfred Adler (1876–1910).

Marcus Adler had remarried as well as he had lost his first wife, Emma Hersh. With his new wife, Fanny Myers, he had two sons and six daughters. It was typical of Marcus that he marked the wedding by taking 200 children who attended the Working Girls Sunday School Evening Classes, of which he was president, to Greenwich Park for the day, paying for the outing himself and giving the poor children a good meal and the opportunity to enjoy the rural surroundings.

It was certainly an eventful year. In the autumn the Chief Rabbi, as usual, built his *sukkah* where he ate during the festival. Barnett Abraham's son, Israel, recalled:

> When I first remember it, it [the *sukkah*] was already large and substantial, with a fire stove in it and, if I recollect truly, it was lit by gas. Old Dr Adler received his guests with patriarchal courtliness and the flow of learned discussion and of casual gossip on communal affairs, was ceaseless. A fine feature of the Rav's character – which his son inherits – was his cheerfulness.

The *sukkah* was large enough to invite guests to join him and it was said in the official history of the United Synagogue that he suggested the amalgamation of the three major London synagogues at a *sukkah* breakfast there on 24 September.[12]

Whether to amalgamate the synagogues was a long-standing topic and it was definitely time for Adler's 'Let there be peace – for my sake'. It was a good time to raise the subject again as there had recently been a major row over a member of one synagogue who had moved to another congregation. The synagogue which had lost the member protested, and the member, himself, said it was his decision and he'd join whichever synagogue he chose. It became something of a *cause célèbre* and didn't reflect well on either synagogue management.

A couple of months after the suggestion to amalgamate was broached at the *Sukkot* breakfast, the individual synagogues agreed in December that they would unite. It shows their concern for their independence, however, that the minute book of the Great records that:

> While all the synagogues they represent should be united as regards their pecuniary interest and the arrangement and expenditure of their income and also as regards matters of common concern, the internal management of each synagogue should remain distinct, and existing arrangements should be as little as possible interfered with; and that the scheme for a fusion should proceed on this principle.

The eventual result was the creation of the United Synagogue and many distinguished figures since then have been suggested as the founder of the body. Adler would have been little concerned about who got the credit. As usual, he was primarily concerned with the achievement of his objectives, rather than who received any accolades going. Certainly, he recognized that an amalgamation would be in the best interests of the community. The stronger the organization of Orthodox communities, the more likely they were to grow.

There would, however, be continuing negotiations for another four years until an Act of Parliament was passed creating the United Synagogue, and in these official discussions Adler appeared to play little part. On the other hand, the future interim executive would have as one of its members Henry Solomon, Adler's son-in-law, so it was likely that the rabbi was kept fully informed by both the negotiators and his close relative.

On 14 July 1870 an Act for Confirming a Scheme for the Charities Commission for the Jewish United Synagogues, received the royal assent. After 150 years, the main London synagogues had agreed to amalgamate. One reason why it had been difficult to agree was because there had been a legacy of periodic ill will to be overcome. When the Hambro Synagogue opened originally in 1721 the congregation was excommunicated by the rabbi at the Great, whose new synagogue opened in 1722. Competition from other congregations was not going to be encouraged.

The minister at the Hambro abrogated the excommunication, but the two communities remained at loggerheads on a number of occasions in the future; most notably, as was common, over accusations of the poaching of members. There was more discord in 1761 when the New Synagogue, the third major Ashkenazi synagogue in London, opened and decided, with the Hambro, to support a different Chief Rabbi from the Great. They wanted Meshullam Zalman where the Great had decided on David Tevele Schiff. That rift continued for fifteen years.

In 1834 there was a move towards a sharing of communal burdens when the three synagogues agreed to share communal expenses in the ratio of 50 per cent by the Great and 25 per cent each by the Hambro and the New. They also cast their combined votes for the appointment of Adler, but efforts to take the cooperation further usually came to nothing.

Discussions on getting together had indeed been dragging on for years. In 1859 the board of management of the New Synagogue suggested that amalgamation might be a good idea, particularly as the Board of Guardians had shown that it was possible to work in harmony. The discussions meandered along for years but the Hambro eventually decided that, with a declining membership, it was the wise thing to amalgamate with the Great, and a new committee met to discuss that possibility in 1863.

Those negotiations, however, broke down as well. One stumbling block was that the Hambro wanted to continue to hold weekly morning and evening services, which would have been an unnecessary expense, as worshippers could all be accommodated easily at the Great. The Great vestry wouldn't accept the inevitable cost of accommodating the Hambro's wishes and so the question of fusion remained unresolved. There were also still the arguments about gaining and losing members from each other, and the underlying problem was likely to be that no one wanted to give up their sovereignty.

There were really three elements needed if there was to be a satisfactory federation. The first was a strong recommendation by a powerful but unbiased leader. It couldn't be Sir Moses because he was Sephardi and the Ashkenazi would see any intervention by him as meddling. It could, however, be the Chief Rabbi.

The second prerequisite was for sound and diplomatic leadership of any new body, and there was now a good candidate in Lionel Louis Cohen, who had been heavily involved in the creation of the Board of Guardians, served as an MP and was a rising star at the Great. He was a prominent banker and became Manager of the London Stock Exchange.

The third need was for someone to do the day-to-day work. Here, there was a new secretary at the Great, Dr Asher Asher, a physician who had come from Glasgow and was to prove a tower of strength in the future. Asher knew how to make an impression: his application for the position was sent in both English and Hebrew.

The work on amalgamating the London synagogues moved towards completion. Legal advice was obtained and it was decided that the best route would be a bill in Parliament sponsored by the Charities Commission. Adler still remained well in the background. With powerful city figures arguing over the minutiae of synagogue bureaucracy, his concern was to ensure that the new body agreed to continue to use the traditional Polish and German *minhag* and that it reconfirmed his total authority in religious matters. Both of these points were approved.

It took until May 1869 for a full scheme to be presented to the Charities Commissioners, having assured them that all the synagogues had approved its contents. It had been readily agreed that the spiritual authority after fusion would continue to rest with the chief rabbi. The Charities Commission were asked to agree to that stipulation in the forthcoming parliamentary act. This, however, came at an awkward moment.

At the time the government was busily engaged in disestablishing the Anglican Church in Ireland. This would have the effect of abolishing church tithes and ending the Irish church's representation in the House of Lords. With such a reduction in the power of the church, the confirmation of the chief rabbi's sole power to rule on the spiritual concerns of the Jewish community would have been an anachronism. This was particularly the case as the Irish bill caused a lot of dissension. So the clauses of the proposed United Synagogue Act which set out the chief rabbi's authority were deleted.

The solution reached by the synagogues on the question of the chief rabbi's position, was to embody all the clauses which had been deleted by the government in the Deed of Foundation of the new body. Adler's religious hegemony was thereby confirmed, as it had been in the constitution of the Board of Deputies.

With so many 'if's and 'but's it was fortunate that there were two determined characters to nurture the new organisation; Lionel Louis Cohen, who would be the first vice-president of the United Synagogue, and Asher Asher who would serve as its Secretary. Both were recognized as having worked hard on the Board of Guardians and were rightly held in high regard in the community. The Bill was eventually passed in July 1870 and covered the Great, Hambro, New, Central and Bayswater synagogues. Today there are sixty-four synagogues within the organisation, and over 600 staff.

In 1867 Adler persuaded his son, Marcus, to start a Jewish school in Stepney in London. Marcus would remain president until his death 44 years later, and both his wives, Fanny followed by Emma, played a full part in supporting the school through its Ladies Committee. Marcus was a strong support whenever called upon. He was a founder of the East London Synagogue and of the Jewish Religious Education Board.

Within the Jewish community the validity of the second day of festivals in the diaspora was still being debated; so, in the spring of 1868, at the New Synagogue, Adler went on the attack and devoted his half hour sermon to a justification of second days:

> We cannot shut our eyes to the fact that there are some, however small their number may be, who act upon the delusive and specious arguments that are advanced; there are some who imagine that because those arguments are not answered, they are unanswerable. We cannot conceal from ourselves the fact that unless serious attention be drawn to this subject, cavils will lead to doubts and doubts will engender laxity.

He went on to spell out very clearly the original rationale for second days, their history and their continuing justification. He based his views on three principles: that the practice was integral to the historic ritual, that it served as a bond for the Jewish identity, and that it was based on Talmudic tradition. He added that the reason why Yom Kippur didn't last for two days was because it would be dangerous to fast that long. Nothing changed.

The most disturbing national event that year was the attempted assassination of the Duke of Edinburgh when on a visit to Australia. A suitable prayer of thanks for his survival was produced by Adler, but it had been a near thing as a bullet had lodged in the Duke's back. A happier prayer he decided to compose marked the victory of British forces in Abyssinia, where a number of hostages were rescued.

Adler continued to be very concerned about *shechitah* and took a very active interest in even the smallest communities when the subject came up. In 1866 the Aldershot congregation appointed a *shochet*, but decided very soon that he wasn't up to the job. They wanted to dismiss him but Adler would not agree until he had, personally, interviewed the man. Then he approved the dismissal and arranged for a replacement, who came from the Oxford community. Adler told Aldershot it would cost them 82p a week rather than the 75p they had been paying before, and the Rev. Jacob Cohen stayed in post for the next twenty-two years.

It was in 1868 that the Chief Rabbi's hegemony in religious matters was questioned in the law courts for the only time in his ministry, and it was over *shechitah*. He was sued for damages by a Dutch butcher named Moses Schott. The plaintiff had come to London from Holland and set up as a butcher in Whitechapel, selling non-kosher meat. He then went on to sell kosher meat as well, which brought him to the attention of the Beth Din and Adler.

Although it might seem surprising that a Jewish butcher should sell non-kosher meat, if there isn't enough demand for the more expensive kosher variety, the only way to make the business viable is to sell non-kosher meat to non-Jews as well. This is still the practice, for example, in parts of Australia.

Adler refused to give Schott a licence and announced that all his meat was *trefah* (non-kosher). He did, however, tell Schott that he would give him a licence if he opened the shop in Islington, further North from Whitechapel, explaining that in the East End supply exceeded demand. Schott refused to move and, lacking a licence, his business in Whitechapel plummeted and he had to close down. So he sued for damages.

The case came up in the Court of Exchequer before Judge Baron Martin and a jury at the Guildhall on 20 December. According to *The Globe*, the next day the chief witness called for Schott was David Woolf Marks from the secessionist synagogue. Schott obviously believed that if Adler and Woolf had different views on ritual matters, they would disagree on *shechitah* as well and Marks would speak in his favour. This didn't happen. Marks said in court that the Chief Rabbi was the ultimate authority for the granting of licences to sell kosher meat and also for deciding whether meat was kosher or *trefah*. Indeed the court held that: 'It was the bounden duty of the Chief

Rabbi to tell any Jew that such meat is trefah.' Baron Martin accepted this view and stopped the case, saying that Adler had acted within his rights, and indeed it was his definite duty to decide whether the meat was kosher.

Nobody pointed out, however, that Adler had offered Schott a licence if he opened his shop in Islington. The case should have hinged on whether Adler had the right to decide where a shop could be opened. The Jewish legal view was that a shopkeeper shouldn't compete with an existing business. It would seem very unlikely that Judge Martin would have ruled in favour of Adler if the case had been presented to him in that way.

Adler didn't give evidence and was well satisfied with the result. The *Methodist Recorder* criticized the whole process of *shechitah*, but the overall press comment was favourable to Adler. One argument at the time was over whether animals should be stunned before slaughter. Adler said 'No' and the argument continues to this day. The fact remains that, properly performed, as it always is, there is no scientific evidence that pre-stunning is less painful to the animal than *shechitah*.

It was at the same time that a new charity was founded of which Adler was happy to become the patron. This was the Society for Providing Poor Strangers with Meals on Sabbath and Festivals, and it used its funds to provide three good meals on those occasions to anyone who applied. It followed the usual practice of making appeals through the newspapers and in the published lists could always be found the guinea (£1.05) donated by Adler.

Notes

1. *Jewish Chronicle*, 26 May 1854, p.200.
2. *Jewish Chronicle*, 25 September 1857, p.1160.
3. *Jewish Chronicle*, 11 September 1857, p.1141.
4. Ibid.
5. *Jewish Chronicle*, 8 July 1859, p.5.
6. David Feldman, *Englishmen and Jews: Social Relations and Political Culture 1840–1914* (New Haven, CT and London: Yale University Press, 1994).
7. Adler papers, 1860, London Metropolitan Archives.
8. *Sunderland Times*, May 1862.
9. Derek Taylor, *British Chief Rabbis, 1664–2006* (London and Portland, OR: Vallentine Mitchell, 2007), p.319.
10. *Jewish Chronicle*, 21 December 1866, p.6.
11. Benjamin Artom, *Sermons* (London: Trubner & Co., 1876).
12. Aubrey Newman, *The United Synagogue, 1870–1970* (London: Routledge & Kegan Paul, 1976), p.8.

11

National Figure

As Britain became a more egalitarian society the subject of education achieved a higher priority on the government's agenda. In 1869 the National Education League pressed for free, compulsory and non-religious education for all children. At the time the government was giving £800,000 a year to the church to provide schools, but it wasn't anything like enough, and many parts of the country had an inadequate number of, or even no schools.

If the situation was to change, Adler was concerned for how this might affect Jewish schools. When he went on pastoral tours, he never failed to inspect the schools of the Jewish communities. In June 1869 he went off to the North East again and inspected schools in Newcastle, Manchester, Sheffield and West Hartlepool. He spoke about the move towards compulsory education, though he pointed out that education had always been compulsory with the Jews.

In 1870 Adler handed out the prizes for the children at the Deaf and Dumb Home. This institution, financially supported by Baroness Mayer de Rothschild, might only have fourteen children, but the Dutch head teacher had brought the skill of lip reading to London from his home in Rotterdam. The children were not just taught sign language, and to William Van Praagh belongs the distinction of introducing lip reading into Britain.

Adler had been invited to give evidence to the parliamentary committee, headed by the Duke of Newcastle, which was preparing a report on the future of education in the country. The resulting 700 page Blue Book covered the subject very thoroughly and the opinions of Moses Angel were an integral part of the analysis.

As far as Adler was concerned, the future 1870 Education Act achieved only some of his objectives. In the bill, Jewish voluntary schools could carry on unchanged but there would be no government financial backing for them. He was happy that Jewish children at state schools would be excused attendance on Saturday and on all the festivals and they would not have to attend Christian religious instruction classes. Their schooling would, however, end before they were 14, which was Adler's proposed minimum age; the schools would teach 5–13 year olds. He also wanted schooling to be compulsory: '2,000 years ago our sages already made provisions for compulsory education, schools and gratuitous instruction'.[1]

Adler was not in favour of religious classes out of school hours on a Sunday. He believed: 'the children learn there but the catchwords of their creed without being impressed with it, or having the soul called into activity'.[2] He was also dismissive of curricula which only taught the three 'R's – reading, writing and arithmetic. He told his audiences that for Jewish children it should be the three 'P's – Psalms, Prayers and the Pentateuch.

The state schools were, nevertheless, going to be far more sympathetic to the religious needs of Jewish children than the nation's public schools for at least the next 100 years. If the government protected Jewish children from non-Jewish religious tuition, the same had not applied to the Factory Extension Act in 1867. This made the plight of the Jewish poor even worse. The bill made working on Sunday illegal and created the six day week. Which was splendid except that the Orthodox Jews didn't work on Saturday and lost Friday afternoons in the winter when the Sabbath started in the mid-afternoon. The inevitable reduction in their already pitiful wages when Sunday working was made illegal was disastrous. There were prosecutions when the Act was disobeyed, but the magistrates on finding the defendants guilty, still expressed sympathy for their plight and wouldn't award costs against them. The Board of Deputies and Sir David Salomon MP lobbied the government to introduce a new bill to enable Jewish workers who observed the Sabbath to work on Sunday. This was finally agreed in the Workshop Regulation Act in 1871.

For the poor, the situation was even worse on the Continent where cholera and famine were now resulting in terrible hardship. One consequence was that the Alliance Israelite Universelle in Paris appealed to all Jewish communities to adopt Russian Jewish children and Adler asked the Board of Deputies to pay for at least ten of them. The Board prevaricated.

In 1870 a magnificent new synagogue was opened by the seceders in Upper Berkeley Street near Marble Arch in London. The possibility of using the occasion to heal the breach between secessionists and the Orthodox was widely bruited. There was some hope that Adler would attend the consecration and that he, or Haham Artom, might carry one of the scrolls round the synagogue. Adler refused, however, to attend the ceremony because he was still insistent that the second day of festivals should be reintroduced into the new synagogue's services and that was a red line for him when it came to the question of recognition of the secessionist community. Many of the most prominent Orthodox leaders did attend, like Anthony de Rothschild and David Salomon, but pleas for reconciliation were rejected by the Chief Rabbi.

The same would be the case after Adler's death. The service was, therefore, conducted by David Woolf Marks, Albert Löwy and Philip Magnus, the three secessionist clergy. It was ironic that the press report on the consecration was alongside a notice from Adler, authorising a layman to conduct services on the High Holy days in a boarding house in Margate.

The Chief Rabbi was not well in the winter of 1871, but the health of the Prince of Wales was far worse as he had contracted the typhoid which had killed his father. Adler prepared a special prayer for his recovery, as was also done by the heads of the other religious denominations. Prince Edward's wife, the future Queen Alexandra, wrote to Adler that his prayer had been 'a comfort and a stay to her during her great trial.' That this apparently harmless act of multicultural concern was still capable of being criticised in *The Times* illustrates the continuing sensitivity of the media to faiths other than the Church of England:

> Considering, indeed, the dangerous nature of the Prince's illness and the importance of his life, as is now felt, to the church and nation, it may occasion some surprise that the Jewish synagogue should have been allowed to anticipate the National Church in offering special prayers for his recovery.[3]

The Times did not seem to recognize that unless the Christian Sabbath moved back to Saturday, the Jewish synagogues would always be a day ahead in their services. That had been true for more than 1,000 years. It was in the fourth century CE, that the Emperor Constantine first adopted both Christianity and the traditional sun worship for the Roman Empire and moved the Judaeo/Christian Sabbath to the day of the sun. Regardless of the controversy, Edward recovered.

The Times, perhaps inconsistently, was also unhappy that the Chief Rabbi was not at the service of thanksgiving at St Pauls Cathedral. Haham Artom attended, as did Celestine Adler, but the Chief Rabbi declined. The newspaper gave its readers the explanation, but without much confidence. It was simply that a Cohen cannot be in the same building as a dead body, and a lot of famous people were buried in St Pauls. That is, of course, why Cohens attend funerals, but never enter the chapel during the service. As Adler was a Cohen he, as usual, abided by the *din*.

It was no better within the Jewish community. Whatever decisions were made, there would continue to be a body of opposition. In particular, there was never a shortage of criticism on the Letters page of the *Jewish Chronicle*. The Board of Deputies was a particular target for supporting this concept or opposing that idea. Adler continued to try to hold the fort at home and all over the Empire.

In 1873 the St Kilda's congregation in Australia decided they wanted changes to the ritual. For agreement, they contacted Dr Samuel Mayer, Adler's successor in Hanover, rather than the Chief Rabbi in London. When Adler asked why he hadn't been consulted, one honorary officer was honest enough to say that they hadn't thought they would get approval if they took that route. Mayer declined to intervene.

As his own health improved, the chief rabbi undertook a pastoral tour to Belfast, Edinburgh and Glasgow. As usual, he examined the children in the synagogue schools and spoke from the pulpits. In Belfast the services were held in the home of Martin Jaffe, son of Otto Jaffe, who built up the largest linen exporting company in the province.

There was no Belfast synagogue, but Adler was not going to neglect any group of Jews for want of expensive buildings. This was in spite of the fact that the Belfast minister, Joseph Chotzner, had taken up his position without asking Adler's approval. Adler was more concerned with the community forming a congregation of the British Empire.

As usual, the reaction to the pastoral visits was very positive. One leader writer commented:

> We observed with gratitude the expedient course taken two years ago by the Chief Rabbi in making a pastoral visitation to various country congregations. The excellent effects of this provincial tour have become daily more palpable. That visit gave an impetus to the erection of synagogues, and the establishment of Jewish schools. It infused new life into our provincial communities. We hope that pastoral visitations will pass into precedents. If metropolitan duties or other causes prevent the Chief Rabbi from making periodic pastoral visitations (and it is easy to understand how difficult, inconvenient, and onerous such visitations must be to him) we think that a pastoral circular letter might be issued with advantage to the congregations under his ecclesiastical supervision.[4]

He went on:

> The advantages of personal intercommunication are obvious in another respect. The visits of a Chief Rabbi offer distinct assurance that all communities under his charge are equally regarded by him, and that his care and supervision are not confined to the grand and rich synagogues of the metropolis.

Adler went on his travels again when he opened the new South Manchester Hebrew Congregation Synagogue in 1873. There was a splendid banquet in the evening and it was noted that the Chief Rabbi 'received quite an ovation'. All was not sweetness and light, however, as the report of the opening made it quite clear that 'The officers of the Old Congregation were not there'.

The Adlers worked as a family. The Chief Rabbi would preach at the Bayswater Synagogue to support Hermann, and hand out the prizes at the Stepney Schools to support Marcus. Hermann was always available to stand in for his father, as he did in 1872 at the consecration of the West Hartlepool synagogue and in handing out the prizes at the Working Girls' Sunday Evening Classes. The Chief Rabbi still carried out a very heavy schedule, though, which was now affecting his health to a greater extent than before.

There was also a new communal organization now. It was back in 1871 that the Anglo-Jewish Association was founded. This was a reaction to the good work done by the Universal Israelitish Alliance on the Continent on behalf of oppressed Jewish communities. The Anglo-Jewish Association would give birth to branches in many parts of the world, but it was not initially popular with the Board of Deputies. Working for overseas Jewish communities had always been their responsibility and, like so many other organizations, they sought no competition.

In fairness to the Board of Deputies, they were a body elected by the Jewish community, while membership of the Anglo-Jewish Association only involved the payment of 25p or more a year as a subscription. The officers of the AJA were elected by the existing members. The good and the great joined up, and these included United Synagogue ministers and the Haham, but Adler did not take a key position. He was asked to be a Vice-President but told the new body that he would only do so if they came to a working arrangement with the Board of Deputies.

He was already the sole spiritual authority of the Board and the United Synagogue, but there was no guarantee that he would be offered the same authority on the AJA. It was particularly unlikely as David Woolf Marks was also an AJA member. Adler would support the AJA's work on behalf of oppressed Jewish communities abroad, but he kept his distance otherwise. The annual meetings of the AJA did not list him as attending.

In 1878 the relations between the Board of Deputies and the Association had improved sufficiently for them to form a Conjoint Foreign Committee and work together on helping overseas communities in difficulty. Both bodies would provide seven members and the Chair would alternate. This made it possible for the progressive members to take a greater part in the activities of the community.

The hidden agenda for some of the members of the Anglo-Jewish Association was to obtain a position of influence in the community through a kind of upper-crust Jewish Old Boys' Association. Their intentions were entirely honourable and they did a lot of good work. It was a fact, though, that they could achieve their status in the AJA without the possibly embarrassing result of actually standing for election. If they wanted to join, they would be accepted.

The absence of a perceived need by the Chair to obtain the approval of the membership at large for contentious policies would reach its culmination in 1917, when the AJA President, along with the President of the Board of Deputies, would write to *The Times* to oppose the idea of a Jewish National Home in Palestine. The then Chief Rabbi and the president of the United Synagogue would have to fight hard to prove that this was not the view of the entire community. The beneficial result of their efforts would be the Balfour Declaration, and the Conjoint was discredited. Whether the community did, in fact, want a National Home at the time remains questionable. There were comparatively few members of the Zionist Federation.

Back in July 1871, the Reform movement in Germany held a Synod in Augsburg which seemed to reinforce Orthodox concerns about where their philosophy could be headed. It was the old problem that, once started, it was never possible to see where the changes would finish. It was agreed at the meeting that if a child was not circumcised, it would still be Jewish if it had a Jewish mother. Furthermore the regulations about not riding on the Sabbath were abrogated. The laws concerning *agunah* and *yibbum* for widows were also abolished.[5] At the same time, David Woolf Marks was attempting to paper over the cracks, telling an audience in Edinburgh that: 'The new movement produced bitter feelings and angry excitement [but] time and mature reflection have now arranged all intemperate feelings.'

When the secessionist ritual was compared with traditional orthodoxy, there was still a great deal with which Adler would take issue. For example, in the *Amidah* prayer the invocation of punishment on slanderers – which demarcated Jews from Judaeo-Christians – was now omitted. When the Book of Esther was read on Purim or the candles lit on Chanukah, the section which declared that the Almighty had commanded the practices was also left out. Congregants were not called to the Torah, and instead of the singing of the *hazan*, the service was declaimed by the minister. These alterations could be considered minutiae, but there were no precedents for them.

People's everyday problems were often worse. The plight of Jewish widows was, perhaps, not of great concern to Sydney Waterlow, the Lord Mayor of London in 1872/73, but what he was very worried about was the medical care of the poor. While public health and factory acts were being passed to try to improve their conditions, the access of the poor to hospital treatment was negligible. The hospitals were in grave need of investment as well; in 1874 St George's Hospital would have to be closed for three months to get rid of the rats.

So Waterlow decided to create a Metropolitan Hospital Sunday Fund and to solicit support from all the religious bodies in the UK. He was backed, among other worthies, by the politician W.H. Smith, the first woman doctor Elizabeth Garrett Anderson, and Florence Nightingale. He was anxious to have Jewish representatives on the Council and Adler and Marks both agreed to serve.

Adler was more than delighted to help and apparently had no objection to working with Marks. He called a meeting at his home in January 1873 to discuss the request with the senior members of the new United Synagogue. It was agreed that the Chief Rabbi would compile a special prayer and form of service for the designated date in June, and forms would be sent to members to enable them to donate in advance. At the synagogue service their names would be read out, which was always a good idea for the fundraisers, as it was easily noticeable when a name wasn't read out.

Waterlow's eventual major charity was naturally created from small beginnings and the *Jewish Chronicle* initially reflected, perhaps pessimistically, that the results in the synagogues did not compare too favourably with the amount collected at the service in St Pauls Cathedral.

The condition of poor Jews in the East End was, of course, made very much worse if they fell ill. The one hospital which would never turn them away, even if they couldn't afford treatment, was the London Hospital. Within the building were four Jewish wards where the patients could get kosher food and where their religious needs were understood. The two men's wards were called the Rothschild and the Goldsmid and the two women's wards Hannah and Esther. When Queen Victoria visited the hospital in 1876, the Chief Rabbi was prominent on the receiving line.

In January 1874 the delegates of the Board of Deputies finally agreed a new constitution which included approval of the election of representatives of Upper Berkeley Street. Montefiore initially resigned as President, but was persuaded to continue in office. He finally gave up in August on the grounds of ill health. One issue which had been discussed at length before the new constitution was agreed was the role of the chief rabbi. There was a strong move among the senior lay members of the Board to change the wording of the constitution on this point.

They questioned whether the Board should be 'governed' in religious matters by the chief rabbi and Haham, or be 'guided' by them. They favoured 'guided' but the delegates, who had the final say, did not want any change and 'governed' remained in place. It was another sign of the high regard in which Adler was held.

What the majority of the delegates recognized was that Adler could lend status to Jewish communities. When he went to consecrate Middlesbrough Synagogue in 1874, the local council treated him with great respect. The mayor even came down to the station to see him off. Without the Chief Rabbi, the new communities were just small groups of foreign strangers with eccentric habits. With the Chief Rabbi at their head, they mattered. For his part, the Chief Rabbi encouraged them to integrate with the local citizenry wherever it was possible. He was fully behind Hermann who, when he consecrated the new synagogue in Newcastle in 1880, told the congregation to get themselves a minister who spoke English.

The ebb and flow of Jewish communities continued. By 1872 when the Chief Rabbi went on holiday to Great Yarmouth, he found a synagogue but no congregation. The old shul was opened again to mark his visit, but the Jews had deserted most of East Anglia; the congregations in Kings Lynn, Cambridge, Yarmouth and Ipswich had departed and the Norwich community needed £500 to avoid bankruptcy.

Sadly there would be no old age for Benjamin Artom. Adler had presided at his wedding in 1875 and it was naturally a very happy day, though Adler wouldn't stay for lunch; he explained that he had ten or twelve more marriages to perform that afternoon. Four years later, in 1879, the Haham suffered a major heart attack from which he never recovered. At the end the *Jewish Chronicle* revised its original rather negative opinion:

> There was in his influence, especially upon the young, something essentially vivifying ... The unceasing efforts of an active and intellectual mind to impart to his flock the many lessons to be derived from the Jewish faith ... to explain the bearing of Judaism on the most religious and philosophical questions of the day, must have left a deep impression among his Congregation ... His noble presence, his burning words, his stirring exhortations will be sadly missed.[6]

Adler soldiered on during those years with the support of the Dutchman, Joseph Vangelder, as his personal attendant and librarian. The relationship would last until the Chief Rabbi's death, and Vangelder was always an important part of his entourage.

The new United Synagogue had to consider what their role was in relation to other Jewish bodies in London. One was the Beth Hamedrash, whose building and finances were in need of reorganization. The original house in Smiths Buildings was in a deplorable state and in 1872 it was proposed that its operation should be transferred to the United Synagogue and be situated in the Hambro Synagogue.

This recommendation was, however, rejected and the United Synagogue declined to take over the organization. One problem for the Beth Hamedrash, as a place of learning, was that a noisy manufacturing company nearby disturbed those who wanted to sit and study. The subject came up again in December 1874 and this time the United Synagogue agreed to take over the responsibility. The old building was leased out for £500 a year and a new building was put up near the Great Synagogue. £2,000 was raised for its construction and equipment and the Beth Din moved there. The Chief Rabbi agreed to the change and continued to give his biweekly expositions on the Talmud. The new building created a much better atmosphere for dealing with Beth Din cases, which everybody agreed were of major importance. Solomon Hirschell's creation was now able to work in much more pleasant surroundings.

In 1875 Adler produced his most important work, *Netinah Lager,* a commentary on the *Targum of Onkelos*. He had it published in Vilna because he felt there would be worldwide interest; few people in Britain would be sufficiently knowledgeable to appreciate it. Onkelos was a Roman, the nephew of General Titus, who converted to Judaism in the second century CE. At the time the use of Hebrew in the Holy Land was declining and it was being replaced by Aramaic. Onkelos translated the Hebrew Bible into Aramaic and Adler set out to review the work, to test its accuracy. It was a monumental task and if the Chief Rabbi's health suffered in his 70s, it could well be because of the effort required. It was an important work: 'In Yemenite Jewish communities to this day *Targum Onkelos* is recited by heart as a verse-by-verse translation, alternatively with the Hebrew version of the Torah in the synagogue.'[7] The publication of the *Targum of Onkelos* increased Adler's post bag considerably as scholars wrote to examine and query aspects of it.

In his 80s Adler would work on a similar mammoth task, the *Ahavat Yehonatan*. The manuscript was completed by the time of his death but had not been published at the time.

There was one other most peculiar incident in 1875 which affected the Chief Rabbi. The *Jewish Chronicle* reported a meeting of the Portsmouth community in November of that year when a resolution was passed to write to him, saying:

> That the Jewish inhabitants of this borough express their unbounded gratification and pleasure that the attempt on the life of the Rev. Dr

> Adler, chief rabbi, was by the intervention of Providence, frustrated, and they fervently hope that a life so useful to the community at large may be spared for many years to promote the moral and religious welfare of the Jews of this country.[8]

The Editor of the paper was in a quandary when he heard of the letter: 'We give insertion to the resolution as requested, but we cannot help expressing our surprise at the proceedings since no attempt on the life of the rev. gentleman, as stated before, was made.'

This was only partially true. The events to which the Portsmouth community were referring had occurred at the Great Synagogue during the afternoon service on Friday, 29 October. In the congregation was a Christian who had also attended services at the Central and was known to its minister. This individual had been recently released from an asylum.

During the service at the Great he pulled out a fully loaded pistol and announced that voices had told him to kill all the Jews. Bravely, one of the congregation sitting near him wrestled the gun from his hand and he was handed over to the police. The result was that he was returned to his family and presumably to the asylum.

Whether the assailant intended to begin a massacre by shooting the Chief Rabbi was never established but Adler was in the synagogue and might well have been the target. The story was picked up by both national and provincial newspapers all over the country but the Editor of the *Jewish Chronicle* chose to play it down. Probably in order not to give ideas to others who were equally demented.

One perennial problem for the community was the working conditions of immigrant Jews in the East End. Their numbers expanded by emigration from Russia and the attractions of the new socialist thinking led to attempts to obtain better conditions in the numerous sweat shops. While Adler had sympathy for the Jewish workers, he was also keenly aware of the antagonism to sweated labour among those non-Jews who might find their employment threatened by the competition, or their wages undercut.

He was in good company in being concerned about the possibility of the working classes turning to socialism. The Marquis of Salisbury, who would become prime minister, had said in the House of Commons in 1866 concerning giving them the vote: 'I have heard much on the subject of the working-classes in this House which I confess, has filled me with feelings of some apprehension.'[9] The victims were widely portrayed as the potential aggressors. They might be tempted to: 'pass laws with respect to taxation and property, especially favourable to them, and therefore dangerous to all other classes.'[10]

The socialist movement in the East End was led by, among others, a young Jew called Aron Lieberman (1849?–80) who tried to spread Socialism but was also a strong secularist. To Lieberman, Judaism as a religion was outmoded, and to emphasize their irreligiosity, his followers went so far as to hold an annual ball on Yom Kippur, and to demonstrate outside synagogues carrying ham sandwiches. He formed a Hebrew Socialist Union to try to get the Jewish workers to act more in unison. They could easily be portrayed as the danger Salisbury was worried about.

As a result Adler became particularly concerned about the likely reaction of the British Establishment, which might be persuaded to pass an Aliens Act to restrict the number of Jewish migrants fleeing from persecution on the Continent. Trying to keep out foreigners has a long history in Britain, but has only had very limited success. Almost everybody originally comes from an emigrant family, if past records are examined with sufficient care.

The solution, as far as Adler was concerned, was to form an alternative organization, and this was inaugurated in the East End in 1874 as a Jewish Working Men's Club. Hermann Adler agreed to be one of the founding committee. The long battle to avoid an Aliens Act was fought all the way up to 1905, when such a measure was passed in the last days of the Balfour government.

Adler also opposed the preachers who he considered were criticizing those of his ministers not being sufficiently Orthodox; the immigrant *maggidim* who came to the East End were sometimes rather divisive. Adler wanted them to get permission from his office before preaching. Many of the smaller East End synagogues wouldn't submit to this supervision. As the *Jewish World* reported:

> It is surprising with what pertinacity this gentleman [the Russian Maggid, Zvi Hirsch Dainow] defies the charge of the Rev. the Chief Rabbi, that he not be permitted to preach unless under ecclesiastical sanction. The Maggid is represented to us as being a man of portly and noble presence, a king among men, eloquent, impressive in his didactic teachings, and a person of the greatest intelligence and mental capacity. His influence among his countrymen is extraordinary.[11]

Adler's constraints were not popular in much of the East End. Eventually Adler allowed Dainow to preach, but not in synagogues under his direct control. The problem, disappeared when Dainow died in 1877. The call for much greater orthodoxy was, however, widespread among the East European immigrants and would be a greater challenge to the longer established community after Adler's death.

Adler was an old man now, but despite his limitations he still left a lasting impression when he visited provincial communities. A reporter for the *Liverpool Daily Post* went to synagogue to hear him and reported that he was:

> A prelate, a venerable and graceful divine, whose utterances on public occasions are duly chronicled in the London newspapers along with those of the preachers at St Pauls, Westminster Abbey, etc. ... At his present age pathos is his leading or at any rate his most impressive characteristic. He mounts slowly and with an appearance of failing sight to the rostrum ... His voice is tremulous although sonorous, and a strong German accent gives his speech a careful and almost anxious deliberation to which the idea of tender pleading attaches ... he never fails to implore his flock most plaintively to be true to the model of Judaism which is known as Orthodox ... there is in his manner no vehemence, nor even rapid fluency, but there is evidence of deep feeling and genuine meditation.

In the pulpit Adler developed techniques that proved especially effective. He didn't need glasses almost until he died, and he sought the maximum effect on an audience he would only be addressing once. The journalist emphasized that preaching was a relatively recent innovation in Jewish services, and this would have made the occasion even more impressive.

This was the impression Adler gave, even if he was, in truth, far less fragile than he appeared. If necessary, he could still be authoritarian. To Adler every Jew in distress remained potentially his responsibility. In 1877 a father had gone to prospect for diamonds in South Africa, and his family had reneged on their promise to look after his two sons. As a result they had been taken to the Swansea Workhouse and were likely to be converted. When Adler heard of the case, he entreated the family to fulfil their responsibilities but to no avail. As a consequence he instructed the wardens of the Swansea community to remove the lads from the workhouse immediately and put them in the home of the Swansea minister. As the *Jewish Chronicle* reported, it was his direct personal intervention which made the synagogue act.

The Chief Rabbi's authority had come under threat again at a Council meeting of the United Synagogue in 1876. This time the subject was the appointment of a dayan and Adler was asked to define the appointee's duties. These, he said, were the exercise of rabbinical office, the control of *shechitah* and the arrangements for Passover and conversion. He also had to have *semichah* and speak good English. On being asked if the United Synagogue employed anybody with such qualifications, the Chief Rabbi said flatly that they did not.

At this point there was a heated discussion about whether the Chief Rabbi was right in his assessment. There was a motion to defer the subject for six months, as against accepting his ruling, but eventually this was defeated by twenty-four votes to fifteen. The size of the opposition would have been a disappointment to Adler, although those who voted to accept his ruling made it very clear that they regarded his authority as beyond question and severely criticized those who questioned it.

The problem for Adler in his old age, however, was not just that there was no English minister he regarded highly enough to appoint to the Beth Din. He was also conscious that the East End Jews were very concerned that whoever was appointed should be up to the standards expected on the Continent. Any appointee would be under scrutiny, because strict Orthodoxy was the one criterion by which the poverty stricken East End could claim to be superior. The idea being that the West End Jews might be wealthy, but they were inferior in their levels of observance. With Adler's worsening health, there had to be an alternative dayan who could hold his own against such criticism. Hermann was able to take over some of his father's responsibilities on the Beth Din, but he wasn't an exceptional Talmudic scholar, and he certainly wasn't of the same standard as the *dayanim* on the Continent.

With the vast increase in immigrants from the pogroms in a few years time, the problem would become more acute. On the Continent a Beth Din was asked to give advice on many aspects of life and the immigrants expected the same from the London Beth Din. More people needed the licences provided by the Beth Din. Where an hour or so on Mondays and Thursdays had once been sufficient to deal with the matters brought to their attention, it was now more like three or four hours. Furthermore it would become necessary to sit on three evenings a week as well.

One solution was the co-option of Jacob Reinowitz (1818–93) whose son-in-law was the Manchester minister, Susman Cohen. In 1876 Cohen had persuaded Reinowitz to accept a teaching role in the East End, and over the next few years he earned a reputation as a Talmudic teacher par excellence. Reinowitz was also from Poland and had been appointed a dayan in his home town, at the age of 28. He served in that capacity for thirty years, so his experience could hardly be better. Adler asked him to become a dayan in London and he served as such until his death.

A dayan had a superior status to a minister, so it would have been expected that the financial rewards would be greater as well. This was far from the case. To keep his family, Aaron Levy had needed to be a scribe as well, writing by hand the Torah scrolls which contained the first five books of the Bible. Spiers ran a boarding house for Jewish boys at University College

School, and according to the *Jewish Chronicle*, Reinowitz 'was allowed to subsist on a miserable pittance given grudgingly by the United Synagogue'.[12] The actual figure was £50 a year, though Lord Rothschild improved on this by providing the same amount. The dayanim could hardly have been held in higher regard by those who knew them if they had been given the marks of status they deserved. They were still officially reverends, rather than rabbis; the rabbinical title was still solely restricted to the chief rabbi. They were still not allowed to consider cases outside London which remained solely in the chief rabbi's province.

Even allowing that Adler wanted to prevent challenges to his authority by placing his office on a pinnacle, the cost to the dayanim seemed out of proportion to the nomenclature. There was absolutely no question of Levy, Spiers or Reinowitz giving decisions which were not strictly according to the *din*. They all had *semichah* and their credentials in that regard were impeccable and unassailable.

They were also, all of them, highly regarded by those who had need of the Beth Din. The humanity of their decisions, the care and attention they gave to each case, and the courtesy with which they dealt with the petitioners, made the Beth Din a highly respected court for the community.

If no English Jew was yet capable of becoming a dayan, there had certainly been progress in some of their ambitions. Simeon Singer was determined to get *semichah* and, after studying with Reinowitz, learned under Isaac Hirsch Weiss and completed a strenuous three-year course. Hermann Gollancz was another and he went abroad for the certificate, because Jews' College still had no curriculum for the granting of *semichah*.

Both ministers were known in future, however, as reverend, rather than rabbi. Nothing changed there, to Gollancz's great annoyance. Only when he went to Leeds for *Shavuot* and was called up to the Reading of the Torah could he be addressed as rabbi. In his own Bayswater Synagogue, he would not be given the same appellation. As he would be knighted in the future, there would, at least, be some compensation.

As long ago as 1872 there had been adverse criticism in the press on the situation; comments like: 'Must a man go to Breslau to learn to be a rabbi?' In 1883, however, it became necessary for Jews' College to offer a three level course if they wanted to be affiliated to London University. The third level would indeed lead to *semichah*, but it would be fifteen more years before a college graduate received the award.

The Chief Rabbi was a good Rosh Beth Din. He exercised his authority with his usual care and courtesy. His first words to the petitioners continued to be 'What can I do to help?' He was at the service of communities all over the world. For example, in 1876, he declared kosher meat in Australia to be possibly *trefah* (forbidden) because he was not, personally, able to supervise the skill of the slaughterers. This aroused a lot of criticism but Adler had no alternative if a suitably qualified rabbi was not available in the Antipodes, although this changed in 1883 when Rabbi Dr Joseph Abrahams became minister of the Melbourne Hebrew Congregation.

What was a great disappointment to him was the decision a few years later to close down the Jews' College school and concentrate in future on educating ministerial students.One of the main reasons for this was that Jewish families were moving out of the City and the school was no longer favourably situated for them. The school had also failed to attract middle-class children whose parents could pay the fees, and the college's financial position was unsustainable if the school continued.

Adler also had to contend with a long bout of illness in 1879, although he had recovered by the High Holydays in the autumn. His doctors were insistent, however, that he must now leave London in the winter for a healthier climate. He settled on Brighton.

In June 1879 the Central Synagogue board of management considered making changes to the ritual in Shabbat and festival services. Having talked widely about what they felt appropriate, they were approached by other London synagogues to suggest that they be consulted as well. The Central agreed and a conference was convened in October to which all the London synagogues were invited. That conference took place at the Central and all the London synagogues, except the Hambro and the New, sent three delegates each, usually their honorary officers. The New had originally agreed to join in the discussions but withdrew.

The Conference of Delegates proceeded to discuss changes to the ritual in great detail, though none of their ministers were invited to be present. Some might, however, have discussed changes with their ministers before attending. Nevertheless, not to have invited the ministers even to join the meetings, if not actually to preside, on a purely religious matter, suggests an unacceptably low view of their learning and status. The ministers was seen as servants to the community, rather than its leaders, as they were so often on the Continent. The press was not allowed to be present at the meetings either.

The delegates made the point that it wasn't just the ritual that they wanted to review but the decorum in synagogues as well. They also wanted weekly rather than monthly sermons. In presenting their conclusions, they made it clear, however, that nothing would be agreed without the approval of the Chief Rabbi and that his decisions would be binding.

The eventual list of recommendations was extremely detailed. It was divided into two classes; there was one set which the honorary officers considered would not need the approval of the seat holders in the synagogues, because they were not considered contentious. Another set were more arguable, and these they felt should be approved by the individual congregants. The report was published in March 1880 and the Chief Rabbi considered each of their recommendations before coming to his own conclusions in a letter he sent out in May of that year.

By this time the Chief Rabbi had been permitted to delegate many of his responsibilities to Hermann, in view of his ill health. In November 1879 he had reluctantly written to the United Synagogue that he was not fit enough to carry on with his full schedule of work. The United Synagogue officers fully understood his fragile condition, because he had been away from his office for a number of months that year. He was 76 and the expectation of life at birth at that time was 42.

With only a few grumbles, it was agreed to appoint his son, Hermann, as delegate chief rabbi. It seemed to some delegates that it was giving Hermann a head start to becoming chief rabbi in the future, but he was so highly regarded for the work he had already carried out as the minister at the Bayswater Synagogue and principal of Jews' College that this seemed unimportant to the majority.

As the Council of the United Synagogue recorded when he was appointed:

> If Dr Hermann Adler were entirely unconnected with the Chief Rabbi by the near tie of relationship, his great learning and high abilities, his conciliatory disposition and the manner in which he has succeeded in gaining the affection of a large and important congregation would designate him as eminently fitted for the discharge of the important duties from which Dr Adler [Nathan Marcus] is compelled to seek relief.[13]

There was, however, another reason for Hermann Adler's popularity with the leaders of the community as the choice to be his father's delegate. Early in his career, he had shown himself very willing to defend the Jewish position against non-Jewish critics. In 1865, soon after he had assumed the Bayswater pulpit, he had taken on Bishop Dr John William Colenso, a South African missionary, who had argued against the divine origin of the Torah. Hermann's book on the subject, written in conjunction with the same Dr Abraham Benisch who had assessed his father's credentials to be elected chief rabbi twenty years before, was entitled *A Jewish Reply to Dr. Colenso's Criticism of the Pentateuch*.

He had also taken up arms again on behalf of Judaism in 1878, when he had very publicly tackled one of the foremost anti-Semites in the country.

Professor Goldwin Smith had been Regius Professor of Modern History at Oxford from 1858–66. He was a noted academic but he was also an atheist. As such, he attacked Judaism in books and in periodicals like the prestigious *Nineteenth Century*. In the July 1878 issue, however, there was a response by Hermann Adler in the magazine refuting Smith's arguments and defending the faith.

Hermann even tackled the thorny issue of intermarriage, describing it as a 'self-denying ordinance'. As against Goldwin Smith's insistence that the Greeks had influenced Christianity and not the Jews, Hermann insisted that Judaism had taught monotheism and moral law by precept and example. As a natural consequence, he was highly praised in the Jewish press for his 'moral courage and literary ability'. It was said to be the first time that a Jewish ecclesiastic had taken up the cudgels on behalf of his religion and it raised Hermann's profile and reputation beyond that of a minister at the Bayswater synagogue and an assistant to his father.

Hermann's article, with its careful and thorough attack on Smith's paper, offered a new dimension to those who were considering prospective candidates to take over after his father. The Chief Rabbi, for all his communications with rabbis on the Continent, for all his responsa to congregations as far away as America, and his advice to ministers throughout the Empire, had never openly engaged with British anti-Semites. That he left to the Jewish lay leaders, like Sir David Salomon, or it would be handled by Sir Moses Montefiore on his travels abroad.

The Chief Rabbi's reticence on this issue might well have arisen from his experiences in Hanover. There, the ineffectiveness of complaints, the unfairness of anti-Semitic legislation, and the long history of discrimination, had all suggested the futility of taking on the anti-Semites. Rolling with the punches was normally the best that could be achieved. Coming to England, he felt well out of it. That was, with very rare exceptions, the way he wanted it to be.

He would very happily cooperate with the non-Jewish world on initiatives like Hospital Sunday, but he would not fight it unless an aspect of the *din* was under threat. Hermann was offering a bolder public relations approach; potentially, he could be the voice of the emancipated British Jew.

Notes

1. Year Book VII, 1962, Leo Baeck Institute, p.307.
2. Ibid.
3. *The Times*, 6 December 1871.
4. *Jewish Chronicle*, 12 May 1871.

5. *Aguna* concerns the result of a husband not giving a divorce to his wife. *Yibbun* was a law that a childless widow couldn't marry again until her husband's surviving brother married her, or renounced his right or duty to do so. Rabbinic pressure is now brought to bear on a recalcitrant husband to grant a divorce.
6. *Jewish Chronicle*, 10 January 1879, pp.8–9.
7. Wikipedia.
8. *Jewish Chronicle*, 12 November 1875, p.525.
9. Owen Jones, *The Establishment: And how they get away with it* (Harmondsworth: Penguin, 2014), p.5.
10. Ibid.
11. *Jewish World*, 10 July 1874.
12. *Jewish Chronicle*, 19 May 1893, p.5.
13. Council of the United Synagogue 1879.

12

Semiretirement

After his appointment, Hermann took up his father's position on the Beth Din, conducted or sanctioned the marriages, drafted correspondence, attended the Council of the Beth Hamedrash and oversaw *shechitah*. Nevertheless, on a subject as important as the ritual, the Chief Rabbi remained very much in charge and had to be consulted on a regular basis. It was a strain for him because the individual synagogues believed their recommendations were all fully justified; the New West End Synagogue alone listed twenty-eight changes they would have liked made. Adler, however, was not going to give way on anything he considered essential. As he wrote: 'I have sanctioned those modifications which do not impair the integrity of our *Book of Common Prayer* and do not infringe upon *dinim* prescribed in the *Shulchan Aruch*.'[1]

He also told them that some of the recommendations were against the *minhag* (traditional practices) and others he wouldn't accept at all. Adler's decisions on the form of the ritual could be criticized by radical members of the community at both ends of the spectrum, but overall he had both taken the middle path and kept to his principles. His *via media* would be generally popular and his rationale understood: 'No public man who has done his work earnestly, will stultify his public life by departing at last from the principles which have been its mainspring.'[2] As he also clearly pointed out that the changes had to be in accordance with the integrity of the existing prayer book, he gave himself the maximum latitude to reject what he felt unlawful.

On rare occasions, in his response to the conference delegates, he said that he accepted the suggestions with reluctance. He had, for example, often criticized the continuation of the practice of *shnoddering*, with its announcements of charity gifts by those laymen given synagogue honours. He recognized, however, that the conference claim was correct that these donations helped to keep the synagogues financially afloat. He had stopped the auction of honours way back in 1847. The conference justified keeping the *shnoddering* interruptions to the service by pointing out the changes to a 'high standard of qualification in its ministers, and therefore remunerating them on a scale unknown to earlier generations'.[3] In which case, one might ask why the ministers weren't invited to attend the original conference and why the *dayanim* were so badly paid.

The synagogue delegates were trying, as they said, to simplify the service, by which they meant shortening it. One of their recommendations for festivals was to stop reading the Biblical books associated with them; the Song of Songs, for example, is read on Passover and the Book of Ruth on Shavuot. These take some time, but the recommendation to abandon them was summarily rejected by Adler.

He also insisted that the prayers for the religious leaders in Babylonian times, which are said during the Shabbat service, be retained in deference to their massive contribution to the maintenance of the faith, even if their contribution had been made well over a millennium before.

Minor changes he did approve and the reasons for his decisions were explained in the near thirty recommendations which he ensured were to be put to the congregations. On one particularly contentious issue, he insisted that the initial Kol Nidre prayer be retained. The argument against it was that Jews were accused of using it to get out of oaths given in a court of law. Adler pointed out that the oaths referred to in the prayer were between man and G-d and not man and man. He said: 'To do so may strengthen the false and baseless inferences and would be interpreted as an admission that our forefathers and existing congregations not under my jurisdiction, do intend by Kol Nidrei to absolve themselves from the binding oaths taken in a court of justice.'[4]

He did introduce new prayers for mothers attending synagogue for the first time after childbirth and for mourners in their homes. He agreed that mourners in synagogue should say *Kaddish* in unison, rather than separately. He sanctioned reducing the multiple repetitions of some prayers, allowing them to be said only once.

He also agreed that when congregants were called up to the Reading of the Torah, that their surnames could be added to their Hebrew names; for example, there were likely to be a number of Abraham ben Josephs and people liked to be recognized. There were new prayers to be said when visiting graves. There was still to be no three-year cycle of reading the Pentateuch, the first five books, though there were some ancient precedents. Adler retained everything of importance. The times of services, which many wanted to start later in the morning, were not to be altered. He did leave it to the individual congregations to accept or reject his recommendations, but there was little likelihood that many communities would gainsay his decisions.

At the end of his letter he made another key point; that what mattered even more than the minutiae of the prayers was the decorum of the services, the concentration of the congregation on its devotions, and the responsibility of the individual to actually attend services. Although divine worship in church was much more practised than it is today, the attraction of a less rigorous, more secular approach to life was increasingly gaining support. Adler saw the movement as akin to the philosophy of socialism; he was not in favour of revolutionary ideas.

The reactions to the Chief Rabbi's rulings were generally positive and the respect for his overall authority continued to always be emphasized. After thirty-five years in office, the judgement on Adler was one of overwhelming approval. This was the crucial point and the one which settled the community into the Orthodox approach it still has today.

Adler had given the whole subject of alterations to the ritual his full attention. For their part, the United Synagogue would decide to abolish the rank of Free Members in 1879, but only by not agreeing to create any new ones. The existing Free Members would retain their privileges throughout their lifetimes.

Adler's decisions did not just apply to his own generation; they became standard practice when incorporated in the *Authorised Prayer Book*, which he supervised in detail until his own death ten years later, when it was effectively complete. While it is still called the *Singer Prayer Book*, it was really the Adler Prayer Book.

So Adler retired to his home in Brighton and left most of the chief rabbi's bureaucratic tasks to Hermann. His health fluctuated but he was carefully looked after by Celestine. When she went away for occasional breaks, the task fell to his daughter, Rebecca, who was 15 in 1880, a bright youngster and devoted to her father. The climate in Brighton suited Adler very well. He always referred to it as Dr Brighton and would walk on the sea front with great pleasure. He continued to give lectures in his study at his home and the Sabbath and Festival services in the house were well attended. The chief rabbi would still officiate on rare occasions; in 1881 he conducted the marriage of Marcus Samuel, the founder of Shell Petroleum, to Fanny Benjamin.

He was also a prominent public figure in Brighton. When a meeting was held in Brighton to protest against the treatment of the Russian Jews, the Mayor specifically asked the Chief Rabbi to come. He was equally called on for less important matters; one lady wanted a recommendation for a Hebrew teacher for her child. Another family had decided to send their son to a good school in Germany; could the Chief Rabbi suggest a suitable school and a Jewish family where he could stay? In 1883 he sent a cheque for £20 to the Brighton Synagogue Hebrew classes. Would he confirm that the local wine merchant's drinks were kosher for Passover. No, he wouldn't, much to the annoyance of the retailer.

Hermann might be the Delegate Chief Rabbi but his father's friends were still going to come to the fountainhead. There was reconstruction going on at the New West End Synagogue and the minister, Simeon Singer, wanted to know if the synagogue should be reconsecrated. No, said Adler, it wasn't necessary. There was a vast amount of personal correspondence and Adler continued to deal with it. He was not always very happy with the Jewish leaders: 'Adler's letters sometimes refer rather caustically to someone identified in Hebrew with the letters *resh shin* ... he meant Lord Rothschild, president of the United Synagogue.'[6]

Even in semiretirement, every important question continued to be submitted to the chief rabbi. In 1883, for example, there was a meeting of the Association for the Diffusion of Religious Knowledge. The press reported that the curricula for the classes had been produced by the committee. Hermann Adler took the opportunity to make it very clear that, while the committee's comments had been very welcome, the decisions on standards had been produced by the chief rabbi and only by the chief rabbi.

On a separate issue, the question arose of whether a cohen could serve on a coroner's jury. Before the inquest it was customary for the jury to view the body and *cohanim* were prohibited from being near a corpse. Should they then refuse to serve or did their public duty take precedence. Adler said their public duty came first.

Though Adler now seldom left Brighton, he was still a national public figure and his support for good causes was still sought. He was happy, for instance, to agree to be a founder of the London Society for the Prevention of Cruelty to Children which later became the NSPCC.

He continued to take a keen interest in the progress of the schools, sending Simeon Singer to represent him on tours of inspection. He lent his authority to Michael Friedländer, the principal of Jews' College, when he produced a new copy of the Bible with the wording in parallel columns of English and Hebrew. This could be purchased in twenty-five monthly parts for 15p a section.

One of his concerns was that the United Synagogue dragged its feet when it came to support for Jews' College. He had to rely on his friends to make the case but without much success: 'No budget night of the olden days would have been complete without an amendment by Sir Adolph Tuck[7] to the proposed meagre grant to the College.'[8] In 1881 a Building Fund was started for better premises for the college. It was estimated to cost £3,000. The United Synagogue was only asked to contribute £100 but even so the motion scraped through by twenty-three votes to seventeen.

His interest in the Holy Land continued unabated. He was an enthusiastic supporter of a new Zionist movement, Chovevei Zion, which was founded in Germany after the Russian pogroms started in 1881. B the time Adler died, it had over 1,300 members in London. Colonization was always going to be difficult, though; Marcus wrote in 1884 to advise the community that the Turkish government were averse to the concept as they did not want their authority threatened by Europeans.

There were other problems the Chief Rabbi continued to tackle. For example, there was an understandable wish for the flood of new immigrants into the East End to keep a low profile and not to attract attention; if the East End was quiet, more Jewish refugees could enter Britain despite the ongoing movement, which was gaining some support, to pass an Aliens Act to exclude them. The adoption of a low profile was, therefore, a defence measure and there was one public display of Jewish practice which Adler eventually decided should be played down. This was the ceremony of *Tashlich* which occurs on the afternoon of the first day of the New Year. The custom is to take pieces of bread, as representing the sins of the year, and throw them in a river or stream, to cast them out. In 1874, and for some years thereafter, a large number of East End Jews went to Customs House Quay to perform the ceremony. It was a very public demonstration, which aroused some unwelcome publicity, and eventually, in 1883, Adler issued an official message, asking that Customs House Quay be avoided for the purpose. It was letting the side down. As he said: 'Our foreign brethren ... must not bring discredit on their generous or freeborn British brethren by these unpleasant vagaries.'[9]

His view was in contrast – though it would probably have been long forgotten – with the beliefs of his predecessor, Solomon Hirschcll who, in the earlier part of the century, would go from his home in the City to the Thames to perform the *Tashlich* ceremony. As he walked in his full canonical robes to the river, Jews would hurry to join the procession until the traffic was almost brought to a halt by the crowd which gathered behind him.

Adler did not advocate the abolition of the practice. In discussing Adlerism, critics have said he did, as part of a case that he was moving towards the practices of the church. The Chief Rabbi merely wanted the flow of Jewish immigrants not to be disturbed by attracting unwelcome publicity. The letter from his office says nothing about changing the practice of *Tashlich* itself.

Adler's influence on the newcomers from the pogroms in Eastern Europe had to be created from scratch and this wasn't easy. Many well-qualified European rabbis had escaped persecution as well, and they were unaccustomed to being answerable to a chief rabbi. Many also came from backgrounds in their homeland where the standards of Jewish observance were higher than in Britain. Adler had proved the rationale for his overall spiritual control over the years, but the newcomers were being asked to accept a system which was strange to them.

Adler still remained the point of contact on Jewish religious matters with the government. As late as 1885 a Bessarabian woman wrote to Queen Victoria to solicit her help to get her son back from Montreal. The palace passed the letter to the prime minister, Lord Salisbury, and he passed it on to Adler.

The long and warm relationship with Moses Montefiore continued in full flower, but both men had indifferent health and it became more difficult for them to visit each other in their Brighton and Ramsgate homes. Montefiore kept in regular touch by letter, writing in an increasingly shaky hand until he had to dictate his letters to his secretary. There would be exchanges of presents, which in Montefiore's case, would usually be described as a souvenir of his late wife. In June 1881, Montefiore wrote:

> My dear and highly esteemed Mrs Adler,
>
> The receipt of your valued favour of the 5th inst. has afforded me sincere pleasure and I thank you most heartily for your good wishes, which I most ardently reciprocate, and for the very handsome and acceptable present which accompanied it. The handkerchiefs are most beautifully embroidered – indeed I have never seen any to equal the fine needlework there displayed. Be assured, my dear Mrs Adler, that I appreciate most highly this mark of your kind remembrance of me, and shall ever value them as a memento of one for whom I entertain the highest respect ... With best wishes and respectful regards,
>
> Believe me, Very truly yours,
>
> Moses Montefiore.[10]

For his part, Montefiore would mark festivals with cheques for £100 for Adler. In terms of today's money that would be about £9,000. In March 1883, for example, he wrote:

> My dear Mrs Adler,
>
> The approaching anniversary of our Purim Festival affords me the gratifying opportunity of which I, with very much pleasure, avail myself to tender to you, our esteemed Chief Rabbi, Dr. Adler, and your family, my ardent wishes that you may, in the full possession of every blessing, enjoy many many happy returns of the Festival. I sincerely hope you are all quite well and have not suffered from the extremely changeable and severe weather we have had of late. May I ask you to

> do me the favour to accept with my best wishes, the enclosed Souvenir Cheque for £100. With my kind remembrances to esteemed Dr Adler and your family....

Montefiore also asked the Chief Rabbi to distribute gifts to the poor; one Chanukah it was the very practical provision of warm blankets. It was hard to reciprocate adequately and so Adler was delighted to have the opportunity to write a special prayer for Montefiore's Centenary Service, though his own poor health prevented him from attending it. Hermann did the honours instead.

The plight of the Jews in Russia, who had become subject to murderous pogroms, decided Adler to dedicate a Shabbat in February 1882 to their troubles. He composed a special prayer for the occasion and asked that collections be made to help relieve their co-religionists. On the day over £3,000 was pledged in synagogues all over the country, of which £1,300 came from the Hermann Adler's Bayswater Synagogue. In today's money £3,000 is over a quarter of a million.

In December 1883 Adler wrote his will:

> I have been very ill and near death, but Almighty God in His mercy has so far restored me to health that I am able, though inadequately, to write. Being in Brighton, and no longer surrounded by members of my family, I feel bound to lay the following religious duties to the hearts of my children, grand- and great-grandchildren with the earnest wish that they may always observe them, and thereby keep my memory fresh and green.

He says that he talks more about religious than moral duties, only because it is the religious duties which are more likely in his day to be neglected. He suggests they read a Psalm or other chapter of the Bible every day, possibly after morning prayers. He also urged that they keep the Oral Law and suggested reading a commentary on the Torah, even in English. He said that he had given up hoping that all his family would be fluent in Hebrew. He was, however, a founder of a society for the revival of Hebrew, of which the German rabbi, Eliezer Lipmann Silbermann, was the chief protagonist. Silbermann produced the first weekly newspaper in Hebrew in 1856 and is acknowledged as the founder of Hebrew journalism. Adler was a keen supporter.

In his will Adler held that the home was the most important Jewish institution and the centre of Jewish life. He told his children to keep *kashrus* and to tell their children to observe it outside the home as well.

> Do not listen, my dear children, as regards the Law, 'Thou shalt not seethe a kid in its mother's milk', to the criticism of the so-called Neologians. [In Britain a neo-Karaite tendency who asserted that the law must be taken literally. Adler believed this would be senseless.] Depend upon it, from the very time of its promulgation, it was expounded and carried out in its extended sense. Depend upon it.

Adler pointed out that there are rules for which we don't know a reason – *chukkim* – but that all the *mitzvoth* have beneficent motives. Being scrupulous and honest in business is a *Kiddush HaShem* (a sanctification of the name of the Almighty). He warned them to shun usury: 'Whatever your calling, shun, oh my dear ones, every kind of usury, for usury still constitutes, alas, the malignant canker which sullies the fair name of our nation.' Shabbat must be kept: 'Distinguish it with a better meal, better dress. Everybody must rest.' The parents might examine their children on Shabbat to see how they were getting on in their religious studies. There should, however, be no business, writing or riding on Shabbat. Lastly they should always be good Jews and Jewesses with firm morality and strict observance the keynotes of their lives.

He left bequests to a wide range of family and friends. £10 each went to Michael Friedländer, the head of Jews' College and to Adler's two fellow-members of the Beth Din, Jacob Reinowitz and Bernard Spiers. His books were to be divided between the children, but Hermann was to have first choice of Hebraic and rabbinic works.

His daughter Sarah was left the 18 carat Australian gold cup which today is on loan to the Victoria and Albert Museum. Jeanette inherited his second largest Sefer Torah and Minna the smaller one, together with its silver decorations and a silver coffee pot. Ida received his filigree Chanukah lamp and two silver candlesticks. Lionel Louis Cohen and Henry Harris were each left a silver cup. Marcus also received silver candlesticks and Hermann a silver soup tureen. Elkan had a smaller Sefer Torah and musical candlesticks. Carl Lehfeldt, Celestine's brother, was left a diamond mourning ring and the trustees would give Rebecca's future husband, Harry Heilbut, a silver goblet. Adler's grandsons, Maier and Naphtali Stern, received £100 each and Joseph Vangelder £50. Rev. Dr Kahn who had married Jetta Stern, his granddaughter, was left £30 and the other grandchildren received £2 each to buy a memento.

Nor were his favourite charities forgotten. The Provincial Ministers Fund received £20, and £10 each went to the Jews' Free School, Jews' College, the Jewish Hospital and the teachers' college in Hanover. There were also donations to the Brighton Synagogue and the Jewish Board of Guardians and

£15 to a yeshivah in Jerusalem. Probate was eventually set at £12,589, which is the equivalent of a million pounds today.

Looking back on his ministry, he would recognize the wide gulf that had now grown up between the Orthodox and the Reform in America. In 1885 the Reform had set down their position vis-à-vis Biblical Judaism: 'Today we accept as binding only its moral laws, and maintain only such ceremonies as elevate and sanctify our lives, but reject all such as are not adopted to the views and habits of modern civilization.'[11]

In Adler's communities throughout the country and overseas, 'modern civilization' had to be measured against the Oral Law. For example, in Adler's time, one third of working women were employed as servants and put in a six and a half day week. They only got Sunday afternoon off. In contrast, the Fourth Commandment in Biblical times gave them the whole Sabbath day for themselves; a six-day week, promulgated thousands of years before. Modern civilization had gone backwards, just as it would take many more years to catch up with the Biblical regulations which had, effectively, abolished capital punishment.

Sir Moses Montefiore died on 28 July 1885. Jemima Guedalla, his niece, sent a telegram to Adler: 'Dear Sir Moses died most peaceably at half past four this afternoon.' Celestine Adler, who always signed her letters CA, replied:

> My dear Mrs Guedalla,
>
> My husband and I have felt very keenly the loss of our dear and illustrious friend, Sir Moses. To you, who have ever shown towards him a devotion beyond all praise, his loss can well appear, as it is to all of us, an irreparable one. It must, of course, afford us all some melancholy sort of satisfaction that his end was so peaceful, like that of some grand Jewish patriarch of Bible times, and that the whole world unites to praise him. The Doctor feels very bitterly his being unable to attend the funeral, and it needed the strongest persuasion on my part to prevent his going, but we dared not let him incur the risk of the excitement – I am sure you will forgive his absence ...
>
> Believe me, yours very sincerely, CA.

The Chief Rabbi insisted, however, on being present at Montefiore's memorial service and this was the last occasion on which he appeared in public. He did produce an order of service to mark Queen Victoria's Jubilee at the Great Synagogue in 1887 but he wasn't well enough to attend himself. That year he also missed the unveiling of his portrait, painted by Solomon Alexander Hart and hung in the Vestry Room of the Great Synagogue.

April 1887 saw the opening of the Anglo-Jewish Historical Exhibition which took place at the Albert Hall in April 1887 and reflected the community in all its various forms. Adler lent the organizing committee his copy of Haham David Nietto's *De la Divina Providencia*, and from the Exhibition came the idea for the formation of the Jewish Historical Society of England. For the Adler family, though, the year had its personal tragedy as Marcus' wife, Fanny, died after a lengthy illness. She was only 49 but she had both cancer and a tumour on her liver.

As the decade progressed, Rebecca, or Beck as she was known in the family, continued to care for her father in her mother's absence. Celestine herself was not well, but she naturally expected to be kept informed of the position at home and Beck wrote her detailed letters. She posted one before a Shabbat which read:

> Darling Mother, I write these few lines to wish you and your host and hostess a very very happy Shabbat ... Dr Pocock says he is very glad you have gone. The change will do you good (DV). He thinks dear father very well ... We enjoyed our dinner immensely. Father came twice. We had hot fowl stewed in its own gravy. This afternoon I went to order two pigeons for our Monday dinner ...
>
> Fondest love and kisses from Beck

It is unlikely that Adler had many financial concerns in his old age. Adler continued to receive fees for marriages being solemnised in many synagogues. In December 1881 the United Synagogue office sent him £17.85 to cover seventeen weddings between October and December. Apart from the support of Montefiore, he would also have had the backing of his eldest daughter Sarah's husband, Henry Solomon. An extremely charitable man, Solomon was listed in the first *Jewish Year Book* as being associated with thirty-six commercial and charitable institutions. In support of his father-in-law, he served as treasurer of Jews' College for forty years and was also treasurer to the Chief Rabbi's office.

It was Solomon who introduced the use of steel pens into business. He became Chairman of the Ocean Railway & General Accident Assurance Co. in 1901. As the Ocean Accident & General Guarantee Co., it would be the first casualty insurance company to have a £1 million premium income. Solomon was also a director of four gas companies and warden/president of the New Synagogue. Minna's husband, Jacob Israel, was also a very wealthy man as his family owned one of the largest department stores in Berlin and he was a commercial adviser to the Emperor.

In 1888 Elkan visited Egypt. He had become a lawyer and had developed a passion for books and travel. As he became known as a noted bibliophile, he agreed to chair the Jews' College Library Committee and held the office for many years. He also built up his own library of about 2,500 manuscripts. He is best known for being the first to recognize the importance of the Cairo Genizah. This is a room in the Ben Ezra Synagogue in Cairo without a door, just an opening half way up one wall. Its purpose was to store worn-out material on which there was Hebrew writing, because nothing in *loshen kodesh*, the holy language, could be destroyed according to the *din*. Anything in Hebrew was thrown through the gap, particularly worn-out, heretical and disgraced documents. This went on for 1,000 years between about 870 CE and the late nineteenth century. Elkan Adler went to Cairo again in 1896 and arranged with the government to bring back to Britain approximately 25,000 fragments of material. It was only about seven and a half per cent of the total, and Solomon Schechter would arrange to bring back nearly 200,000 more fragments later in the same year. Not surprisingly, work is still continuing on assessing the information the material in the Genizah provides about Jewish life in the Dark and Middle ages, up to modern times.

The years were drifting by. Sir Moses had passed away, Becky got married and went to live in Amsterdam, Hermann was acting as delegate chief rabbi and Jeanette was married to the chief rabbi of Hamburg. In 1887, though, Marcus lost Fanny.

In Brighton in the autumn of 1889, the Chief Rabbi was now 86 but showing little sign of slowing down. He was busy writing a commentary on *Ahavat Yehonatan*, which was a work in the same form as his Targum commentary on Onkelos. He had seen all his children marry under the *chuppah* to Orthodox Jews and he had been blessed with numerous children and grandchildren. He would have considered the enlarged family as one of his great successes in life. He continued to hold an early Sabbath service at the house, as he had done throughout his ministry and he didn't lack for visitors.

The community suffered one embarrassment at that time when Sir Henry Aaron Isaacs was elected Lord Mayor of London. Sir Henry, who had been largely responsible for the building of Tower Bridge, was delighted to be elected, but extremely embarrassed by the fact that the Lord Mayor's procession would be, as usual, on a Saturday and he would be expected to ride in the Lord Mayor's coach. Sir Henry was a warden of the Hambro Synagogue. Every effort was made to get the celebrations delayed till the Monday, but the City Fathers stood firm and Sir Henry reluctantly agreed to ride in the carriage rather than walk to the Mansion House on the Sabbath. The President of the United Synagogue, Lord Rothschild, warmly congratulated him on his appointment and Adler stayed diplomatically incommunicado in Brighton.

It was the kind of conflict Jews in the Diaspora often had to face between civic and religious demands, which Montefiore had been anticipating half a century before. It was why he had always been suspicious of the unalloyed advantages of emancipation and Sir Henry's dilemma showed how right he was.

On 27 November 1889 *The World – A Journal for Men and Women* printed an article in its series 'Celebrities at Home'. It gives a fine picture of the life of the Chief Rabbi as it drew to a close.

> In an unpretentious house on the right hand side of the modest thoroughfare, lying between Queens Gardens and the Western Road, the venerable ecclesiastic whose jurisdiction is more extensive than that of Her Britannic Majesty (for the spiritual authority of the Chief Rabbi is still acknowledged by the Hebrews of the Transvaal) is passing the peaceful evening of an eventful life ... There is nothing save a clump of neatly-clipped shrubs to distinguish Dr Adler's dwelling from those of his neighbours, but the reminiscences of the hale octogenarian who welcomes you presently with the dignified courtesy of a bygone age to his plainly furnished oratory, overlooking a tiny grass plot fringed with evergreens, begin with the march of Napoleon through Hanover on his way to Moscow.
>
> ... it is almost impossible to believe [the rabbi] who rises briskly from the table at which he is working without spectacles on his Biblical Commentary, to tell you that, thanks to the invigorating air of 'his best friend Dr Brighton' he could fast for twenty five hours on the Day of Atonement, and was once more able to observe the Feast of Tabernacles by taking his meals in an al fresco bower, according to the time honoured traditions of his faith.
>
> The carpet which covers the floor is worn by the feet of many worshippers, for Nathan Adler's chapel-study has been regarded for some years past as a place of pilgrimage, and it is considered a high privilege to take part in the service which he celebrates there every Saturday. On a bracket-desk close to the window are placed the *Tefilla* [Phylacteries], the *Tehillim* [Psalms] and the *Mishnajoth* [Jewish law] – the three devotional volumes always used by the Chief Rabbi.
>
> Just opposite, on the other side of his writing-desk, is a curtained cupboard on walnut-wood surmounted by the Tablets of the Covenant, which serves as an *Aron Hakkodesh* or 'Sacred Ark' and contains a number of ancient 'Scrolls of the Law' carefully wrapped

up in gold brocade, with chased '*yad*' or 'pointers' attached to them by silver chains. Many of these valuable 'Scrolls' were presented to Dr Adler by prominent members of his flock in London; but he especially values one written at Wilna [Vilna], given him by his old friend, Sir Moses Montefiore ... Dr Adler's theological labours necessitate the constant use of many works of reference. *The Speaker's Commentary*[12] and Mr W.H. Lowe's Mishnah[13] are within easy reach of his hand, and he regards them with quite as much reverence as the more ponderous volumes of Rabbinical literature spread out before him.

He takes you to his bookcase to see the Wilna edition of The Talmud, the gift of his children, and Sir Moses Montefiore's Portuguese Forms of Prayer, and calls his faithful Dutch servant, Joseph Vangelder, who officiates at once as valet, librarian and private chaplain, to bring Sir Anthony de Rothschild's silver tureen; the cup made out of the first gold discovered in Victoria, sent to him in 1852 by his brethren in the Colony as a 'token of the high esteem in which he is held, and to mark their sense of his indefatigable exertions in the holy cause of religion and education', the *tallith* or prayer scarf woven for his special use under the direction of his son-in-law, Jacob Israel, Commerzienrath[14] in Berlin; the curious silver ornaments, known as *Klei Kodesh*; and the three-centuries-old Missal of the Hagadah used on the evening of the Passover.

Your host is expecting a visit from his son and assistant, Dr Hermann Adler, who has during the past ten years discharged his public duties in Finsbury Square. Although the Coadjutor Chief Rabbi has crossed swords polemically with Dr Colenso, Mr Goodwin Smith and Professor Max Muller[15] he always consults his father on important points of business; and when he arrives Dr Adler will be able to illustrate the comprehensive character of their high office, which has a social and judicial aspect quite distinct from its purely religious attributes.

Meanwhile Joseph is directed to show you Mr B.S. Marks's striking portrait of the Chief Rabbi ... the faded portrait of Sir Moses Montefiore gazing at his wife's portrait ... and the embroidered trophy containing portraits of Dr Adler's children, grandchildren and fourteen great-grandchildren, arranged by his daughter, Mrs Stern, the widow of the Chief Rabbi of Hamburg.

When you return to the oratory on the first floor, the Chief Rabbi has put away his MS book filled with 'Rashi' characters, as distinctly written as if he were a student of twenty. When he was transferred from Hanover to London in 1845, the 'restrictions' born of ignorance and superstition were in full force, and he has many stories to tell of the great emancipation battle ... he saw Sir David Salomons take his seat at Westminster 'by force', he listened to the judicial decision which won for Baron Martin the name of 'Good Samaritan', and when he sought an interview with an Anglican Bishop, to put the case of his much-persecuted race before him, he was met by many profuse apologies for the inability to converse in Hebrew! Times have changed since then, and the position of the Jews in 1889 is very different from what it was in 1845.

When his daily portion of the Commentary on Jonathan ben Usiel's Targum[16] is accomplished, Dr Adler falls back on lighter forms of literature. He even pleads guilty to an occasional novel, but just now is busily engaged with the *Jewish Quarterly* ... points with undisguised satisfaction to the presence of three Hebrew articles ... forty five years ago such topics ... would have excited far less interest than they do at present, nor could the Editor of the *Quarterly* have been induced in the 'forties' to devote more than a third of his available space to purely Jewish subjects.

... He was installed in London as Dr Hirschell's successor and, with Mr. Alfred Wigan's[17] assistance, acquired so complete a mastery over the English language that his sermon on the Crimean War Fast Day was described as 'instinct with the fire of an ancient prophet'. Dr Adler has compiled many learned theological treatises, but the poetic eloquence of his prayers on public events, from the birth of Princess Christian in 1846 down to the joint thanksgiving for victory in Abyssinia and the escape of the Duke of Edinburgh from assassination, may possibly take a firmer hold on the minds of the general public.

... He afterwards moved to Finsbury Square which is still the Chief Rabbi's official residence. It was here that Sir Moses Montefiore paid him his last visit when well advanced in the 'nineties', and, turning the key on his juvenile host, then nearing the 'eighties', tripped lightly down the stairs in order to prevent his old friend escorting him to the door.

... The Chief Rabbi is explaining to you the exact functions of the 'Beth Din' or ecclesiastical court over which he presided for so many years, when the arrival of his son with the week's letters, puts an end to his narrative. A dozen abstruse points of ritual must now be discussed in detail.

The wants of a congregation in the backwoods of British Columbia have to be duly considered; an earnest inquirer is most anxious to learn the precise rendering of that most perplexing text about a deceased wife's sister in the eighteenth chapter of Leviticus according to the new German version of the Pentateuch.

Lord Salisbury has referred to the Chief Rabbi a petition addressed to the Queen by a Bessarabian Jew to send back his son-in-law, who is supposed to be in Montreal; and the questions concerning succession are scarcely less intricate than those relating to ceremonial. When the reports about new synagogues at Hammersmith, Hampstead, Nottingham and Northampton and the Jews' College have been gone through there will still be several decisions of the Hebrew Courts of Arches[18] to revise; several epitaphs on deceased worthies have also to be drafted, and there are equally large bundles of correspondence relating to the propriety of Lord Mayor Isaacs using his state-coach on Saturday,[19] and the progress of the Russian refugee students at Geneva. Dr Adler and his son have a great deal to settle before nightfall.

... The Chief Rabbi of today is something more than the head of the Hebrew faith throughout the British Empire. The extent of his dominions gives him a power very much akin to that of the Pope, and Rabbis in all parts of the world have come to regard the offices in Finsbury Square as their Vatican, with the little house at Brighton as its annexe and sanctum sanctorum.

Dr Adler's manifold occupations necessitate his rising at an early hour, and his only luxuries are *The Times*, a brief siesta and an occasional game of chess. The air of Brighton is his principal medicine; and on fine days strangers turn to gaze at the venerable old man, in the garb of a country clergyman, enjoying the sunshine on one of the Queens Gardens seats, or walking leisurely towards the pier, accompanied by a joyous group of great grandchildren.

... The era of legal emancipation has also been one of material prosperity and progress, and no living man has contributed more to all that has been achieved for the well-being of those whom he always calls his 'brethren' than the patriarch who now affectionately bids you farewell. You have scarcely quitted the oratory when Nathan Adler commences to peruse, with eyes undimmed by age, the first of the papers carefully arranged before him by his son, who has inherited so large a share of his characteristic energy, strength of purpose, and administrative ability.

It was in 1889 that one of his last links with his time in Hanover came to an end. The Duchess of Cambridge died that year at the age of 91. Adler was now approaching 87 and the end was near. He drove along the sea front on

Friday, 12 January 1890, looking as ever like a country clergyman. He made *havdalah* at the end of Shabbat on 13 January but on the following Sunday week he was very poorly. He continued to study the Talmud and was strong enough to sign a letter congratulating his grandchild on giving birth to a new great-grandchild.

Adler's Hebrew birthday was on 21 January and he died that morning of heart disease. It is always considered a blessing to die on your birthday and he passed away at his home in Brighton at a quarter to nine in the morning, after laying *tefillin* and saying his morning prayers. His sons and daughters had been with him all the night before, as had Joseph Vangelder. His *Ahavat Yehonatan* remained unfinished.

The *tahara* (the ritual cleaning of the body before burial) was carried out by the Chief Rabbi's sons, but he had given specific instructions that Dayan Spiers and Dayan Reinowitz, his colleagues on the Beth Din and friends from the Beth Hamedrash, should be invited to participate. Coincidentally, he died on the same day that the Sephardi Haham, Moses Gaster, married Leah Lucy Friedländer, the daughter of the Jews' College principal, at Bevis Marks. They delayed their honeymoon in order to attend the funeral at the Willesden cemetery, and met the train carrying the body at London Bridge, together with the honorary officers of the United Synagogue.

Lord Rothschild was too ill to attend, but a magnificent wreath from the family arrived 'with every mark of respect from Lord Rothschild and his brothers.' The police cleared the streets round the station and the funeral procession went to Willesden via the Great Synagogue and Bevis Marks. It was a very long procession and the passers-by stood silently as it passed. Many Jews from the City and East End walked all the way to Willesden.

There was a very large attendance. Dr Azriel Hildesheimer came especially from Berlin. There were also condolences from the chief rabbi of France. Adler was buried in the white clerical dress he wore for Rosh Hashanah and Yom Kippur, with his head supported by earth from the Holy Land, which his children had brought back from their visits to the country in earlier years.

Adler's passing was regretted throughout the Jewish community. There were memorial services all over the country. While he had always defended the Orthodox approach to Judaism, he had still managed to do so without alienating large sections of the Reform congregations, and his work as the *Av Beth Din* was held in high regard in the East End.

The following Friday, the *Jewish Chronicle* said in its editorial:

> For ten years fading health had made him for most of his flock a memory rather than a reality, but it was the memory of a good old

> man who practised the Judaism he preached and who loved his community with a truly paternal love. The very bravery with which he clung to his official duties and his literary occupations, in spite of the infirmities of advanced age, had something pathetic about it which still further strengthened the admiration and affection in which he was held.[20]

This wasn't the man *The World* had met just a few months before his death, but it was the public image in the community.

Hermann Adler was a shoo-in to succeed his father and was installed on 23 June 1891. His pleasure at taking office was, however, marred by no less than four unhappy deaths that year. In February his stepmother, Celestine, died at the age of 69 with Elkan at her bedside. She was nearly blind because of the effect of cataracts and had suffered from gout for many years, as well as heart trouble and kidney disease. So her death was not as great a shock as that, only a month later, of her daughter, Becky, who was only 26.

Hermann's sister and the mother of three small boys, Rebecca was married in 1887 to a Dutch merchant and was very popular as a kindly and sparkling personality. That is well proven by the letters she wrote when she was looking after her father in Brighton towards the end of his life. Unhappily, after giving birth to her third child, she contracted puerperal fever and died soon after, on the same day as her son was circumcised.

Carl Lehfeld, Celestine's brother also died at the age of 81. He had been a very prominent Berlin physician and was awarded several Prussian knighthoods. In December that year another relative, Henry Solomon, died of erysipelas. Today it is easily cured with penicillin, but, as with Frederick the Great, it was fatal before the great invention, and carried off one of the most charitable of men in the Jewish community. Sarah, his wife, died at 77 in 1907, mourned by her nine children, and equally highly regarded for her charitable work.

1891 was really a very bad year. One of Adler's most noted protégés, Rev. Henry Berkowitz, also died. He had come to London at the same time as the Chief Rabbi and Adler employed him to teach his children, so that he became part of the household. When he left, he started a school in Gravesend and, with it, a synagogue which he financed entirely on his own, and which the Chief Rabbi consecrated. So popular did he become in the town, where he founded a soup kitchen and worked hard for the old people, that he was elected Mayor in 1887. He never forgot Adler's kindness to a young immigrant and they remained firm friends over the years.

Joseph Vangelder ended his life in a Home for Aged Jews in Hackney. He remained devoted to his Judaism, as was noted in July 1898 when the residents of the home were invited to a garden party. Vangelder turned down the invitation on the grounds that he doubted whether garden parties were permitted during the Three Weeks, an annual mourning period to commemorate the destruction of the Temple in Jerusalem.

The relationship of Adler and Montefiore had been instrumental in establishing the Chief Rabbi's unquestioned authority, but Hermann Adler had a more difficult task in replicating it with the leaders of the United Synagogue. In April 1890 Lord Rothschild, as president of the United Synagogue, was asked to call a conference to see whether all the various strands of the Jewish community could agree to come together under the nominal headship of Hermann Adler. This came to nothing as the Sephardim and the Reform did not take up the invitation, though the new Federation of Synagogues took the opportunity to link itself closer to the older United Synagogue body. Hermann Adler objected strongly to the whole idea. He made it clear that that he would accept no limitation on his powers and that included being independent of the Beth Din. He was particularly aggrieved at the suggestion that there should be a council of the various sections of the community to advise him on spiritual matters.

This idea of an advisory council would come up on future occasions, as it had in 1844, but the lay leaders never managed to bring it into play. In 1890 the Executive of the United Synagogue gave in.

Notes

1. *Jewish Chronicle*, 23 June 1880, p.4.
2. Ibid.
3. *Jewish Chronicle*, 5 March 1880, p.11.
4. Adler papers, London Metropolitan Archives.
5. Ibid.
6. Rabbi Raymond Apple, Nathan Marcus Adler lecture.
7. From the family who popularised the Christmas card, postcards, cardboard jigsaw puzzles and Valentine cards.
8. Israel Finestein, *Scenes and Personalities in Anglo-Jewry 1800–2000* (London: Vallentine Mitchell, 2002).
9. Adler papers, London Metropolitan Archives.
10. A good deal of Adler's correspondence is housed in the archive of the Jewish Theological College in New York. The letters reproduced in this chapter are from that source.
11. Rabbi Raymond Apple, Lecture to the JHSE Israel branch, 2014.
12. A thirteen-volume commentary on the Bible and Apocrypha commissioned by the Speaker of the House of Commons, John Denson, the work of thirty top Church of England scholars, spanning eighteen years of work in nearly 8,000 pages. It was written to defend the truth of the Bible and refute its critics.
13. Cambridge University Press, 1883, edited by Rev. William Henry Lowe, Christian Hebraist and Lecturer of Hebrew at Cambridge.

14. A commerzienrath was an honorary title used in the German Empire to denote a commercial advisor to the Kaiser.
15. Critics of Jews and Judaism.
16. *Targum Yehonaton* was an Aramaic translation of the Prophets. Adler's unfinished commentary was similar to his work on *Targum Onkelos Netinah Le-Ger.*
17. Alfred Sydney Wigan (1814–78) was a successful actor-manager in various theatres in London.
18. The Court of Arches is the Court of Appeal of the Church of England at Canterbury. Therefore, the Hebrew Court of Appeal refers to the Beth Din.
19. Sir Henry Isaacs became Lord Mayor of London in 1889.
20. *Jewish Chronicle*, 29 January 1890.

13

Epilogue

In his last years in Brighton, Adler had plenty of time to review his career and he would have been pleased if he could have read the obituary in the *Jewish Quarterly Review* in February 1890.[1] It said:

> Dr Adler's private and official life was the realisation [of his programme]. He was himself an example of true and genuine piety; taught in impressive sermons the truths of our religion; took a lively interest in the educational institutions of our community; watched over the places of worship, and preserved in them the spirit of devotion and attachment to the Law; promoted the amalgamation of the Synagogues under his jurisdiction into the United Synagogue; and lastly became the object of love and veneration, not only to his own congregation but to all who had the opportunity to come in contact with him.
>
> In evidence of this statement I quote from 'A tribute to the Memory of the Venerable Rabbi, from a Member of the Berkeley Street congregation (*Jewish Chronicle*, January 29th 1890):-
>
> 'However differently some of us may have been trained in our views of Judaism from the conceptions which he (Dr Adler) represented, all of us who are attached to our religion and our race feel that in him has passed away one of the purest and one of the most cultured exemplars of them which the present century has produced as man as well as an Israelite and a Rabbi, the personality of Dr N.M. Adler reflected those finer emotions of the ancient faith which are sadly becoming more and more rare. He was ready to recognize fellowship with any other Israelite in whom he perceived a devout intention, even though he might differ from a particular method. He never repelled one – he invariably attracted. He represented Judaism in England in a manner that we all rejoice about when we contemplate it. The Chief Rabbi of England is now a household word, known throughout the country among every denomination, and associated with scholarship, with profound piety, and with dignity which command the universal regard of all sections of Englishmen.'

Even for an obituary, this is pretty high praise, but what Adler might have particularly appreciated is that the *Jewish Quarterly Review* missed the central point, which was that Adler was a very tough operator in his chosen field. He was also an outright winner when it came to achieving the great majority of his objectives. It's all very well being a man of true and genuine piety, taking an interest, and watching over synagogues, but if, at the end of the day, your flock heads off in a different direction, you have failed in what really matters. Adler, from his earliest days, had been taught how to win.

He was brought up in a world where Jews suffered discrimination, where they were regarded as second class citizens at best, and where there was little they could do about the oppression. For over sixty years Adler was the chief rabbi in Oldenburg, Hanover and Britain and the Empire. The treatment of the Jews was much worse in Germany than in Britain, but when he arrived in 1845 there was still a need for the right approach to Jews and Jewish problems in the United Kingdom. The problem was made greater because the community expanded largely through penniless migrants from the Continent.

In spite of the problems, Adler improved the status of his congregations throughout the country, and never lost an important battle within his community. During his lifetime he saw the position of the Jews improve in all three jurisdictions where he was the spiritual leader. It was true that power might always lie with others in non-spiritual matters, if they wished to exercise it; the rulers, the great families, the wealthy and famous in his own community.

If he was going to win, he had to disarm the opposition. He had to be a consummate diplomat and that, indeed, was what he became. He set out to earn love and veneration at least partly to disguise the fact that his influence was not based on wealth or family connections. He said as much in the sermon he gave at his installation in the Great Synagogue.

The reason why he has been nearly forgotten is equally clear: he didn't care if somebody else got the credit for his achievements. He offered the bauble of credit as a way of disarming opposition to his wishes. It was well known that if there were serious disagreements within the community, Adler was likely to appeal 'Let there be peace for my sake'. Everybody could then agree, and get the congratulations for enabling there to be peace.

Another way of dealing with the situation would have been for Adler to say 'Do what I tell you'. It would have had the same effect, but it would have led to a great deal of resentment and would have helped to create an opposition party. Those who disagreed with Adler during his ministry were more likely to grumble than to seek to get him overruled.

One of the clearest examples of his methodology is the order of prayer and the content of the prayer book in services throughout the Jewish community to this day. They are to be found in the Singer Prayer Book and Simeon Singer is famous throughout the English speaking Jewish world for its creation. Only the truth was that almost every part of the book was supervised by Adler, until he died just before it was completed. He provided Singer with the protection of the authority of the chief rabbi's office but he did more. Singer, himself, in the first edition of the book, acknowledged: 'As it was practically complete before the death of the late Dr N.M. Adler, it was enabled to receive, and to be issued with the stamp of his sanction and authorisation.'

Singer has always been given the credit but it was described as 'The Authorised Daily Prayer Book'; Adler got the version he wanted which would become the standard all over the country. The first edition even had a dark blue cover, so that it resembled the Book of Common Prayer to be found on the pews of English churches. Acceptability by association.

When the forms of service were reviewed by a powerful lay body in 1879, ten years before the Singer publication, Adler had only agreed to changes on relative minutiae. Very occasionally he said he agreed to minor changes with reluctance, but the vast body of the rules and regulations remained untouched and are enshrined in the book. In giving way, Adler could make the case that he was flexible, but Jewish law and tradition were safe in his care. Singer wasn't in any way the decision maker, and wouldn't have expected to be in Adler's last years.

The Singer Prayer Book was one of the last of his great achievements. As he had always wanted to coax the synagogues to his way of thinking, before the prayer book it still meant that many groups had practices which were unique to their congregation. The difficult question was how to bring them all into line without being dictatorial. Anything which came from his office could be criticized as such, but Simeon Singer was the new generation, just over 40, the minister of the prestigious New West End Synagogue, a rabbi in his own right, the apparently modern image and very popular. He was also totally reliable, loyal and dependable.

If the new prayer book carried Singer's name, rather than Adler's, there was a better chance of it being accepted. Moreover it was a book, not a set of rules. The statutory service was enshrined in the book, but not the *minhag* of the individual community, so the book could be a force for unity. Which, effectively, was what happened time and again.

The authority of the office of chief rabbi was massively strengthened by Adler's ministry. The only serious campaign to undermine it came in Manchester, but the attempt by Schiller-Szinessy to create local chief rabbis in the provinces came to nothing. Such officials would have been popular with the provincial lay leaders, who would have expected a greater degree of influence as a result, but they would have fatally undermined the power of the potentially varying decisions which would have emerged. Over the years Adler's title evolved as part of Britain's ecclesiastical leadership. Where Henrietta's death certificate had identified him by the ancient title of the High Priest of the Jews, Celestine's simply described him as the chief rabbi; but regardless of his title, Adler was increasingly seen as the Jewish authority figure.

At the outset of Adler's ministry, it was settled that only the chief rabbi could make decisions on religious questions for the provinces. Not even the London Beth Din had the authority to do so. Moreover, his decisions were binding. Adler might have appealed for their approval on the grounds that they would bring the community peace, but if that hadn't worked, his decisions would still have been the decisive factor if he chose to enforce them. There were a few occasions when he temporised, particularly in Manchester, but normally a word from him was sufficient.

For almost his entire ministry in London, the acknowledged lay head of the community was Sir Moses Montefiore, but Montefiore never tried to make religious decisions without obtaining Adler's rulings and giving them his full support. In the same way, many worthies got the credit for the creation of the United Synagogue, but it was Adler who had nudged the disparate leaders of the constituent synagogues into agreeing to coalesce into a united body.

The sticking point of its creation in the first place was not its desirability and logical rationale; that could hardly be denied. It was the likelihood that, if it came about, there would be congregational leaders who might lose some of their sovereignty. Adler fully realized the importance the lay figures attached to their status. So long as they got the credit, and as long as Adler's decisions could be justified with the authority of the *din*, the Honorary Officers might grumble about aspects of the services they disliked, but at the end of the day, it would be no more than that. Unfortunately, some lay leaders behaved like petty tyrants and Adler was the only religious figure who could stand up to them.

The local ministers of the congregations remained the servants of the communities, inadequately paid and treated with less than the courtesy and respect which applied to the vicars of the Church of England. Such authority as they possessed rested to a large extent on the power of the chief rabbi, and the respect and affection which he won from the communities by hard work, good judgement and great learning, did raise the status of the local religious officers.

Although Adler made some progress in the status and learning of his ministers, one Principal of Jews College, Adolph Büchler, admittedly not well known for the temperance of his language, described the clergy as: 'half-baked products of unsuccessful training imposed upon a helpless congregation'.[2] Solomon Schechter, another trenchant critic, who would eventually take over the Jewish Theological Seminary in New York, called the average British minister:

> The most hard-worked man ... labouring under a cruel system, reducing man to a mere plaything of politico-economic forces ... rapidly losing touch with the venerable rabbi of Jewish tradition, whose chief office was to teach and to learn Torah. With us the duty of learning ... seems to be of the least moment in the life of the minister ... In his capacity as full Reverend, he is expected to divide his time between the offices of cantor, prayer, preacher, bookkeeper, debt-collector, almoner and social agitator ... Occasionally rumour spreads about some minister, that he neglects his duty to his congregation, through his being strictly addicted to Jewish learning. But such rumours often turn out to be sheer malice.[3]

Adler had to hold the line and, certainly, he didn't always win when trying to marry Jewish and British law. He also lost battles with the likes of Sir David Salomon. At the end of the day, though, he won massively more than he lost and he achieved his major aims. In view of his health, it could have been suggested that he stand down in 1879 rather than simply delegate some of his tasks to his son. This was never suggested. As long as he lived, the vast majority of the community wanted him to remain in office. This, in itself, was a very high compliment.

In 1891 the United Synagogue Council commented that: 'The visitation of Provincial Synagogues and Schools is exclusively the function and duty of the Chief Rabbi, as is the visitation of a diocese by its bishop.'[4] It was a convenient analogy but, of course, Adler had not been taught by the church. In England he continued to carry out the pastoral duties of a German Landrabbiner, accepting responsibility for the well-being of all his congregations

Even when his objectives were likely to be nullified by the government, Adler often found a way round. The United Synagogue Act did not grant the chief rabbi the ultimate authority in the community. The Deed of Foundation of the United Synagogue, which emerged as a consequence, did. The Marriage Bill might have forbidden the marriage of an uncle and a niece; marriages of that nature were, therefore, arranged overseas.

It wasn't just in his public life that Adler was a winner. He had two exceptional wives and his eight children all survived him. What was more the offspring became strong supporters of Orthodox institutions. The office of chief rabbi is very much a full-time job. It is difficult to find the time for the children as well, as some other chief rabbis discovered to their infinite regret, but there was no backsliding in the Adler family.

What was more Adler ensured the continuation of his policies by masterminding his succession. When the time came, Hermann Adler was the obvious choice to take over from his father. In addition to all his other sterling qualities, he was only a few years away from being born in England. It would only be because of the untimely death of Hermann Adler's son, Rev. Solomon Alfred Adler, that the family dynasty didn't have the chance to continue. It ended a family connection with the British chief rabbinate which had included every occupant of the office since the first, Aaron Hart, in 1705. All had been descended from the Dutch rabbi Zevi Ashkenazi.

If Hermann Adler had a weakness, it was the general perception that he was more at home in the West End than the East End. He was an expert at fitting in with the Establishment – Edward VII called him 'My Chief Rabbi' but he was too grand a figure for the impoverished masses in the East End. He certainly tried to reach out to them. At the memorial service in 1893 for Dayan Jacob Reinowitz, the synagogue chosen was in the East End and, as most of the congregation were from abroad, Adler gave his sermon in Yiddish. It wasn't just to communicate better; it was to try to prove his membership and affiliation with the Jews who were becoming the numerical majority of the community. In the East End, however, he was simply not considered 'one of us'.

Yiddish was a source of embarrassment for those who worked so hard for full emancipation. Lord Rothschild, the head of the United Synagogue, was just one of the lay leaders who would have preferred Yiddish to become a dead language as soon as possible. He would tell the delegates electing a new chief rabbi in 1912 that the sooner the 'slang and jargon', as he saw it, of Yiddish was eliminated, the happier he would be.

It was unfair on Yiddish; as a language it is no different from any Western tongue, in that it has a very varied parentage in Greek and Latin words, as well as Hebrew, Aramaic and German. The real objection, which few would honestly protest, was that it was associated with poor people – and it was, therefore, considered common.

In spite of the kind words of the Upper Berkeley Street member about Adler in the *Jewish Quarterly Review*, the progressive movement's strongest opponent was the Chief Rabbi. Communities like Upper Berkeley Street had many attractions. Some of the most important Jewish families were members; the services were shorter and more decorous and the statutory religious demands on the members were less onerous. It was an attractive option.

On various occasions throughout his ministry, Adler crossed swords with David Woolf Marks. Marks put forward arguments based on his reading of the Bible and the Talmud, while Adler defended Orthodox Judaism. The case for the progressive movement needed, however, to be based on the community's acceptance of an untraditional approach, and a socially unacceptable move by congregants to a smaller and less significant grouping.

Few people considered themselves intellectually capable of judging the arguments. They were faced with two powerful advocates, both of whom had attractive personalities. Even Hermann Adler was impressed by Marks. He spoke of:

> The power, the fascination and the earnestness of this eloquent preacher ... Far beyond the fascination of his speech was the fascination of his personality and the kindliness of manner ... And then how great was the power he wielded in his contact with those outside our community.

Where Nathan Marcus Adler scored over Marks was within the wider Jewish world. He wasn't a university professor but he could help his communities in very many ways and Marks couldn't offer them anything other than a case for amendments to the ritual and the *mitzvoth*. If Adler had been less supportive of his congregations it might have been enough, but when he was consistently described as revered, it was because he had made sure that so many members of his flock were in his debt. Paradoxically, Adler's approach was itself suspect in the eyes of large number of the immigrant community.

It was different overseas where large segments of the German and American communities changed their allegiance from Orthodox to Reform. That didn't happen in Britain or the Empire and it hasn't happened since Adler died. In his lifetime, besides Upper Berkeley Street and the small congregation in Manchester, the only Reform synagogue to emerge was in Bradford; the specific result of the upbringing of the majority of the members on the Continent. Even so, Bradford didn't follow the practices of Upper Berkeley Street.

During his lifetime David Woolf Marks was rewarded for his oratory with much respect, but he did not gain a large following in the community for his views. He lost out to Adler and, as the *Jewish Chronicle* said after the Chief Rabbi's death:

> Had a man of smaller ability and with a less commanding personality occupied the rabbinic chair, it is probable that the wholesale reform and the undesirable extravagances that characterise American Judaism would have found their way into our community.[5]

To an extent, it is true that the failure of the secessionists to make much impact was achieved by Adler turning a blind eye to infractions in the carrying out of the law. The *din* covers almost every area of life. There are rules, for example, about clothing; the subject is referred to as *shatnez*. There is no reference to it in the *Jewish Chronicle* until 1957, but it is just as important a commandment as any other. Adler would state the law, but he would only criticize those who failed to live up to what were generally considered the essentials. As a diplomat, he always tried to involve the individual congregations in considering and approving his decisions. They became joint decisions rather than edicts, but in reserve there was always the appeal for peace.

To the outside world there was surprise at the extent of his jurisdiction. *The Times*, reporting his funeral, pointed out that even areas outside the Empire acknowledged his authority, like the Jews in the Transvaal and the treaty ports in Japan. His constant aim to make and keep the peace in the British community also came in for much praise: 'His personal influence was steadily executed to induce the seceders and the larger body to work together for charitable purposes, and there is no bitterness in the schism now.'[6]

There were areas where he could only lay and nurse the foundations. Education was one of these. The development of schooling for the children within the communities was always high on his list of priorities. He would have preferred to have been the ultimate religious authority in all of them. He didn't achieve that with the largest school, JFS, but it was looked after by the Rothschilds and grew mightily throughout the century. If that hadn't been the case, he might not have accepted the situation so readily.

His Jews' College School was a failure because the community wouldn't support it. Nevertheless, the number of day schools attached to synagogues increased widely during his ministry and he persuaded many of his provincial supporters to finance their operations. The credit for the growth of Jewish faith schools today is rightly given to Rabbi Dr Solomon Schonfeld and Chief Rabbi Immanuel Jakobovits, but they were building on foundations first laid down by Adler.

Ironically, where he was less successful was in obtaining financial support for his own office. This was really, of course, the responsibility of the lay leaders of the community to produce, and a report for the United Synagogue in 1871 highlighted the shortcomings:

> There were in all 27 congregations who, at the outset, promised to contribute: five metropolitan, 21 provincial and one Colonial. Of these originally contributing Congregations, 9 Provincial and one Colonial have ceased to pay ...; four congregations which contributed later, have also ceased to do so. There are several congregations who pay irregularly, and only 11 Provincial Congregations whose payments are as regular as the Metropolitan Congregations ... There are no fewer than 21 provincial and 15 Colonial Congregations participating in the benefits of the Chief Rabbi's supervision who have never contributed to the fund.[7]

The situation had hardly improved twenty years later when the United Synagogue returned to the subject in 1891. As everybody knew, though, there was little the United Synagogue could do except appeal to the consciences of the missing supporters:

> The contribution made by the Council towards the maintenance of the Office of the Chief Rabbi is far in excess of what the United Synagogue should be called upon to pay, and the Executive Committee venture to express the hope that Congregations will respond in a becoming and liberal manner to the appeal which they propose should be addressed to them.[8]

To a considerable extent, the United Synagogue appealed in vain. Whether communities contributed to his office or not, however, Adler was always going to help any congregation if he was asked to do so. It was also to his advantage that he arrived in Britain at the same time as the development of the railways which made it much easier to get around the country. This meant that the Chief Rabbi didn't have to remain a distant figure in London. Adler visited his communities, raised money for them, found them officials and settled their differences.

He also benefited from arriving at a time when Prince Albert had made German culture more fashionable. Adler's efficient, bureaucratic approach fitted in well with this trend. It is often forgotten that Britain's traditional ally was Germany. The battle of Waterloo was won because the Prussian army turned up in the nick of time. It was France against whom Britain clashed for much of the eighteenth century and the Napoleonic wars.

Allied to all these factors were the points the *Jewish Quarterly Review* made. Adler was a fine speaker, a thoroughly approachable leader, a kindly man and a friend of the poor as well as the rich. He would be found in slums as well as in mansions.

Adler also set down the wide scope of the chief rabbinate for those who came after him to follow; as the committee appointed to find his successor said:

> Synagogues outside the United Synagogue ... are constantly calling upon the Chief Rabbi to use his influence in the collection of funds towards building new synagogues and towards the purchase of Cemeteries, inviting him to consecrate their edifices and to examine their schools. They participate in all the advantages of the Chief Rabbi's supervision; he communicates with them on all celebrations which have communal interest; they write to him continually concerning their local affairs; they invoke his decision on religious questions; they rely on him to find and examine suitable officials as Preachers, readers, teachers, and *shochetim*, and they appeal to him for his advice on every conceivable occasion.[9]

There have been two concepts associated with Adler; *Minhag Anglia* and Adlerism. The term *Minhag Anglia* does not appear in the *Jewish Chronicle* until 1924 when it is discussed by Rabbi Arnold Mishcon in terms of the Sabbath evening prayers and the relevance of *piyutim* (liturgical prayers).[10] There is no suggestion that a new form of organization, still less Judaism, had been created by Adler.

So long as the *din* remained paramount, Adler was prepared to accept a wide range of unimportant *minhagim* (local practices). Adler laid the foundations for the majority of the middle-of-the-road Jewish community in Britain to remain in the Orthodox fold, but his method of achieving this was widely misunderstood. In 1891 the *Jewish Chronicle* summed up the prevalent belief that the Adlers:

> gave their name to a regime, to an era ... The system of Rabbinate which had long come to be known as 'Adlerism', the keynote of which was the close consolidation of religious government and the concentration of ecclesiastical control ... If, therefore, 'Adlerism' had its faults and its drawbacks ... it has formed a basis on which can now be safely laid a system more fitted to Anglo-Jewry as it is.[11]

In suggesting it was empire building on Adler's part, the view was unfair. Before Adler's time there were few sizeable Jewish communities outside London. The centralization of ecclesiastical control had hardly been an issue when almost all the Jews lived in the capital. Chief rabbis like Aaron Hart, Hart Lyon and David Tevele Schiff were always happy to give advice and help to provincial communities, but they were, basically, London rabbis, paid by the London congregations and working primarily on their affairs.

Centralization became necessary in Adler's time for many reasons: primarily, to ensure that rulings on Jewish status in provincial communities were acceptable around the world; to facilitate career paths for synagogue officials around the country and elsewhere in the Empire; to help raise money for new buildings and to encourage local charities. With the expansion of the community to many new parts of the country, if Adlerism hadn't existed, it would have needed to be invented.

If Adlerism was anything, it was a flexible Orthodox Judaism designed to keep the community Orthodox and together. Adler considered it far more important to achieve that, rather than to insist on high standards of observance. The *Jewish Chronicle* anticipated changes in religious government or ecclesiastical control in the future, but it wouldn't happen. The system would remain intact, simply because the *din* and traditional Judaism wouldn't alter.

Some very peripheral changes did occur. In appearance Adler was often compared to a country clergyman, as against wearing the flowing robes of his predecessors, but there is nothing in the *din* against adopting the ecclesiastical robes of the general community. Clerical garb in England originally took its model from academic dress and, with regard to Jewish ministers, David Tevele Schiff adopted that style of dress first. The traditional names of the synagogue officers were anglicized in Adler's time, so that *parnassim* became wardens, *k'leikodesh* became clergy, *hazanim* were called precentors and *shammashim* became beadles. In Adler's time it became permissible for the pulpit to be separated from the *bimah*, the reading desk. It made the proceedings easier to see and hear, though it might still be difficult for those in the ladies gallery.

The wardens in many synagogues would take to wearing top hats and, on Yom Kippur, might even put on evening dress. The ministers would be clean shaven with neatly trimmed beards, as against the traditional full beards of old-time continental rabbis, but the ritual was safe with Adler. As the minister of the East London Synagogue, Joseph Frederick Stern, said: 'The clerical garb of the Adlerian minister was as much a symbol of social service as of the teacher.'

The system became known much later as *Minhag Anglia*, but nothing fundamental was altered. The community simply admired the British and wanted to be like them, as long as the ritual remained within the *din*. From the time the Ashkenazim started to arrive in the late seventeenth century, they had retained the German and Polish ritual, and that didn't change.

As far as the expression *Minhag Anglia* is concerned, a *minhag* is a firmly established Jewish procedure. *Anglia* is the late Latin name for England. So why *Anglia*? Why not English *Minhag*? The title of Minhag Poland is used. Because in Victorian times, Latin was the yardstick for culture. It distinguished the class act from the humdrum. Used for all the Establishment's mottos, taught in all the best schools, it didn't matter how clever you were, if you couldn't pass the Latin exam (Littlego), you couldn't get into Cambridge. An appreciation of Latin was one of the passwords to social acceptance, because it belonged to the upper classes and didn't mean a thing to the man-in-the-street.

Put '*Minhag*' and '*Anglia*' together in Victorian times and you get a pretentious attempt to divorce the procedures of British Jewry from the perceived lower-class attributes of the followers of the specifically German and Polish rites in the East End. *Minhag Anglia* is said to be epitomized by the *Singer Prayer Book*, but the foreword to that book acknowledges that it is based on those continental traditions, as the prayers always had been among the Ashkenazim in Britain.

The upwardly mobile members of the Ashkenazi Jewish community didn't want to be associated with the East End. They were anxious to divorce themselves from their poverty-stricken family origins. Their common dislike of Yiddish, despite its very rich literary heritage, was based on their anxiety to be accepted as equals by their fellow citizens. Certainly, speaking fluent Yiddish was not likely to be an advantage if they wanted to join a London Club or get an invitation to a society party. Jackie Mason is right when he says that many of his co-religionists do not like his humour because it is too Jewish. This inferiority complex was quite unnecessary; the laws of Judaism had been setting civilized standards of behaviour when most of the other cultures in Biblical times had been primitive in the extreme. Adler would have had little time for the concept of *Minhag Anglia*. In fact, the expression '*Minhag Anglia*' does not appear in the *Jewish Chronicle* index during Adler's ministry.

He was in office in Britain long enough to become an institution and, if he is often forgotten today, there is still Adler Street in the East End of London named after the family. The results of his work, though, are still very much to be found in the community he served with such diligence. 'He was instrumental in maintaining the nominal loyalty of the overwhelming majority of Anglo-Jewry throughout the Victorian period and was able to serve as the community's unchallenged spiritual leader for over 40 years.'[12] As far as the 'nominal loyalty' was concerned, for Jews there was always the chance to do better tomorrow. During his ministry that possibility was down to Nathan Marcus Adler. The core influence of Adler on the Jewish community in Britain has lasted for over a century since his death, even though he has been largely forgotten. It is a result that would have delighted him.

In assessing what he achieved, the first consideration must be the very low level from which he started. Even after being in office for five years, there were still only 3,000 Jews praying in synagogue on the Sabbath in 1851. In spite of all the lip-service that was paid to the desirability of home-grown religious leaders, there still wasn't anyone born in England who was fit to be made a dayan after Adler had been in office for twenty-five years.

Furthermore, the vast majority of the Jewish middle classes wouldn't send their youngsters to the new Jews' College and the general level of observance of the *mitzvoth* was equally low. The financial help he got from synagogues for his educational efforts was pitiful. A very considerable proportion of the original community were more interested in being accepted as equals by the general population than they were in perpetuating traditional Judaism.

Adler's achievement was to ensure the community didn't buckle under these disintegration pressures. It was to lay a solid foundation on which his successors could build; a foundation of more synagogues, more schools, better ministers and a more committed community.

The wording on his grave sums up his standing and the way he successfully trod the line between his British and Jewish responsibilities:

> In Memory of the Very Revd Dr Nathan Marcus Adler. For forty-five years the revered and beloved Chief Rabbi of the United Hebrew Congregations of the British Empire. His soul returned on high on January 21st 5650.

Notes

1. *Jewish Quarterly Review*, February 1890, p.378.
2. Annual Report, Jews' College.
3. 'Four Epistles to the Jews of England', *Jewish Chronicle*, 27 December 1912, p.18.
4. Aubrey Newman, 'The Chief Rabbinate and the Provinces', in Jonathan Sacks (ed.), *Tradition and Transition: Essays Presented to Chief Rabbi Sir Immanuel Jakobovits to Celebrate Twenty Year in Office* (London: Jews College Publications, 1986), p.219.
5. *Jewish Chronicle*, 30 January 1890.
6. *The Times*, 24 January 1890, p.5.
7. Newman, 'The Chief Rabbinate and the Provinces', p.219.
8. Ibid., p.222.
9. Ibid., p.219.
10. *Jewish Chronicle*, 21 March 1924, p.18.
11. *Jewish Chronicle*, 21 July 1891.
12. Steven Singer, *Orthodox Judaism in Early Victorian London, 1840–1858* (New York: Yeshiva University, 1981).

Appendix A

Nathan Marcus Adler Genealogy

Great Uncle David Tevele Schiff (1722–91) British Chief Rabbi.
Issaachar Beer Adler married Jente Rothschild.
Marcus Beer Adler (c.1745–1834) married Rebecca Frankel (1767–1861), daughter of the Chief Rabbi of Hanau.

Marcus and Rebecca had:

> Beer Marcus (1784–1866), who married Esther, daughter of Rabbi Hirsch Worms, sister of Henrietta
> Gabriel, Chief Rabbi of Schwarzwald (1788–1859)
> Nathan Marcus Adler, Chief Rabbi of England (1803–90)
> Hundchen who married Jacob Budge.
> Hermann
> Benjamin

Nathan Marcus Adler married Henrietta Rachel Hitzel Worms (1800–53). Henrietta was the sister of Baron Solomon Benedict de Worms, father of Lord Pirbright. She was the daughter of Jeanette von Rothschild, sister of Nathan Mayer Rothschild and niece of Nathan Mayer Rothschild. Jeanette's father was Meyer Amschel Rothschild.

Nathan and Henrietta had:

> Sarah (1830–1907), who married Henry Solomon.
> Jeanette (Yenta) (1832–c.1900), who married Rabbi Asher Stern, Chief Rabbi of Hamburg
> Minna (1833–1906), who married Jacob Israel, Berlin linen factory and general merchant
> Marcus (1837–1911), who married Emma Hersh and Fanny Myers (1838–87)
> Hermann (1839–1911), who married Rachel Joseph and succeeded Nathan Marcus Adler as Chief Rabbi

Nathan Marcus Adler's second wife was Celestine Lehfeld (1821–91), sister of Dr Carl Lehfeld.
Nathan and Celestine had:
Ida (1859–1933) who married Magnus Levie Schaap
Elkan (1861–1946), solicitor, bibliophile and communal leader
Rebecca Judith (1866–1890).

Appendix B

Nathan Marcus Adler's Inaugural Sermon, when Installed as the Chief Rabbi at the Great Synagogue, London on 8 July 1845

(Translated from the German by Dr Barnard Van Oven)

My Beloved Brethren,

It is with a mind deeply moved by mingled feelings of bashfulness and timidity, that I commence my first address to you; and if you will reflect on the great change which the last few days has wrought in my position, you will acknowledge that such feelings are fully justified. But ten days since, I stood in my native city; my words were addressed to the ears and hearts of those who had known me from my youth, and who were cognisant of every particular of my life and my labours.

I, too, could rely on their attachment and could lay claim to their love. But this day I stand up, for the first time in this great capital of the world, a stranger in the midst of a strange assemblage, whose love I have yet to gain – in the midst of a congregation which comprises men and women, on whom the eyes of all Israel, nay of all the world, are now resting, who constitute the pride and the hope of my people. Must not such a scene make me feel abashed?

There, too, I addressed my hearers in their mother-tongue. My words could not be misunderstood. They passed direct from heart to heart, from mind to mind; but here I am as yet constrained (until practice shall conquer difficulties) to speak to you in the German language. How easily may my words be unfavourably received, how readily miss the road to your hearts; and shall such thoughts not make me tremble? Or if I cast my looks backward, and reflect that I am now in a place where so many pious, learned and noble men have already spoken, taught, striven and laboured, amongst whom I will only name my uncle and predecessor, who for forty years guided his flock with faithfulness and love – whose name and wisdom are still cherished in Israel [David Tevele Schiff] – must not such reflections make me anxious.

Or if I look onward, and reflect that I enter upon a sphere of action, on the due performance of which the spiritual welfare of so many thousands, both near and far, depends – of parents and of children, of great and of small; and if I measure against those many and high duties the feebleness of my powers, the narrow limits of my capabilities, must not my heart be most deeply and solemnly moved – must I not feel myself fearfully embarrassed to select the best mode of address? But I put my trust in Him, who, from my youth upwards, hath ever been to me a staff, a support, and a help.

I put my trust in Him who most delighteth to give aid to the feeble, because so shall they, by his power, become strong. I put my trust in Him who said to the priest 'And they shall put my name upon the children of Israel, and I will bless them'. I put my trust in Him who said unto Jeremiah, 'Fear thou not for I am with thee'; who, through the mouth of the wise, recommends 'to cast thy mental bread upon the waters'; to 'give a portion to seven, and also to eight; for thou knowest not what evil shall be upon earth'.

I trust in those friendly expressions with which you have but just now gladdened my heart. I trust that you will meet my timidity with love; and so add to my weak words a force and power which I am unable to give to them. Therefore, I beseech you, allow me shortly to explain, 'With what purpose, and with what hopes, a minister enters on the duties of his sacred office.'

These purposes and hopes are expressed in a passage of the prophet, Zechariah, which impressed itself strongly on my mind when you honoured me by your choice. 'Thus saith the Lord of Hosts, If thou wilt walk in my ways, and if thou wilt keep my charge, then thou shall also judge my house, and shalt also keep my courts; and I will give thee admission to walk among those that stand by.' After the prophet had been promised that the Lord would renew the splendour of the first temple in a second – after the prophet had already in spirit beheld that temple, the splendid golden ornaments, the candelabra, and the numerous lamps, then did the Lord show to him by what means the glories of the new temple should be brought about – by the high-priest Joshua.

The prophet saw how he would be inducted into office – how his filthy garments would be removed, and his clean vestments put on – saw how his opponents would point to his wants, defects, and imperfections – how the Lord would reprove them, and put forward the high-priest as a brand rescued from the fire. He saw how the angel placed on his head a fair mitre, the symbol of priestly virtue, and said unto him, 'If thou wilt walk in my ways, and if thou wilt keep my charge, then thou shalt also judge my house, and shall also keep my courts; and I will give thee admission to walk among those that stand by.'

Although, my beloved brethren, I am far from daring to compare myself to the high-priest, Joshua, yet I resemble him in his imperfections, for which you must make all due allowance, if I am to fulfil my sacred and important office. I resemble him in the sacred commission given. The words of the text contain all the sacred duties of the high-priest of former days, and which are, with suitable circumstances, to be fulfilled by the minister of our time, as well as the hopes which he hath to cherish. And even I, my brethren, enter on my new office with the following purposes:

1. To walk in the ways of G-d.
2. Truly to maintain His law.
3. To superintend the institutions for education.
4. To watch over the places of worship.
5. And lastly, with a deep hope that I shall make my way into your hearts.

O let my words be deeply implanted in your hearts, that they may there blossom and produce fruit, even sevenfold.

1. To walk in the ways of G-d.

The minister of this day, like the high-priest of old, enters on his office with an intent to walk in the ways of his G-d. In which of the ways of the Lord is man able to walk? How is a feeble mortal, son of earth, able to imitate the Deity? Is it in power? Human power is but weakness. Is it in wisdom? Human wisdom is but folly. Is it in strength? The human arm reaches not far. Is it in justice? Man drinks often of injustice as though it were water. It is only through the goodness of G-d, and his love towards all his creatures, that man can learn to understand, and, as far as his weak powers allow, to imitate him. When the man of G-d desired to know the ways of the Lord, and said 'I beseech thee, shew me thy glory'. G-d answered him, and said, 'I will make all my goodness to pass before thee'.

This, the love of G-d, which is made manifest in the great laws of nature, as in the small ones which affect us personally – which preserves order alike in the great circles of the universe, and in the narrow limits of the circumstances around us – which displays itself in the holy law, in all that it commands or forbids, permits or demands (for all tend alike to promote the welfare of mankind) – this love it was the duty of the high-priest, and is now the duty of the pastor, to know and to proclaim, to seek for, and to inquire into.

Three books which are laid open to his researches, the book of nature, the book of history, and, above all, the book of the law, must be his constant study. He must read in them day and night, must learn them by heart, and take them to his heart. And if man is permitted to acquire but the first elements of this knowledge, the first syllables, or a few letters only, even that will afford him means of comprehending the depth and grandeur of Almighty love, and will lead him onwards to that which is the beginning and end of all wisdom, the fear of G-d. And if man is permitted to perceive but one branch of the tree, but one spark of that flame, but one arm of that stream, by that portion he may judge of the whole, by that single one he may judge of all combined. But he must, as far as he is able, go in the ways of the Lord – he must move about in the commands of G-d; and must, like the priest, love peace and seek for peace.

But how shall the pastor succeed in his efforts, if his own life be not an example – if he point out a path which he does not follow? Can it be more than a false appearance, if his sermons, his knowledge, his labours, are opposed to his actions, or if his deeds and his words stand in opposition to each other? Can he recommend and procure mutual love and peace, if his own conduct be not that of love and charity – if he do not, like a true follower of Aaron, strive to promote peace? How shall he gain followers to the duties of religion, if it is needful that he himself be reminded of them? Ere thou seek to take the splinter from another's eye, remove the mote from thine own.

No, he must himself tread in the desired pathway of the Lord. He must adorn himself before he can adorn others. He must so conduct himself as to make knowledge honourable – he must be filled with sacred love before he can recommend it to others. It is only where warmth of feeling exists, that such warmth can be communicated – only where the spirit of life pervades, that it can be excited, or burst forth in others.

He must cast off his unclean garments before he puts on the clean vestments of others. In one word, investigation and activity, word and deed, conviction and conduct, must go hand in hand; and then surely and silently they will do their work.

And I, my beloved brethren, have a settled purpose to go before you – to lead your footsteps in the ways of the Lord, and to walk therein as I have done from my earliest youth. The expression may sound perhaps too boastful to you; nay, it must sound so, if I did not add to it, that it is for you not only to resemble me, but rather to surpass me. When the prophet, with the tongue of fire, was asked 'Whom shall I send, and who will go before us?' then he replied 'I will go before thee'; so I do not venture to assert, that in all the pathways of the Lord I will go before you. Many of you may, will, can, and must, surpass me; but I have taken upon myself the holy resolve to walk in the ways of the Lord, and to guide your steps in the ways of love and peace.

2. Truly to maintain his law.

The minister of this time, like the high-priest of old, enters on the duties of his office with a purpose to watch over all sacred things. It was his duty, as you know, to keep watch over the law, spiritually and actually, from without and from within. The sacred things, the ark and table of the covenant, the showbread, etc. were entrusted to his care. Under his direction the Levites officiated (guardians also of the holy things); but he had also to watch them spiritually, and to determine between things permitted and forbidden, common and holy, clean and unclean. His duty was to protect them from injury, so that no one should, as it were, devour the sacred things.

Man turns to his pastor in all positions of life – in joy and in sorrow – in times of happiness and of misfortune – at the beginning of life and at the closing hour. In his contests against the general enemy, as well as against the inroads of disease; and this is, in many respects in these days, the truly priestly calling – He should be, he must be, the watchman, the guardian, the preserver of the holy law.

It is indeed, very arduous, to take good care of it when some rest their hopes on rapid innovation, and others steadfast adherence to whatever time has sanctified, even although it should be contrary to the law. It is indeed difficult, very difficult, to take good care of it while urged on by some to constant advance, and implored by others to remain immovable. It is indeed difficult in such circumstances to find the golden mean. But if he be seriously resolved to do his duty to G-d and to His holy law, then will he place himself in the watchtower, preserve the sacred inheritance undimmed and uninjured, secure it from all injury, and defend it from every attack.

Yes, on every change in life – on entering the congregation – the celebration of marriage – at the coming in and at the going forth – his voice shall be raised to declare, to watch over, to protect, and to promote the commands of G-d.

In all important circumstances he will judge according to his fullest knowledge, and direct conscientiously. He will distinguish the false from the true, the bad from the good, the wrong from the right, the dark from the light – he will stand between the living and the dead, and bid the religious pestilence to cease. But he will take every thing seriously in his heart, all names inscribed on the tablet of his breast – he will, in all cases, consult the law as the *Urim* and *Thummim* of old; and as that oracle speaks and decides, will he judge and determine.

Yes, my beloved brethren, I also do purpose to become a guardian of the law, to protect, promote and advocate it. This may seem to you grandiloquent boasting; yea, it must seem so, if I did not add, that even should such escape me, should I lack power to bring my purpose to its complete fulfilment, one thing I cannot want – one thing which man has, above all other gifts, at all times within his reach – and this is a holy will. The will to become a pious guardian in the true spirit fills me, rushes and throbs through all my veins; and therefore my G-d will vouchsafe to me the fulfilment of the prescribed task.

3. To superintend the institutions for education.

The minister enters also on his office with the purpose to govern G-d's holy house. All know that the term 'My house' did mean the Temple, within whose walls in the inner and innermost courts, the priesthood was employed. These brought the various offerings of sin or praise. It was their duty to guard against any faulty offering, any strange fire, which the Lord had not commanded being introduced, that the fire on the altar of the Lord be duly fed and never extinguished, to take care that the light should be burning from evening until morning outside the curtain which hung before the Ark of the Covenant; in a word, it was their duty to take the charge and care of all within the house of G-d.

If in these days the pastor would fulfil those duties of the priests of old, his labours must be directed to another house of G-d; he must erect the temple in other places; and these are the establishments for education. He must strive to make every house become a house of G-d – to make every father and mother a priest to light up the divine fire in the infant breast; remove those clouds which conceal the most holy G-d from that youthful mind wherein He so much delighteth to dwell. He must guard against any strange fire being introduced, and watch that the true flame burn clear and bright from morning until evening, and from evening until morning.

Home is the first and most important school; there example works more effect than precept, and bad example more powerfully than good. He must take charge of G-d's house. Those are the establishments for education, whether preparatory or high schools – whether he establish them or improve them – whether he found or support them – whether he call them into being or uphold their existence; so that, a pious spirit pervading all classes, may pass from the school to the domestic home, from the home into the business of life – that, by means of the lispings of infancy, the kingdom of G-d may be upheld, and by means of the voice of the scholar, the moral world.

The true houses of the Lord are the institutions for instruction, in which priests and teachers, directors and guides, instructors of youth and of the people, should be educated, so that they may attain to the highest degree of religion, and remain endued with the greatest knowledge and piety until their G-d call them to His service; the institutions for those who are to undertake the priestly office, who although seemingly poor, are yet rich in their endowments.

It is his duty to have a care in such institutions that the holy Law be and remain the one Sun whence all rays of light emanate, and to which they return; that the Law be the light of all other knowledge and science. Your children may learn to know every tree and flower that grows, from the cedar of Lebanon to the hyssop on the wall, but they must know and recognize Him who has created all. They may speak and use many foreign languages, as is fitting for so distinguished and powerful a nation, whose ships are found throughout the world, and in whose dominions the sun never sets; but they must use and love that one language in which G-d made himself known, which whether in tears or in laughter, in joy or in sorrow, in pleasure or in pain, belongs to our innermost selves, and expresses our sentiments and feelings. Your children may study the records of all people, especially of their native country; but their own history must not be a sealed letter, a closed book to them; in a word, it is the duty of the pastor to superintend and to take care of establishments for education – to direct what should be taught and how – so that a spirit of true piety and wisdom may be diffused throughout all schools and pervade all homes.

And I, my beloved brethren, do purpose to superintend your establishments for education; this sounds boldly – it would be bold if I did not add, 'That G-d supporteth the weak'. It is not power, it is not number, but the spirit of the Lord which commands success. Can you, I may ask, stop the revolving sails of a windmill? You answer, no; surely no. But I say, take hold of the springs, the innermost springs; and not only any one of you, but a mere child, can arrest its course and set it in motion. Truly, the task I here prescribe to myself is difficult; but my G-d demands this good service from me, and that raises in me a confident hope that I shall succeed.

4. To watch over the places of worship.

The minister enters on his office with the purpose of watching the forecourts of his G-d.

You are aware, my beloved brethren, that whilst in forgiveness – the solitary mourner for lost and loved ones, that he may find hope and comfort. Here too the joyous shall come to pour forth his gratitude, the happy to express his delight.

Therefore it is the duty of the pastor to watch well the forecourts, to have a care that they accomplish their holy purposes, that every thing be banished from G-d's holy house which might prevent holy respect and decorum, which might diminish holiness and devotion; and also, that nothing be permitted to enter there which is contrary to the holy law.

Therefore it is the office of the pastor to take upon himself the anxious duties of these holy places, to make known the commands of the Lord in their purity – to direct attention to the holy writings – so that the light of the law may shine forth not only within this place but without also, giving light and warmth in the business of life, so that the pious purposes resolved on by him may be thus brought into happy fruition.

And I, too, my beloved brethren, have the purpose to watch over your forecourts, to take charge of your synagogues, to have a care above all that all honour and respect due to holy places be not diminished. It is also my purpose, fearlessly and without hesitation, to lay before you the word of the Law, unclouded and pure even as the wise have transmitted it to us, as our ancestors have taught it to us, as the noblest minds have presented it to us.

It is therefore my purpose to explain it in different houses of the Lord, now here, now there, so that none shall be void of instruction; and so to strive that it may be more studied, be better known, and more easily brought into actual use in the affairs of life; so to strive that our love for our fellow man may flourish, prosper, and increase, and prejudices disappear. This sounds again boastfully: it would be so if I did not rely on that G-d who has proved Himself to thousands, who assuredly knows that I seriously seek to serve Him. He will support me and give me help to accomplish the duty which I have prescribed to myself.

5. To make my way into your hearts.

But the minister of these times, like the high-priest of old, enters into his office with the earnest hope of winning his way to the hearts of his flock: 'I, said the Lord, will give you admission to those that stand there'. This expression has many meanings.

The Lord would give Joshua admission to the assembly of priests, who previously had only observed his unfitness and imperfections, his faults and crimes, but not his capabilities – admission to the hearts of his contemporaries, the distinguished men, upon and by means of whom he should act, and bring about the great designs of G-d – admission finally to the angels above; there, where man mounts from step to step, from power to higher power, from height to greater height, to receive the reward of all his labours.

The pastor equally requires this hope, this reliance on the love and confidence of his flock. Then, say, my beloved, if this love be absent, this confidence be wanting, this assurance be denied, how can he labour in his vocation, or even produce small fruits? Would not his powers and his willingness be exhausted by vain efforts to attain the wished-for object? If their hearts are closed against him, and the way to the springs of life and thought, to the mind and to the heart, be barred against him by the fiery sword of distrust, how shall he begin, prosecute, or accomplish the arduous duties of his calling? How uneasily must he walk in the ways of the Lord, if he fears that every step he may take will be mistaken, misunderstood, and falsely judged?

Will he be able to judge correctly, to determine rightly, and to make smooth the difficulties which occur in the various and manifold circumstances of his office, if he has to fear that by acquiring the love of one he may lose that of another? How can he improve the existing institutions, how establish sacred places, if mistrust impede his course – mistrust in his words, labours, and occupations; or if haste and impatience desire and demand of his works that they should be like the rod of Aaron, which was no sooner planted than it bloomed, budded, and bore fruit? How can he make the houses of G-d the scenes of his labours if he have to fear that he shall be thought to say too much here, too little there?

No, the hope that he will gain admission to the hearts of his congregation, that he will be met and supported by them with feelings of affection, is indispensable to the pastor if his labours are to be rich with blessings and are to endure. His conduct, his life, his labours must be such as shall make him worthy to become of the number of the noble and angelic above; but they must reciprocate his love. Heart to heart must be the watchword. And this, my beloved brethren, this is my hope, that I may win admission to your hearts; and the more honestly, the more zealously I have determined to devote my exertions to your service, wholly and unreservedly – the more does my soul desire to gain your love and confidence; for without these your expectations will be disappointed and unconquerable difficulties will frustrate my endeavours. I hope all from your love; that you will aid me by counsel and support, by help and action, and will bear me onwards in love and confidence.

But how can I doubt your love or confidence? Have they not summoned me from the small house of my fathers? Have they not placed me here this day? Have they not, on my arrival here, before inauguration in my office, given me proofs of kindness? All these great antecedent preparations are to me but friendly pledges and promises of future goodwill. Well then, let us make a covenant – a durable covenant to all you now here present, and to those absent ones to whom I equally hold out the hand of brotherhood. I pledge myself that I will walk in the ways of the Lord, that I will keep guard over the holy Law, that I will direct your schools – will watch over the fore-courts of the Lord. I feel assured that you will meet my efforts with trust and confidence; and I will strive to justify your confidence, and, yet more, to gain the approval of the Almighty; so that, when dust shall return to dust and my ashes shall rest amongst you, my soul shall gain admission to my ancestors and predecessors who amongst the angels rejoice in the heavenly reward of their earthly labours.

With this hope, join with me in the prayer which, in your language, I will address to the Lord.

Prayer

Father of all, who hast called me from my country, my kindred, and my father's house, unto a land which Thou hast shown me; who didst put love into my heart, even when a boy, for a country which is great in power, great in boundless extent, great in prosperity yet greater beyond all other nations upon earth by her character and liberty, listen mercifully to the prayer which I deliver for the first time in this holy place.

Lord of Lords! whose kingdom is the kingdom of the whole universe; who leadest the king's heart as rivers of water, bless with Thy best blessing our gracious Queen. Thou hast submitted to her sway nations of different languages, of different persuasions, in different quarters of the globe; whose hearts beat loyally towards her, because she is righteous, benevolent, and merciful towards all without distinction. She is a pattern of all noble virtues, a pattern worthy of imitation; protect and shelter her precious life; preserve her from all sorrow and grief, and be pleased graciously to bless all the members of the Royal Family.

My mind reverts to one, the defender of innocence, the promoter of science and art, the helper of the afflicted, the friend of all that is good, righteous and noble; who once in my native country spread happiness around, and now continues the same noble conduct here, grant to all of them to enjoy the fullness of delight, that they may see the prosperity of their house increase more and more; lead them by thy hand from glory to glory.

Father! who dost requite every one according to his actions, be merciful to the councillors, to the nobles, and to all commissioned to execute the command of our sovereign: send down upon them Thy spirit, the spirit of council and might, the spirit of love and knowledge; reward them for their actions in having put down some of the barriers which, until now, separated brother from brother, citizen from citizen. May the happy success of their measures be the reward of their endeavours, and may their cares be alleviated by the consciousness that they have promoted the prosperity of the people.

Fountain of all goodness! who hast preserved peace in this country, continue I pray Thee, to maintain it in future; let mercy and truth meet together, and righteousness and peace kiss each other. Bless all – all who labour for the prosperity of their native country – all who serve it with their strength and activity, with their arm or their sword, with their body or their mind; grant that science and art, diligence and industry, order and prosperity, virtue and piety, may grow and increase.

Shepherd of Israel! Bestow Thy heavenly grace upon all the congregations which Thou has entrusted to me. I am far from some of them, but Thou art nigh unto them. Grant that the covenant may be blessed which they have made with me; grant that they may enjoy Thy favour in their synagogues and schools, and in their institutions of love and charity. Look down, O Almighty and Everlasting G-d, upon the congregations of this metropolis, which form the centre of the others. Bless the presidents and the officers, the superiors and the inferiors, the strong and the weak, the healthy and the sick, the rich and the poor. Let Thy blessings be shown in the increase of their comfort, in the unanimity of their pursuits, in the prosperity of their houses, in the welfare of their children, and in the tranquillity of their minds.

Give me strength from Thy might, a cheerful spirit and holy ardour to lead Thy people with righteousness and fidelity, to set forth Thy true and loving word in my life and doctrine, that I may walk in thy way, that I may keep Thy charge, judge Thy house and keep Thy forecourts, until the law come from Zion, and the word of G-d from Jerusalem. Amen.

Appendix C

Writings of Nathan Marcus Adler

The late Ruth P. Goldschmidt-Lehmann was the librarian at Jews' College in London for many years after the Second World War. She compiled the list below of the writings of Nathan Marcus Adler. She didn't suggest that the list was complete, but included all the writings she had seen for herself. They illustrate the large number of areas in which the Chief Rabbi participated, though few of his works were published. Ms. Goldschmidt-Lehmann was a dedicated researcher and a first class librarian.

1829 Inaugural sermon, Oldenburg Synagogue.
1836. Sermon to celebrate William IV's birthday.
1843 Paper as an expert witness in Frankfurt.
1845 Letter to the community accepting the office of chief rabbi.
Reply to the address of welcome.
Installation sermon.
Inaugural sermon at the Hambro Synagogue.
Sermon in the Great Synagogue, based on Jeremiah.
Letter to the wardens of the Chatham Synagogue.
Circular to congregations asking for information about their communities.
Sermon at the New Synagogue, based on Isaiah.
Address to the children of the Jews' Free School.
Sermon at the Western Synagogue (in German).
Sermon at the Great Synagogue, based on Deuteronomy.
Address at the examination of children at the Jews' Orphan Asylum.
Letter to the president and members of the Edinburgh Synagogue.
Sermon at the Fenchurch Street Synagogue.
Sermon at the Great Synagogue, based on Zechariah.
Sermon at the Great Synagogue on Yom Kippur.
Sermon at Crosby Square Synagogue on the first day of Succoth.
Sermon on the first visit to the Maiden Lane Synagogue.
Sermon at the Great Synagogue on the duty to parents.
1846 Sermon at the Crosby Square Synagogue.
Sermon at the Fenchurch Street Synagogue.

Prayer for the Russo-Polish Jews.
Prayer for the success of Sir Moses Montefiore's mission to Russia.
Sermon at the Great Synagogue.
Prayer of thanks for the success of British troops in India.
Sermon at the Great Synagogue.
Address to the children at examinations at the Jews' Free School.
Order of service at the synagogue of Jews' Hospital for the support of the aged.
Address at the Jews' Hospital anniversary.
Prayer of thanks for the safe delivery of Princess Helena.
Lecture at the Great Synagogue.
Letter to the Port Philip, Australia congregation thanking them for their good wishes.
Letter to the Sydney, Australia congregation, thanking them for their good wishes.
New Year sermon at the Great Synagogue.
Address at the opening of the Western Jewish Girls' Free School.
Prayer for the alleviation of the famine in the country.
Approving the conferment of the title of Hever (Honoured individual) on Mr Israel Levy of Manchester.

1847 Laws and Regulations for all the Synagogues.
Form of service for the day appointed by the Queen to be observed as a general fast and day of humiliation (to pray for an end to the famines in Ireland and the Highlands).
Sermon at the Great Synagogue on the general fast day.
Sermon in Hanover.
Speech in Birmingham.
Letter to the president of the Birmingham congregation.

1848 Thanksgiving for the good harvest.
Thanks for the testimonial received from Birmingham Cohanim.
Letter of thanks to Metropolitan synagogues for relief for foreigners.
Sermon at the Great Synagogue, based on Ecclesiastes.
Prayer for the continuance of peace and tranquillity (as against revolutions on the Continent).
Sermon at the Hambro Synagogue on second day of Passover on the Oral Law.
Address at the Jews' Free School.
Sermon at the consecration of the Canterbury Synagogue.
Speech at the examination day at the Western Jewish Girls' School.

Speech at the opening session of the Jews' and General Literary and Scientific Institution.

1849 Sermon at Bevis Marks Synagogue.

Letter of thanks for being made an Honorary Member of the Jews General Literary and Scientific Institution.

Sermon at the consecration of Norwich Synagogue.

Prayer for the cessation of the cholera epidemic.

Sermon at the Great Synagogue for the cessation of the cholera epidemic.

1850 Sermon on a visit to Portsmouth.

Letter to the Secretary of the Marriage Commission.

Address at the third public examination at the Western Jewish Girls' Free School.

Address at the funeral of Baroness de Rothschild.

Sermon at the Great Synagogue, based on Micah.

Address at the opening of the lecture session of the JGLSI.

Address at the laying of the corner stone of the Manchester Hebrew School.

1851 Speech at the anniversary dinner of the Jews' Free School.

Sermon at the Maiden Lane Synagogue.

Sermon at the Western Synagogue.

Speech at the inauguration of the Jews' School in Cheetham Hill, Manchester.

Address at the fourth public examination of the children at the Western Jewish Girls' Free School.

Order of the service at Ramsgate Synagogue after repairs.

Sermon at the New Synagogue, based on Zechariah.

Sermon at the Hambro Synagogue.

1852 Address at a public meeting to discuss the founding of a college.

Lecture at the Great Synagogue on the life of Moses.

Discourse at the Western Synagogue on holiness.

Sermon at the Great Synagogue on immutability.

Address at the fifth public examination of the children at the Western Jewish Girls' Free School.

Letter acknowledging the gift of a gold *kiddush* cup from the Jews in Victoria, Australia.

Sermon at the Great Synagogue on immortality.

Sermon at the Great Synagogue on its consecration.

Lecture at the Great Synagogue.

Sermon at the Great Synagogue on the lives of the Patriarchs.

Sermon at the Great Synagogue on the Maccabees.

1853 Lecture at the Great Synagogue, based on Exodus.
Speech at the fund raising dinner of the Jews' Free Schools.
Prayer of thanksgiving for the birth of a prince.
Sermon at the Great Synagogue on the Revelation on Mount Sinai.
Letter on a proposed mission to China.
Sermon at the Great Synagogue on the return unto G-d.
Sermon at the New Synagogue, based on Leviticus.

1854 Address in Leipzig on the Jews in Palestine.
Sermon at the Great Synagogue on Israel.
Pastoral letter to congregations in Britain.
Letter to Sir Moses Montefiore in support of Jews in Palestine.
Prayer for the reopening of the Exeter Synagogue.
Sermon at the Western Synagogue, based on Exodus.
Sermon at the Maiden Lane Synagogue, based on Deuteronomy.
Address for visit to Exeter, based on Deuteronomy.
Lecture at the Great Synagogue on the transition from fasting to feasting.
Letter to the president of the soup kitchen for relieving the poor during the coming winter.
Sermon at the Great Synagogue on behalf of the poor.
Sermon at the Great Synagogue at Chanukah.

1855 Address at the anniversary dinner of the Portsmouth Hebrew Benevolent Institution.
Discourse at the consecration of the new Central Synagogue.
Sermon at the Western Synagogue on the Ten Commandments.
Letter to the Board of Deputies on the Dissenters Marriage Bill.
Sermon on the reopening of the New Synagogue.
Address at the opening of Jews' College.

1856 Response at the anniversary dinner of the Jews' Hospital.
Letter to the Committee of the Board of Directors of the Jews' Hospital in New York on post-mortem examinations.
Letter in support of the Metropolitan Free Hospital.
Sermon at the New Synagogue on the second day of Passover.
Sermon at the Great Synagogue on the last day of Passover on antipathy to foreigners.
Letter to the Wardens of the Hebrew Congregation in Manchester, on the Manchester Reform Movement.
Sermon at the Great Synagogue on Thanksgiving Day, based on the Psalms.
Letter to the *Jewish Chronicle* on the exercise of rabbinical functions by Dr Schiller-Szenessy in Manchester.

Discourse at the Western Synagogue.
Sermon at the consecration of the new Hebrew Synagogue in Birmingham.

1857 Address at the Manchester Hebrew Synagogue when laying the foundation stone.
Letters to the Board of Deputies on the Divorce Bill.
Order of Service at the Western Synagogue for the consecration to mark its complete repair.
Address delivered in Brighton.

1858 Sermon at the consecration of a new synagogue in Manchester.
Discourse and prayer at the consecration of the new cemetery in West Ham.
Address at the inauguration of the new Westminster Jews' Free School in Soho.
Discourse at the Western Synagogue on Israel's vocation, based on Leviticus
Address at the inauguration of the new building at the Infant School in Spitalfields.
Discourse to commemorate the admission of Jews into Parliament.
Order of service for the consecration of the Maiden Lane Synagogue after repairs.
Sermon at the Great Synagogue for the bar mitzvah of Baron Rothschild's youngest son.

1859 Letter to a Welsh Rector, sympathising for the wreck of the Royal Charter steamship in a force 12 gale off the coast of Wales, which cost 450 lives.
Sermon at the Great Synagogue.
Prayer for the London synagogues for the success of Montefiore's mission to Rome to obtain the reuniting of Edgar Mortara with his family.
Address at the annual meeting of Jews' College.
Reply to a toast at the Jews' Free School 50th anniversary dinner.
Sermon at the Western Synagogue, based on Numbers.
Sermon at Maiden Lane Synagogue.
Letter to the Jewish public to not eat unporged hind quarters.
Sermon at the Great Synagogue on the charities for dispensing food for the poor.

1860 Sermon at the Great Synagogue.
Funeral oration for Samuel De Symons, Treasurer of the Jews' Free School and founder of the Central Synagogue.
Sermon at the Western Synagogue.

Sermon at the Maiden Lane Synagogue, based on Joshua.
Sermon in support of the Syrian Relief Fund.
Letter to the Jewish community on the plight of the Jews in Syria.
Sermon at the Hambro.

1861 Sermon at the Great Synagogue on the first day of Passover.
Sermon at the Western Synagogue.
Letter to the Acting President of the Touro Monument Committee.
Letter supporting the foundation of a publication society.
Form of service for the day of the burial of Prince Albert.

1862 A prayer for the Ramsgate Synagogue and to mark the golden wedding of Sir Moses and Lady Judith Montefiore.
Discourse at the laying of the cornerstone at the Bayswater Synagogue.
Discourse at the Western Synagogue on religious zeal.
A pastoral letter to the congregations in the colonies.
Sermon at the Great Synagogue on the sanctity of an oath.
Funeral discourse at the burial of Lady Montefiore.
Pastoral letter on the forthcoming collection for alleviating distress in the cotton manufacturing districts.

1863 Letter to the London Committee of Deputies of British Jews.
Sermon at the Western Synagogue.
Dedication sermon at the consecration of the Bayswater Synagogue.
Sermon at Maiden Lane Synagogue, based on Deuteronomy.
Address at the funeral of Rev. Barnett Abrahams.

1864 Prayer of thanksgiving for the safe delivery of a son to the Princess of Wales.
Sermon at the Great Synagogue on the Royal Society for the Prevention of Cruelty to Animals.
Sermon at Bevis Marks to mark the return of Sir Moses Montefiore from Morocco.
Prayer of thanks at the Great Synagogue to celebrate the success of Montefiore in Morocco.
Sermon at the Western Synagogue.
Discourse at the annual visit to Maiden Lane Synagogue.
Discourse at the inauguration of the memorial tablet for Rev. Barnett Abrahams.

1865 Sermon at the Great Synagogue on the Morning and Evening Sacrifice. With special reference to the claims of deaf mutes.
Speech at the triennial festival of the Jews' Orphan Asylum.
Letter to Albert and Sassoon Sassoon about the David Sassoon Memorial Fund.

Speech at the consecration of the Southampton Synagogue.
Prayer for the ending of the cattle plague, to be read on Monday and Thursday mornings.
Discourse at annual visit to Maiden Lane Synagogue.

1866 Prayer for Sir Moses Montefiore on his departure for the Holy Land.
Response to Lord Chelmsford's circular about the Report of the Royal Commission on the Laws of Marriage.
Address at the inauguration of the new buildings of the Jews' Free School.
Sermon at the annual visit to Maiden Lane Synagogue.
Address to mark the award of a commemoration scholarship at the Jews' Free School.
Prayer for protection against cholera.
A prayer and thanksgiving for relief from the cattle plague, and for protection against cholera.

1867 Sermon at the Great Synagogue on the proposed society for sabbath keepers.
Sermon at the consecration of the new Borough Synagogue.
Prayer for the success of Montefiore's visit to Jassy.
Discourse at Maiden Lane Synagogue based on Genesis.

1868 Sermon at the consecration of the North London Synagogue.
Response at the Westminster Jews' Free School anniversary dinner.
Sermon at the New Synagogue on the second day of a festival.
Sermon at the Western Synagogue.
Sermon at the Great Synagogue.
Prayer for the preservation of the life of HRH Duke of Edinburgh, and for the success and safety of the Abyssinian expedition.
Sermon at Canterbury Synagogue, based on Deuteronomy.
A lecture at Jews' College on the *Targum of Onkelos*.

1869 Discourse at the Central Synagogue based on 1 Samuel.
Sermon at the German Synagogue, on behalf of the Association for the Diffusion of Religious Knowledge, on Rabbi Akiva.
Sermon at the Old Synagogue, Liverpool, based on Numbers.
Comment on opinions and decisions at German congresses.
Sermon at Birmingham Synagogue.
Address at the inauguration of the Lady Montefiore Jewish Convalescent Home.
Address at Maiden Lane, based on Genesis.
Sermon at the North London Synagogue on religious safeguards, based on Zechariah.

1870 Sermon at the Great Synagogue on the famine in Jerusalem.

Letter to the President of the Board of Deputies on the Elementary Education Bill.
Sermon at the consecration of the new Central Synagogue.
Sermon at the Great Synagogue, based on Jeremiah.
Sermon at the Great Synagogue, based on the Song of Songs.
Sermon at the Hambro Synagogue, based on Isaiah.
Sermon at the Central Synagogue.
Lecture on Rabbi Jochanan ben Zakkai, to the Jewish Association for the Diffusion of Religious Knowledge.
Sermon at the Great Synagogue.
Sermon at the consecration of the Chatham Synagogue.
Address at the distribution of prizes at the Stepney Jewish Schools.
Sermon at the Great Synagogue on the war.
Address at the consecration of the Coventry Synagogue.
Sermon at the re-consecration of the Western Synagogue after repairs.
Sermon at the Great Synagogue.
Sermon at the Great Synagogue on behalf of the Board of Guardians, based on Ezekiel.

1871 Lecture at Jews' College on Rabbi Jehudah the Patriarch.
Sermon on the occasion of the pastoral visit to the North London Synagogue.
Letter to Rev. H.D. Marks on the election of the first Reader at the Great Synagogue.
Letter to the *Western Mail* about the Moses case in Swansea, where the plaintiff couldn't prosecute the case because it was held on Shabbat.
Sermon at the Great Synagogue on the advent of a personal Messiah.
Address during a pastoral visit to Cheltenham.
Sermon in Dublin Synagogue, based on Numbers.
Sermon at Swansea Synagogue, based on Numbers.
Address to the children at the Swansea Jewish School.
Sermon at Glasgow Synagogue, based on Nehemiah.
Sermon at the Great Synagogue, based on Deuteronomy.
Letter to the President and members of the Committee of the Manchester Hebrew Congregation.
Sermon at the dedication of the new Bristol Synagogue.
Prayer for the recovery of the Prince of Wales from serious illness, and for all the Royal Family.

1872 Prayer of thanksgiving for the recovery from illness of the Prince of Wales.

Sermon at the Great Synagogue at the thanksgiving service for the recovery from illness of the Prince of Wales.
Sermon at the Great Synagogue.
Letter to the President and Council of the United Synagogue about the Burial Society.
Sermon at the Central Synagogue on science and religion.
Sermon at the Western Synagogue, based on Numbers.
Address at the distribution of prizes at the Stepney Jewish Schools.
Prayer for the safety of Sir Moses Montefiore on his journey to Russia.
Sermon at the consecration of the new Sheffield Synagogue.
Address at the dedication of the Stepney Jewish Schools.
Sermon at the Bayswater Synagogue, based on Genesis.
Address at Maiden Lane Synagogue, based on Genesis.

1873 A responsa on the *kashrut* of a new breed of chicken.
Address at the distribution of prizes at the Borough Jewish Schools.
Response at the anniversary festival of the Westminster Jews' Free School.
Address at the reopening of the North London Synagogue.
Sermon at the consecration of a new synagogue in Manchester.
Sermon at Maiden Lane Synagogue on the annual visit.

1874 Five volumes of the *Targum Onkelos* printed in Vilna.
Pentateuch commentary.
Address at the consecration of Aria College.
Letter to the Presidents of Synagogues supporting the Bengal Famine Relief Fund.
Sermon at the Great Synagogue on Hospital Sunday, based on Job.
Address at the distribution of prizes at the Jews' Free School.
Sermon at the consecration of the new synagogue in Middlesborough.
Sermon at the consecration of the new synagogue in Princes Road, Liverpool.
Sermon at the Great Synagogue on forbidden food.
Sermon at the Brighton Synagogue.
Sermon at the Great Synagogue, based on Genesis.

1875 Sermon at the Great Synagogue, based on Deuteronomy.
Sermon at the Great Synagogue on Hospital Sunday, based on Leviticus.
Sermon at the Great Synagogue, on the Sabbath.
Sermon at the Great Synagogue, based on Isaiah.

Prayer for the consecration of the new building for the Jews' Deaf & Dumb Home.

1876 Speech at the unveiling of the Michael Henry Memorial tablet at Stepney School.

Funeral discourse for Sir Anthony Rothschild.

Letter to the Council of the United Synagogue about the appointment of a dayan.

Prayer for the laying of the foundation stone of the East London Synagogue.

Letter to the Secretary of the United Synagogue about hasty burials.

Prayer of thanksgiving for the safe return of the Prince of Wales from India.

Address at the consecration of the new *Beth Hamedrash* on the study of Hebrew literature.

Sermon at the reconsecration of the Borough Synagogue.

Discourse at the consecration of the St Johns Wood temporary synagogue.

Sermon at the Great Synagogue on Jewish morality.

Sermon at the Western Synagogue, based on Proverbs.

1877 Dedicatory sermon at consecration of East London Synagogue.

Sermon at the reconsecration of the Hambro Synagogue.

Letter to ministers asking for support for the Indian Famine Relief Fund.

Sermon at Maiden Lane Synagogue on annual visit.

1878 Sermon at the Great Synagogue, based on Leviticus.

Sermon at the Great Synagogue, based on Exodus.

Sermon at the Great Synagogue for Hospital Sunday.

Address at the new synagogue near the Hand-in-Hand Asylum.

Sermon at the Great Synagogue on the death of Princess Alice, based on Psalms.

1879 Letter asking the Council of Jews' College to appoint a chairman.

Letter asking for the memorial prayer to be said for Haham Benjamin Artom.

Letter to the Australian President of the Congregation about the constitution of a Beth Din.

Letter to the Chairman and Executive of the United Synagogue about his ill health.

Letter to presidents of synagogues about the appointment of Dr. Hermann Adler as Delegate Chief Rabbi.

1880 Letter to *The Times* about the General Election scheduled for the seventh day of Passover.

Letter to the Honorary Secretary of the Conference of Delegates about modifications to synagogue services.
Letter to the President of the United Synagogue about his move to Brighton.
Letter to the President of the London Committee of the Board of Deputies about the activities of the conversionists at Mission Hall.
Letter to the Board of Deputies about the scheduled polling day at Southwark on the seventh day of Passover.

1881 Letter to the President of the Westminster Jews' Free Schools apologizing for not attending a meeting.

1882 Letter to the Lord Mayor of London regretting his absence from a public meeting at the Mansion House about the persecution of the Jews in Russia.
Prayer for the Jews in Russia.
Pastoral circular and special prayer for the Jews in Russia.
Letter to the Oxford Vice-Chancellor thanking him for his sympathy for the plight of the Russian Jews.
Address as an expert witness to a Hamburg Rabbi.
Order of Thanksgiving for the success of the army in Egypt.
Joint Signatory to an address presented to the Lord Mayor on behalf of the Mansion House Russian Jews' Relief Fund.

1883 Letter to the president of the Jews' Free School supporting the Building Fund.
List of instructions for Passover.
Letter appealing to Jews not to congregate to perform *Tashlich*.
Letter to Sir Nathaniel de Rothschild regretting his inability to be present at the consecration of the new Jews' Free School building.
His Will.

1884 Letters on *Shatnez* and *Kashrut*.
Letter congratulating the Jewish Board of Guardians on their 25th anniversary.
Letter to the *Melbourne Jewish Herald* on *trefa* banquets.
Letter regretting his absence from the Jews' Free School anniversary dinner.
Pastoral letter to provincial Jewish communities.
Letter to the United Synagogue, recommending a special service of prayer and thanksgiving for Sir Moses Montefiore on his 100th birthday.
Letter to the President of the Sephardi synagogue, recommending a special service of prayer and thanksgiving for Sir Moses Montefiore on his 100th birthday.

Letter to the Presidents of Colonial Jewish congregations, recommending a special service of prayer and thanksgiving for Sir Moses Montefiore on his 100th birthday.

Service of prayer and thanksgiving for all synagogues of the British Empire on the occasion of Sir Moses Montefiore's 100th birthday.

1885 Letter promoting a forthcoming book on the Hebrew calendar.

A prayer for the British forces in the Sudan.

Letter asking for the memorial prayer to be recited on the Sabbath to mark the death of Sir Moses Montefiore.

1887 Service of prayer and thanksgiving to mark the Jubilee of Queen Victoria.

Circular to ministers and wardens enclosing the form of prayer and thanksgiving for the Jubilee.

Letter to Lord Rothschild stating that cremation is against the *din*.

Letter to presidents of Hebrew congregations about the licensing of *mohelim* in provincial congregations.

Letter to Great Synagogue about using a musical instrument on a Sunday during Chanukah.

Letter regretting absence from the anniversary dinner of the Jewish Hospital & Orphan Asylum.

Letter to Moses Angel, Headmaster of the Jews' Free School.

1889 Letter to Eastern European colleagues about the plight of immigrants arriving to seek refuge in England.

Pastoral letter about he Jewish Provincial Ministers' Fund.

Letter to the Hon. Secretary of the proposed Hampstead Synagogue about ritual.

Letter to the President of the Board of Guardians for the Relief of the Jewish Poor.

Additional works which have been noted elsewhere include a volume of sermons in German and English under the title *The Jewish Faith and the Bonds of Brotherhood*. There were several volumes of *derashot* (expositions) which he gave semi-annually to audiences interested in the Talmud. There were responsa and *hiddushim* (novellae) consisting of short notes on the Talmud and *posekim* (commentaries and decisions of the *halachah* especially the Turim, a fourteenth-century work by the Spanish Yaakov ben Asher).

Bibliography

Archive material in the Adler Collection, Jewish Theological Seminary of New York, held by Rabbi Raymond Apple, Jerusalem.

Artom, Benjamin, *Sermons* (London: Trubner & Co., 1876).

Bermant, Chaim, *The Cousinhood: The Anglo-Jewish Gentry* (London: Eyre & Spottiswoode, 1971).

Black, Eugene C., 'The Anglicization of Orthodoxy: The Adlers, Father and Son', in Frances Malino and David Sorkin (eds), *Profiles in Diversity: Jews in a Changing Europe* (Detroit, MI: Wayne State University Press, 1998).

Black, Gerry, *JFS: The History of the Jews' Free School, London, Since 1732* (London: Tymsder Publishing, 1998).

Elon, Amos, *The Pity of It All: A Portrait of the German-Jewish Epoch, 1743–1933* (Harmondsworth: Penguin Books, 2004).

Endelman, Todd M., *The Jews of Britain 1656–2000* (Berkeley, CA: University of California Press, 2002).

Feldman, David, *Englishmen and Jews: Social Relations and Political Culture 1840–1914* (New Haven, CT and London: Yale University Press, 1994).

Ferguson, Niall, *The House of Rothschild: Money's Prophets 1798–1848* (Harmondsworth: Penguin, 1998).

Finestein, Israel, *Jewish Society in Victorian England* (London and Portland, OR: Vallentine Mitchell, 1993).

Finestein, Israel, *Scenes and Personalities in Anglo-Jewry 1800–2000* (London and Portland, OR: Vallentine Mitchell, 2002).

Gilam, Abraham, *The Emancipation of the Jews in England 1830–1860* (New York: Garland Publishing, 1982).

Goldfarb, Michael, *Emancipation: How Liberating Europe's Jews from the Ghetto led to Revolution and Renaissance* (New York: Simon & Schuster, 2009).

Harding, Nick, *Hanover and The British Empire, 1700–1837* (Martlesham: The Boydell Press, 2007).

Harris, Isidore, *History of Jews' College* (London: Luzac & Co., 1906).

Hyamson, Albert, *Jews' College London 1855–1955* (London: Jews' College, 1955).

Jones, Owen, *The Establishment: And how they get away with it* (Harmondsworth: Penguin, 2014).

Kershen, Anne J. and Jonathan Romain, *Tradition and Change: A History of Reform Judaism in Britain, 1840–1995* (London and Portland, OR: Vallentine Mitchell, 1995).

Levin, Salmond S. (ed.), *A Century of Anglo-Jewish Life* (London: The United Synagogue, 1970).

Lipman, Sonia and V.D. Lipman, *The Century of Moses Montefiore* (Oxford and New York: Oxford University Press for the Littman Library of Jewish Civilization in association with the Jewish Historical Society of England, 1985).

Loewe, Louis (ed.), *Diaries of Sir Moses and Lady Montefiore* (London: Jewish Historical Society of England, 1983).

Mann, Golo, *The History of Germany since 1789* (Harmondsworth: Penguin Books, 1974).

Marmur, Dow (ed.), *Reform Judaism* (London: Reform Synagogues of Great Britain, 1973).

Mashinsky, M.L., *Chance Encounters: Stories that are Hardly by Chance* (New York: ArtScroll Mesorah Publications, 2000).

Meola, David, 'Jews in Hanover and their Role in the German Press, 1815–1848' (PhD dissertation, University of Alabama, 2012).

Newman, Aubrey, *The United Synagogue, 1870–1970* (London: Routledge & Kegan Paul, 1976).

Newman, Aubrey, 'The Chief Rabbinate and the Provinces', in Jonathan Sacks (ed.), *Tradition and Transition: Essays Presented to Chief Rabbi Sir Immanuel Jakobovits to Celebrate Twenty Year in Office* (London: Jews College Publications, 1986).

Ornstein, Philip, *Historical Sketch of the Beth Hamedrash* (London: United Synagogue, 1905).

Persoff, Meir, *Hats in the Ring: Choosing Britain's Chief Rabbis from Adler to Sacks* (Boston, MA: Academic Studies Press, 2013).

Pfeffer, Jeremy, *'From one End of the Earth to the Other'. The London Beth Din, 1805–1855 and the Jewish Convicts Transported to Australia* (Brighton: Sussex Academic Press, 2009).

Roth, Cecil, *History of the Great Synagogue, London 1690–1940* (London: Edward Goldston & Co., 1950).

Schama, Simon, *The Story of the Jews: Finding the Words 1000 BC – 1492 AD* (London: HarperCollins, 2014).

Schmidt, H.D., 'Chief Rabbi Nathan Marcus Adler (1803–1890): Jewish Educator from Germany', *Leo Baeck Institute Yearbook*, 7, 1 (1962), pp.289–311.

Seymour, Miranda, *Noble Endeavours: The life of two countries, England and Germany, in Many Stories* (London: Simon & Schuster, 2013).

Sher, David A., 'Chief Rabbi Nathan Marcus Adler', *Jewish Affairs* (South Africa) (December 2015).

Singer, Steven, *Orthodox Judaism in Early Victorian London, 1840–1858* (New York: Yeshiva University, 1981).

Susser, Bernard (ed.), 'Provincial Jewry in Victorian Britain', Paper for a JHSE conference, 1975.

Taylor, A.J.P., *The Course of German History* (London: Routledge, 2001).

Taylor, Derek, *British Chief Rabbis, 1664–2006* (London and Portland, OR: Vallentine Mitchell, 2007).

Taylor, Derek, *Chief Rabbi Hertz. The Wars of the Lord* (London and Portland, OR: Vallentine Mitchell, 2014).

Williams, Bill, *The Making of Manchester Jewry, 1740–1875* (Manchester: Manchester University Press, 1985).

Winder, Simon, *Danubia: A Personal History of Habsburg Europe* (London: Picador, 2014).

Index